ELEVEN BATS

Anthony 'Harry' Moffitt recently retired from the Australian Defence Force after almost thirty years, most of which was spent with Australia's elite Special Air Service (SAS) Regiment as a Team Commander and Team Specialist.

He has served in eleven active deployments, including being wounded in action in 2008. Harry completed his time with the SAS as its Human Performance Manager. He's a Registered Psychologist and runs a human performance consultancy, Stotan Group, working with sports teams, the military and industry. He remains a cricket tragic.

ELEVEN BATS

A STORY OF COMBAT, CRICKET AND THE SAS

ANTHONY 'HARRY' MOFFITT

ALLEN&UNWIN
SYDNEY · MELBOURNE · AUCKLAND · LONDON

Certain names and details have been changed to protect the identities of serving defence force personnel.

Every effort has been made to trace the holders of copyright material. If you have any information concerning copyright material in this book please contact the publishers at the address below.

Allen & Unwin
83 Alexander Street
Crows Nest NSW 2065
Australia
Phone: (61 2) 8425 0100
Email: info@allenandunwin.com
Web: www.allenandunwin.com

 A catalogue record for this book is available from the National Library of Australia

ISBN 978 1 76087 784 2

P. 37 quote from *The Odd Angry Shot*, Samson Productions, screenplay copyright © 1979 by Tom Jeffrey
P. 81 photograph courtesy of thefulltoss.com
All other photographs are courtesy of the author's collection:
for security reasons individual photographers have not been identified
Set in 12/18.5 pt Minion Pro by Bookhouse, Sydney
Printed and bound in Australia by Griffin Press, part of Ovato

10 9 8 7 6 5 4 3 2 1

'WE ARE IT. THERE IS NO ONE ELSE.'

Dedicated to all current and future operators of mission critical teams. I hope this inspires you all to tell your stories, good and bad. To process those extreme experiences and remind you that what you are is only part of who you are. Be daring, compassionate, and look after each other.

CONTENTS

INTRODUCTION

I never heard the explosion.

There must have been an almighty bang, because I was in the air feeling like I had been trampolined off a blanket held at the corners. Looking down between my legs, I saw the driver's seat I had been sitting in and the steering wheel I had been holding. They were floating above the earth, along with the rest of the vehicle, which was now in two halves and, like me, airborne, out of control, useless and powerless. At the apex of my flight, time stood still. But I still can't hear the explosion.

Everything else has the clarity of a slow-motion replay. It was Tuesday, 8 July 2008, early on a typically cloudless morning in Uruzgan Province, Afghanistan. What I do know is that when I landed, my mate Sean McCarthy would be dead, and our interpreter Sammi would suffer injuries so severe he would lose his left leg. As I hung there in the perfect sky, I was still innocent of this knowledge. The only person I thought was going to die was me.

They say your life flashes before you. I have a crystal-clear memory, while I was floating in that eerie silence, of three images side by side, like a row of photographs on a mantelpiece. I had recently started a degree in psychology and I pictured my textbooks, which were in my backpack flying somewhere in the air with me. I wondered if they would be damaged. The portrait in the centre of my imagination was of my wife, Danielle, and my kids, Georgia and Henry. I saw their faces looking up at me. There was no time to process any emotion. All I thought was, *There they are, the most important people in my life.* And to the other side, I saw the Applecross Cricket Club. We had won a grand final a few months earlier and the felt pennant was one of my most prized possessions.

Family, study, cricket. When you're about to die, you learn what really matters to you.

———

My name is Sergeant Anthony Moffitt, though I am known as Harry. For nearly all my adult life I was a professional Australian soldier. I served more than twenty-five years in the Australian Army, including nearly twenty as an Operator and Team Leader in the Special Air Service Regiment (SASR, or SAS as it's commonly called). I completed many operational tours and international engagements, amassing nearly one thousand days on active service in Afghanistan, Iraq and Timor-Leste. I spent roughly the same number of days again working with forces around the world.

Like many Australian soldiers in that period, I have been shot at, blown up, busted and broken, mentally drained, socially dislocated and spiritually, ethically and morally challenged. Unlike many Australian soldiers, I have been on hundreds, maybe thousands, of combat missions in that time. My family rode the rollercoaster, quietly determined to support me, which was not always easy for them given the tensions between warfare and modern social values.

Australia can be a testing place to pursue a profession of arms. In the past, we in the armed forces have been warned against wearing our uniform in public, which was frustrating, if understandable. Many times over my career I have found myself defending 'war' and our defence forces against younger, progressive, educated people, and I don't disagree with their attitudes or even the content of their arguments. I welcome having my thinking challenged, and my position on killing, combat and warfare has changed over the years. No one hates war and fighting more than me, especially as I have seen the results—the torn human flesh, the civilian impacts, and what it does to the minds of those in combat. But I have also seen what extreme ideologies can do, and sometimes we are called to help. I occasionally envy those who enjoy the comfort of seeing the world in black and white. But the world I have seen is not that simple.

During my service, I didn't turn into the quintessential tough soldier: a strong, imposing, striking warrior, hardened in the heat of combat, dark and contemplative, with an air of control and decisiveness. I am skinny, anxious and easily distracted. My journey has been less about combat and courage and more about adventure and the determination to understand and overcome my weaknesses. I merely squeezed everything I could out of my limited resources.

During my years of service, I became known in the SAS for organising cricket games within the unit, in backyards, streets, military compounds and even 'outside the wire' wherever I travelled with combat teams. I was also a playing member, Aubrey King medal-winner (awarded for end-of-season trip shenanigans), and former vice-president of my beloved Applecross Cricket Club over a twenty-year career (and I am still available for selection!). I enjoy travelling internationally to watch Test cricket, and at home I listen to it passionately on ABC or BBC radio. Like many Australians, I am avid about Test cricket in particular, which I consider has much in common with combat operations in its strategic and tactical design, planning and execution. Cricket, like war fighting, involves long periods of thinking and plotting, punctuated by moments of extreme tension and action. Often, nothing consequential comes out of these moments but sometimes they produce the highest drama.

This book is about my life inside and outside the army, and about how I changed as a person during my years as a soldier. It is also about how the game of cricket became a framework around which I was able to better understand my experience and communicate with others. Cricket provided me and some of my fellow soldiers with a purpose when there seemed to be none. An escape when one was needed. A conversation when silence needed breaking. A moment of forgetting the long time we were spending away from family and friends. It even represented a therapy between deployments, when I built not only a career with Applecross but the Moffitt Backyard Cricket Ground, my very own MCG.

Cricket drew teams and individuals closer together, building ties between us and the people in Afghanistan, Iraq and Timor-Leste we were working to protect. It even forged links with some of those we considered our adversaries; in some ways, cricket transcended death itself.

The matches that broke out among us on airfields, in Q stores and on Forward Operating Bases (FOBs) were always a superb balance of competitiveness and 'spirit of the game'. The banter came thick and fast, and was not always politically correct ('You swing like your mother, Harry!' or '. . . like a shithouse door in a thunderstorm!'). Allegiances would form along state lines, which is common in the military, whatever the sport. Organised games of rugby union and league, AFL, basketball and other sports are an enormous component of military culture. But cricket seemed to span all states. I loved how cricket was the broadest church, accessible to every man, woman and child. Break out a match and everyone gets a hit, a bowl, and a chance to catch a lofted shot to cow corner. Cricket can be played anywhere: inside a kitchen, on a two-metre wide strip behind the shitters, or inside an aircraft hangar.

Cricket has been played in many battle zones. Most notably in Australian military history, Shell Green in Gallipoli hosted cricket matches as a ruse to trick the Turks into thinking everything was normal while the withdrawal was being prepared. In the shadows of the Sphinx, soldiers of the Light Horse played cricket before embarking on the assault on Beersheba in 1917. In a famous image, Albert 'Tibby' Cotter, an Australian Test pace bowler, is shown slogging a ball into the Egyptian desert. Cotter was killed in the charge at Beersheba, where he was a stretcher-bearer. He left stardom as a sporting celebrity to join the AIF but, not wanting to fight, chose what was arguably a more dangerous role. He is one of a handful of Australian Test cricketers who served on active duty, and an inspiring figure in my life.

Along my journey, as the importance of cricket impressed itself on me, I decided to keep the objects that gave form to the spirit of the game: the bats we used in these war zones. Over eleven years, the collection grew to eleven bats. It became my habit—more than a habit, a necessary part of my preparation for each trip—to carry a cricket bat to wherever we deployed. It was also my habit to ensure that SAS team members and support staff signed the bats at the end of those deployments.

Our military equipment manifests courage and combat; my odd collection of cricket equipment manifests the humanity of modern warfare, the insanity and tragedy, the fear, the anxiety and trauma, punctuated by occasions of joy and camaraderie and black humour. These bats provide a tangible anchor for what has been a sometimes surreal journey.

Prime ministers have also signed the bats, two governors-general as well as military generals, genuine royals and the Victoria Cross recipients Mark Donaldson and Ben Roberts-Smith.

Perhaps my favourite signatures are from a Timor-Leste deployment in 2006, the names of Xanana Gusmão, Mari Alkatiri, José Ramos-Horta and Alfredo Reinado—particularly these last two. Ramos-Horta's and Reinado's signatures are on the same bat only centimetres apart, a remarkable fact, as less than two years after they signed the bat, Reinado came down from the hills outside Dili, tried to assassinate Ramos-Horta in his home, and was killed during this attempt.

I try not to have favourites, but I value this bat more than most.

Until my retirement, I hadn't thought anyone else might be interested in the stories behind my cricket bats. A civilian friend once said to me over a beer, 'You've got an amazing collection of bats, they should be on display.' Later, while moving house and pulling the bats out of an old box, I wondered if these unique military artefacts might have something to say about the history and commitment of the SAS and the Australian Defence Force (ADF) over the last two decades. From the streets of Mogadishu to the jungles of Timor, the coastal plains of Kuwait to the Hindu Kush of Afghanistan, the western deserts of Iraq to the African and Middle Eastern areas of operations, among many other places, Australian soldiers had certainly seen a lot in this period. And although the SAS only comprised a tiny fraction of the defence force, we had been called on to do a disproportionate amount of the fighting. Perhaps a time would come when these bats could tell my story, and the story of the mates and the regiment I love so much.

The Australian War Memorial expressed an interest in displaying the bats; however, I was not ready to 'donate' them yet, as I wanted the chance to show them off a little. They have been on display at the Shrine of Remembrance in Melbourne and at the MCG Long Room, where I was invited to talk through a few of the stories that accompany each bat. Rather than the typical 'war stories', I preferred to talk about the humour, humanity and psychology of modern combat. I found telling my stories therapeutic. I also liked to emphasise the impact of service on our families, too often forgotten in modern war narratives.

All eleven of my bats have been 'outside the wire' on combat, humanitarian and diplomatic missions and I believe they are inextricably intertwined with the service of Australian soldiers across the ages. Yet cricket is neither life nor war. Sports analogies, while they can carry important meaning, cannot be allowed to trivialise the gravity of fighting in war. Sport is entertainment, combat far from it. Sport is comparatively non-consequential next to the immeasurable after-effects of fighting in war. Sport is fleeting, while combat thunders down the ages. Sport is constrained, combat unconstrained. Sport has rules and an umpire who influences events; combat, most of the time, has neither, and when rules are broken and an 'umpire' steps in, it is a process that often takes place many years after the event. However, that does not nullify the value of sport during times of war. While war is tragic and traumatic and tears people apart, sport is fun, peaceful and brings people together. (When George Orwell described sport as 'war minus the shooting', he was using a rhetorical flourish; sport may indeed be 'bound up with hatred, jealousy, boastfulness, disregard of all rules and sadistic pleasure in witnessing violence', as Orwell described, but, even at its worst, it's still a long way short of war.)

It was war, not sport, that sent me flying into the air that day in Afghanistan in 2008; it was war that revealed what was important to me, and war that asked me how the hell I had got myself into this situation.

SEARCHING FOR UBL

AFGHANISTAN, 2002/03

Among the missions I have been involved in, none has been more demanding or rewarding than the days and nights on foot patrols. From the snow-capped mountains of Afghanistan to the jungles of the Indonesian archipelago, in extreme weather and environments, Special Operations Forces (SOF) conducted our foot patrols in a particular way. Much of it was about alertness and anticipating the unexpected.

But some things you can never see coming.

One of the hardest foot patrols I ever did was my very first in Afghanistan, a ten-day Special Reconnaissance (SR) patrol. Our six-man team had to gather intelligence and perform some 'ground-truthing' in an area of interest near the border with Pakistan. This was late 2002, when Coalition forces had gone into Afghanistan after the September 11 attacks with the purpose of finding Usama Bin Laden and eliminating his Al-Qaeda (AQ) terrorist network and their friends in the Taliban government who had been ruling Afghanistan. Between 2001 and 2002 the Coalition had achieved much of that work, but Bin Laden was still at large.

Our unit's mission was to support US troops in the effort to track down Bin Laden. The SAS's 3 Squadron, from whom we were taking over, had seen significant action. In one incident near the Pakistan border, a group of them had become isolated by AQ fighters in the hills, and, in danger of being wiped out, needed the rest of the squadron to extract them and save their lives.

While I felt stretched tight with tension and stress, getting ready for that first patrol was the realisation of a boyhood dream for me. Ever since the Vietnam War, the Australian SAS had a global renown for these foot patrols, going into the most difficult areas and making it out alive, even after being cornered by the enemy, hundreds of kilometres from extraction support. These foot-patrolling skills defined our unit early in the Afghanistan war, giving us a reputation that would evolve into something of a burden. By the end of the war, I believe we became a victim of our own success.

At Bagram Air Base in Kabul, preparing for the patrol, we were sitting one day in a square concrete room about four by four metres in size, the cement render chipped and falling off the walls, in a battle-damaged old building that was once a Russian Army workshop. There were rusting lathes and other machinery still lying about. Against the walls were our folding cots and shelves cobbled together from Hesco barriers, the compressed wire and fabric material used to protect us against blasts. In the middle of the room was our war table, which we had made out of bits of wood recovered from around the yard, the top covered in laminated maps of our area of operation, larger maps of Afghanistan, and pictures of semi-naked women. On top was a pile of papers detailing the patrol's personal details, next of kin, blood group and other important documents in case of death or injury, reminders of the gravity of our job.

We sat at the war table listening to music—The Externals, Front End Loader and Eminem—while checking and rechecking our kit. Weight was always an issue, and I realised I couldn't carry my copy of Charles Dickens' *Great Expectations*, which I was always reading or re-reading. I broke my copy into four quarters, to spread the weight among the group. It was a habit of soldiers to read books this way, swapping sections with each other, but sometimes it meant you read the story completely out of order.

We talked about the tactics we would be using and what would happen if one of us was killed. The banter ranged into politics and the history of Islam. To keep things light, my good mate Hawkeye baited me with a question: 'Which fucking crusade are we on anyway, Harry?'

A keen student and teacher, I was only too willing to take the bait. 'We're not on a crusade,' I began, explaining that, rather than following Richard the Lionheart into the eastern Mediterranean, we were travelling the same routes as some other great but ultimately failed empires. Genghis Khan had been through Afghanistan, and Alexander the Great launched his invasion through the Hindu Kush from Charikar, just up the road. Northern Afghanistan had become known as the 'land of bones' and 'graveyard of empires', not that this had put off any modern invaders.

Hawkeye, though better read than any of us, was not interested in a history lesson. He said something about us being here to finish the job off. I told him what a redneck he was, and he called me a 'commie pinko leftie' because I felt sorry for the villagers, who seemed to hate us and the Taliban equally.

In retrospect, in 2002 none of us really knew what we were talking about. Our education was about to unfold. We launched from Bagram to Khost military air base, near the Pakistan border south-east of Kabul, where we prepped and tried to find a ride to our destination at a locality called Gag Ghar, on the edge of the border to the east of Khost. There were American CH-47 Chinook helicopters flying in and out, but we quickly realised we were a low priority and gave up hope of hitching a ride. As the Khost base was being attacked day and night, and security was porous to say the least, we were on our toes the whole time. We spent those days gaining intelligence about our patrol destination from the local Afghan forces, tending to our equipment, and trying to avoid getting shot at or bombed. This left us fatigued before our mission even started.

Adding to the strain, there was no reliable food at the base, so we had to live out of our packs, eating our own rations. While there was plenty of water, we were fast running down our food stocks. If we ran out of food, we could find ourselves in trouble, given the extreme physical toll from moving through the mountains day and night carrying our heavy packs.

When it became clear that we would never find a helicopter to insert us, we investigated a less comfortable yet potentially more exciting Plan B. We identified an Afghan 'jingle truck' driver with a satisfactory (though questionable) security clearance to drive us up to our area of operation. This trip was a risk, as the roads and mountains surrounding our destination were dominated by enemy forces who regularly hijacked or bombed both local and Coalition vehicles. Nevertheless, we loaded up in the back of the truck, covered ourselves in hay and old clothes, and put our lives in the hands of this driver. Safe to say, it was an arse-clenching ride.

Our team leader, the 'Chief' Alfred Siaosi—for whom I have a deep respect, admiration and friendship, and who continues to shape me as a soldier, citizen and man—said it would be better if he sat in the front with the driver. This was dangerous, given the Chief's obvious non-Afghan appearance, but someone had to make sure we got to the right place while checking that old mate behind the wheel hadn't filled his pockets on a promise to drive us straight into a trap.

Hidden in the back of the truck, I remember thinking, *Now this is Special Ops all right—like* Hogan's Heroes! But the trip was long and getting bumped around under piles of hay, wondering if you were going to get blown up at any moment or, more likely, skid off the side of the mountain, made us more than a little edgy. We were hopelessly exposed and heading towards extreme danger.

Several kilometres short of our drop-off point, the driver told the Chief that he didn't want to go any further into the 'bad lands'. He was shitting himself. Fair enough, I guess. We might have been safer on foot anyway.

It was now long after sunset, meaning we would be walking with our night-vision goggles (NVGs), giving us an advantage over anyone looking for or at us. As a nimble small team, we were more comfortable like this anyway, and felt as though we 'owned' the night and could deal with any enemy force.

My personal debut into the battlespace was inauspicious. As I climbed out of the truck, I tripped and fell two metres; gun, pack and body thundering into the ground and severely twisting my ankle. I said nothing and tried not to hobble too obviously.

I could blame the weight of the packs we were carrying. When 'Junior' Jim Hardy put his pack, webbing and weapon on the scales before leaving Khost, it came to nearly 75 kilos. We had tried to minimise our weight, and the first thing to go was food. We were conditioned to subsist on less than a fistful of food per day, which, we knew from our preparation, could lead to some of us losing 5 to 10 kilos of bodyweight on a ten-day patrol. The next thing to be jettisoned was toiletries. If you had to take them, toothbrushes were cut down and toothpaste was rationed out to the day.

The priorities in our kit were obvious and simple: optics, communications equipment and long-range weapons. The batteries for the equipment took up more weight. And most important of all was water, of which we carried 20 litres each. On a long trek like this, we might need to drop a cache of water somewhere and hope it was still there when we got back to it. Otherwise, we would be asking another patrol to risk their lives to come up to the mountains, thousands of metres above sea level, and resupply us.

True to our Standard Operating Procedure (SOP) for an insertion, we found a small hollow to hide in, where we sat in complete silence for about an hour after the jingle truck had left. There was sporadic gunfire in our general direction, but none of it was effective, so it was difficult to know if they were aiming at us or just firing randomly into the night. I was convinced it was all my fault: I thought that my heavy fall from the truck had been heard from all the surrounding valleys. I was very anxious and, I am not afraid to confess, a little frightened.

To my right, through the green luminescence of my NVGs, the Chief was brilliantly silhouetted against the tracers of the gunfire and the dim lights from fires in the valley villages below. I took a moment to admire this picture. A big strong man, he was perfectly balanced as he scanned his 'arcs' with both gun and eyes. His poise belied the bulk and weight of the load he was carrying in his pack and webbing—each of our guns weighed the best part of 10 kilograms. The sight instantly calmed me down. Even though I was in my early thirties, older than most combat debutants, my nerves needed settling and I appreciated having a leader I could trust.

Continuing to scan, and looking in the direction in which we were to set off, the Chief placed his hand on my shoulder, squeezed hard and whispered, 'You all right, Hazza? Good to go?'

I nodded slowly, while watching and aiming with my own gun, re-attending to my arcs. 'Let's go, mate.'

And so began a series of some of the toughest nights of my life on that steep terrain we grew to know and love as the 'Ghani Stair-Master'.

———

Before first light, at the end of a night's walking, we stopped to build a 'hide' for the day. This was no easy feat, as the locals could spot irregularities in the landscape as easily as if you suddenly saw a bus in front of your house in the suburbs. The art of making a good hide was not to alter the surrounds, for instance not taking all your covering vegetation from the same bush, stripping it bare and making it conspicuous. In the hide, a patrol of up to six SAS operators had to fit into an area as small as the back of a VW Kombi pop-top. There was no room to stretch out or even lie down straight. Our first day was a nervous one, and we didn't sleep. We were hyper-vigilant, in a place crawling with guys who wanted to kill us. They were somewhere out there; we were sure of that.

Our job was to work close to the border, mainly performing reconnaissance with a readiness for engagement. We were mostly looking for bad guys who were trafficking drugs, arms, information, money and people. The Australian SAS had made its name as a special reconnaissance unit, and this remained our core specialty. We were providing overwatch on a valley into which a US Marine battalion would later land. It took us three nights to hump up to the top of the Gag Ghar mountain. We passed many graveyards, presumably Russian graves from the Mujahideen wars of the 1980s, and many old defensive trenches from those fights.

It was testing to carry so much weight for hours on end, at night and in lopsided terrain on the slope of a mountain. If you fell, you might not stop for hundreds if not thousands of metres, and we had some close calls. The Chief would walk us for forty-five minutes and rest us for fifteen, and then go again. As we climbed higher, we did shorter walking periods. At 2000 metres above sea level you started to really feel the altitude, and it became a vicious cycle: the harder you worked, the harder it got.

In one of our hides, we were discovered—by a herd of goats. They wandered up and started eating the scrub we had picked from high up in a tree. We had actually done the goats a favour, as they had already eaten all the low scrub. To address the ongoing issue of being discovered by goats, scientists assisting Special Forces had created a spray, supposedly smelling of tiger piss, that we were directed to spray on our hides to ward off the hungry and curious animals. The only problem was that the goats didn't know what tiger piss smelt like, as there were no tigers in Afghanistan. Another brilliant idea from the boffins in the lab and the senior leaders who directed them.

As the hours ticked by, the goats nibbled our cover away. 'Fuck off!' I kept hissing at them. If they kept going, our hide would be stripped bare. 'Get lost!' But they didn't speak English.

Inevitably, the young goatherder stumbled onto us. There we were, six men crammed into the rocks camouflaged with chicken wire and scrim which we had painted and dirt-glued onto hessian. We also used umbrellas with local dirt glued on for shade. Which was all good until the poor kid clambered over the rocks and saw us with our guns.

Two options went through our minds: grab him or let him go. (A third option, to shoot him, might have possessed any of us in a moment of fear, but fortunately our nerves and training held.) The Chief decided on option two.

After we waved the goatherder off, we were keen for night to come on so we could move out of there. In early evening, an older man came up to a ridge adjacent to us, lit a fire and began chanting loudly in his local dialect. He may have been told about us by the young goatherder. We wasted no more time getting out. Later, we joked that the old man was probably yelling back down to his mates in the valley, 'They're up here hiding in the mountains! They smell like urine! Come and get them, one of them is old and has a twisted ankle!'

The goatherders did give us some entertainment one afternoon when we were sitting high above a valley floor, watching people and cars go by, reporting on their activity. Scanning the mountains is no mean feat, staring into a valley 20 kilometres long and several wide, rising up from the floor by 600 metres on both sides. Therefore, we came with some serious optics. Hawkeye was on the spotting scope when I heard him unleash a loud whisper.

'Fuck me, you're not going to believe this! There's a guy down there around the back of his house, and I think he is trying to . . . Is he trying to fuck a donkey? No, he is, he's doing it now! Fuck . . .'

I would learn over time that patrols sparked various emotions, but usually within a predictable band. This time, I didn't know whether I was amused, or saddened, or completely weirded out.

'Can I have a look?' 'Slick' Tommy Quick asked.

Hawkeye probably wanted someone to confirm that he wasn't imagining things. He let Slick lean into the scope. Slick looked for longer than you might deem appropriate. In fact, if I wasn't mistaken, he seemed to enjoy what he was seeing. He was audibly marvelling. He turned to us and said, 'Disgusting prick.'

Then he put his eye back to the scope and continued to look.

Hawkeye took another turn, wresting the scope back off Slick. Then they looked at me.

'Harry, you want a look?'

I'd already made my mind up. A patrol usually does everything together, as if you are six parts of one brain. But there are limits.

'No thanks, mate, I'll take your word for it. There are some things a man can't unsee.'

———

Our training had been exhaustive, but nothing could really prepare us for the uniqueness of the experience. Nothing was quite as I'd expected, and these discoveries brought out the full range of emotions: stress, anxiety, delight, wonder, fear . . . and that was just the start of it. On a later patrol, we harboured at Asadabad in a walled village the US had taken over for its tactical advantages, fortifying it and making themselves a stationary target for local insurgents, who obliged by attacking the camp most days. We, the Australian SAS, were more inclined to be a mobile force, but we were required to use their compound as our base for that patrol.

At one of our first briefings, we were shown the 'smart rock', or 'spy rock', another brilliant concept brought to you by the people who made tiger-piss spray. The idea was that a patrol would insert into an area at night and place the smart rock on the edge of a donkey track. The rock, tricked up with video and audio technology, would record activity on the track and do our surveillance work for us. Unfortunately, the locals knew every rock and tree on the tracks they had walked several times a day for most of their lives.

The first local who came by the smart rock picked it up and took it away. No doubt he had little idea he was handling thousands of dollars' worth of military hardware.

As we undertook patrol after patrol, building up experience, we learned that life could be cheap. The US Special Forces had been using an enclosed valley behind the compound as a shooting range to keep their skills up. But there were occasional mishaps, and worse. Range practice was important to keep the soldiers motivated, their skills sharp and their weapons in good order. In one range exercise, the Americans accidentally killed a young local boy with errant fire falling outside the shooting area. His distraught family came down from the hills for an explanation. After negotiations, the Americans paid them around a thousand dollars—life literally had a negotiable price.

Mistakes were not uncommon, and 'blue-on-blue' casualties occurred more often than we wished to admit. One night in 2002, Canadian troops were conducting a complex night range practice when a US F-16, returning from a ten-hour patrol, dropped a laser-guided 500-pound bomb on them, killing four and wounding eight. We also made mistakes, and although we didn't incur any fatalities, we were just lucky. No one was immune to error.

The waste of life was distressing. I learned later that the military would routinely employ CDEs, or collateral damage estimates, to put a number on how many civilian casualties (civcas) might be caused by an action. For example, if we had a high value target, like a Taliban commander, in a house in a village and wanted to kill him using an air strike, the powers that be might allocate a

CDE of 5 (meaning they were willing to tolerate up to five civcas in neutralising that target). I found it hard to comprehend that anyone could think of war in this way. At the time I thought, surely if you put protecting civilians at the centre of your strategy, you would win the war faster and with less damage. I still believe this.

These would be far from the last times I would have my moral values tested.

Danger was ever-present when we were inside smaller compounds. Inside the Asadabad compound, which measured about 100 by 50 metres, were improvised cells for PUCs (People Under Containment), captured enemy commanders and combatants waiting to be choppered back to Bagram, where there was a large holding facility. Presumably seeking to free them, their friends outside often attacked us with rocket-propelled grenades and small arms fire.

The first time it happened to me, we were sitting around chatting over a cup of tea when we heard the whoosh of an object above our heads, accompanied by loud flicking sounds in the trees as a rocket passed a metre or so above our heads, before, seconds later, exploding at the back of the compound. If it had hit any of the trunks or hard boughs of the trees above us, instead of just leaves falling, it might have caused casualties. While gunfire rained in, we rushed to vantage points around the compound wall, which was 3 to 4 metres high, to stand on platforms to return fire. The insurgents would habitually launch such skirmishes just to remind us they were there. Later that year, after we left, that particular compound was significantly attacked and US Special Forces personnel were killed and wounded. It was positioned at the start of a route that became known as the 'Taliban Highway', so called as it was a well-known facilitation route used by the Taliban and Al-Qaeda.

These outbreaks of extreme threat would alternate with moments of extreme surrealism. One of the more mundane jobs in those Special Operations compounds was the burning of the 'shit cans'. Channelling the iconic scenes of soldiers on shit-can detail in Vietnam War movies, I didn't mind doing it—I was following a long military tradition. I took one of the 44-gallon drums, cut into quarters, from the back of the timber shitters. I dragged it out to the edge of the compound, poured fuel in and lit it. The fire threw up thick columns of black smoke that contrasted against the brilliant pink sunset. I climbed up a timber ladder to an observation post on top of the corner of a thick mud compound wall. The scene looked like the set of a *Mad Max* movie. There were the pops of SOF mortars outside, no doubt called in by a patrol who had seen something. You could lose interest in the war for a moment, but the war would never lose interest in you.

Having recovered from the first blast of stench from the shit cans, I lit a cigarette and contemplated the war. Even for such healthy people as Special Forces soldiers, and even if you were a non-smoker like me, a cigarette was common for those 'coming down' moments after a patrol or a firefight, steadying you for a moment of thera-peutic reflection. I stood there, the stars beginning to come out on a beautiful Afghanistan night, with the waft of burning shit in the air, thinking, *How the fuck did you end up here, Harry?*

What were we doing there? The question arose in different forms in different places and times, but I recall a piercing philosophical conversation during that deployment at an American compound on the banks of the Helmand River, near the town of Jangalak, when I crossed paths with an overweight American wearing civvies. Unlike us tough guys who strained to suck ours in, he was not self-conscious at all about his gut hanging over his belt.

'G'day, mate,' I said. 'How you going?'

'Good, thank you, sir.' There was an awkward pause before he said, 'Are you one of the Aussie SAS guys?'

'Yeah, mate.' I offered my hand. 'Harry.'

'John. I'm here with the HUMINT team,' he said as he returned my handshake. HUMINT was an abbreviation for 'human intelligence', or what ordinary people might call spying.

'CIA?' I asked.

'Allegedly!'

I didn't know quite what to say, so I took out another cigarette and offered it to him. He declined but pulled a half-smoked cigar out of his breast pocket. I gave him a light and we contemplated the mountains.

'What a great sunset, eh?' I said.

'Yeah. Pity it's in such a shithole.'

'I don't know, it's a pretty spectacular place, don't you think? The mountains, the valleys and most of the people seem nice.' I was still fresh and seeing the best in everything.

'Only because we've got money and food,' John said. 'There is a whole bunch of real assholes out there. And not all of them are TB [Taliban] or AQ. They wish we would just fuck off. And we will in time. They will win eventually. They have seen the likes of us come and go before, and they know we will eventually go.'

'So you don't reckon we're going to win?'

John let out a guffaw and laughed for longer than seemed necessary. 'No, sir, no fucking way, there is no winning in this place. They are all over us like shit on a stick, Harry. They kill a few of us and then blend back into the locals. There is only one way that we are ever going to have any effect here, or "win".' His fingers motioned the quotation marks. 'And that is if we take the gloves off!'

'What do you mean?' I asked, feeling myself slipping into a scene from *Apocalypse Now*.

'We need to bomb the whole fucking place. You see this valley, it's crawling with TB and AQ. They come in from over the border and use this valley to get down south. We've got a snowflake's chance in hell of changing anyone's mind up here. Being here we are only pissing them off. No, unless we get ruthless, man, we are the ones who are gonna go home having achieved nothing except a bunch of dead buddies.'

John took a puff on his cigar and turned to look me squarely in the face.

'Dead "mates", you might call them.'

He pulled a hipflask out of his trousers, took a belt and offered it to me.

'May as well make the most of the sunset, eh?'

I took a swig and recoiled a little at the strength of the booze, but smiled in polite appreciation. We continued to smoke and scan in silence. There was a mounted M60 at a post beside us, silhouetted by the kaleidoscopic light. Somehow it made a spectacular picture, so I took out my camera and snapped a photo.

'Yeah, bomb the whole fucking place,' John said, continuing his thought. 'But that ain't gonna happen.' He took another belt of his drink and wiped his mouth. 'Because us westerners are just a bunch of pussies. Unless we can take the gloves off, this war ain't never gonna end, Harry.' He spoke as if the entire decision of the conduct of the war, winning or losing, now rested in my hands. 'You see, the more we hurt them the harder they get. The more they hurt us, the weaker we get, the more we infight and divide. They don't care if they die or live, and that is the difference, Harry. For them dying is true glory, and for us it is not. There is glory and honour for them in fighting us. Our humanitarians and lawyers are killing us! We just worry about policy, ROE [Rules of Engagement] and bullshit like that. The enemy have none of that holding them down. All that body armour and heavy shit you guys hump around, well there is a whole bunch of policy that keeps us down in the same way. They fight in dishdash and have no policy or rules.'

Emboldened by the drink and this amazing scene we were in, I ventured to challenge him. 'Why are you here then, John? I mean, if you don't believe in the fight?'

He shrugged. 'Mostly money, and the stories are gonna be heaps more interesting when I am an old man rather than sitting in an office back in the US. You know, the CIA is mostly bullshit. There are only a few of us who really do the yards. The rest of them are all pussies, sitting in an office and then pretending whenever they go out with family and friends. The hierarchy is the worst, no different to the military. Truth is, Harry, the CIA generally fucks up more shit than it helps. Hey, look at this place!'

I didn't know if John was directing my attention to the fucked-up situation or the incredible sunset. I chose to contemplate the latter.

———

In such an existence, with anything from death or a scene of out-and-out weirdness waiting around the next corner, it was important to know how to switch off and relax. Even for me, in my early thirties, happily married with a wife and two young children back in Perth, my state of mind could be rattled by the sheer unpredictability of events, not to mention the physical and logistical difficulties of living in a Spartan military camp in Afghanistan.

Having had no chance for a shower when we were outside the wire, I was keen to have one on our first night back at Bagram. Showers were a rarity on that trip, indeed they were rare in the field full-stop. (I've had mates whose wives would not let them in the family home after returning from long field exercises until they'd found somewhere to shower; once, when I took my pants off after six weeks without a shower, they literally stood up by themselves!) It was coming into winter, when the cold was as extreme as the heat had been in summer. The temperature and humidity were too low even for snow, and hot water was hard to come by. Plastic jerry cans full of icy water were placed next to the electricity generators to heat up. Some generators were three-deep in jerry cans. I went out and removed the can closest to the generator before sliding the next ones in closer. The shower felt like the best I'd ever had.

Back in our workshop, I joined Hawkeye and two other patrol mates, Pigpen and Junior, who were cleaning our machine gun and tinkering. I sat down to join them. Tinkering is one of the great pleasures of the SAS operator. Any time, any generation, anywhere, you are guaranteed to see them retaping, sewing, moving pouches, practising drawing a pistol from a new holster, or fiddling with their kit.

Hawkeye had not come out on the last mission because he had been sick with diarrhoea and vomiting, which meant he had to be isolated very quickly. He was feeling better now, and, as always, I was glad to see him. We were listening to US Radio coming to the end of a bulletin about how the Americans were making great inroads against Al-Qaeda on the border and how confident the hierarchy were that they were homing in on Usama Bin Laden (UBL) and his lieutenants.

'General Rupert [I think that was his name, but I might have misheard] is confident that the US Special Forces are hot on the trail of UBL and are successfully significantly disrupting AQ's ability to fight,' the radio voice prattled on before quoting the general, who said, 'I believe we are close to a position where we will defeat UBL and AQ, and this will only make Afghanistan a stronger country in the long run.'

I reached to turn it off and said, 'What a load of bullshit.'

Hawkeye replied: 'Come on, Harry, you've seen what these Al-Qaeda pricks have been doing. Cutting innocent people's heads off, and most of the AQ arseholes aren't even from Afghanistan. They won't stop until they are in charge or dead, and I know which one I wish upon them. I hope Allah has mercy on them, 'cos I won't.' He might have been channelling CIA John when he got into this mood.

'Mate,' I said, 'the Poms couldn't do it, the Russians couldn't do it and I don't know what drugs the Yanks are on that makes them think they will do it. Look how hard these little fuckers are—tough as old rope. They get around in a dishdash, a chest rig and a gun, while we crawl around with sixty-kilo packs and body armour. Who are the dumb ones?'

This was the cue for Jim 'Junior' Hardy to put in his two cents' worth. The youngest and best-looking of our team, Junior almost always ended up carrying the heavy loads and the machine gun. He was generally quiet, a little naïve, and self-conscious, but in the right mood he was unafraid to challenge the older blokes. He had resolve, loyalty and discipline. The team loved him and pushed him out in front as our best face whenever there were females about. He looked up to the Chief and would follow him to hell itself. Junior's political persuasions were unformed at this stage, but at times he was equally keen to challenge either Hawkeye or me.

'Isn't all this just Muslims fighting Muslims?' Junior asked. 'We're just a side project. I agree we should just send as many of the extremists as we can to Allah and let him sort 'em out.'

'The problem with that,' I said, 'is that it only makes them harder and more resilient, and probably turns the good ones against us. We are getting softer and they are getting harder. Their mycelium network,' I darted my eyes to see if they had suspicions about whether I knew what I meant, 'is spreading to all parts. It is why we are going to lose this war eventually.'

Hawkeye snorted. 'That's a "word-watch" fine for you, Harry, you and your fucken big words. You're so full of shit, you don't even know what half of them mean . . . mycelium? Sometimes I'm not so sure you're cut out to be a soldier, mate, you pinko leftie. Go hug a tree, I'm going to call the trouble and lids.'

I watched him go. Hawkeye and I had grown close in a short time, and we still are. He was our patrol scout, tasked with the dangerous business of going out ahead and testing the ground for our progress. The place was strewn with unexploded bombs and booby traps. He was also a sniper. Even though his politics were further to the right than mine, I sometimes envied his clarity. It seemed to make life easier. He agreed with General George Patton's opinion that 'the object of war is not to die for your country but to make the other bastard die for his'. Hawkeye wasn't without kindness for the underprivileged. He came from the country, and, like me, had a wife and two kids at home. Our wives were, and remain, close friends. We talked about all sorts of things: Hawkeye loved antiquity and the ancient world, but equally he loved talking about the stock market and commodity prices, especially gold and silver, which he traded successfully. He'd made a fair bit of money but was a renowned tight-arse in the unit. The most common line you would hear from Hawkeye was: 'That one cost you two bucks? This one was free, mate!' Just like Darryl Kerrigan in *The Castle*, he responded to many an offer with, 'Tell him he's dreamin'.'

For all his wealth, Hawkeye looked like a hobo, only wearing issued, borrowed or second-hand clothes. 'If you don't shop army,' he liked to say, 'you're paying too much.' But he was an excellent

professional soldier with unmatched martial acumen, endless energy
and concentration, and he longed to build his perfect home in the
country where he could shoot local fauna from his veranda. For
Hawkeye, the war and combat defined him. I wondered how he
would adjust to life after this.

No—I wondered how any of us could.

————

One of the benefits of being back at Bagram was the ability to make
a phone call to our families in Australia. Hawkeye had wandered
out of the workshop, through a tent containing water, ration packs
and other patrol supplies, to the phone area to wait for one of several
old-fashioned landline telephones outside the accommodation huts,
where the soldiers sat in the dirt or on sandbags talking to their
wives. The only concession to privacy was that the phones had
exceptionally long cords, so you could get more or less out of earshot.

Because of the time difference and the desire of soldiers to talk
to their kids at bedtime, the peak phone call period was afternoon,
Afghan time. A queue soon formed around the phones. Due to the
numbers of people waiting for their turn, privacy was compromised.
Young couples having a sexy call were often relayed and broadcast,
not only by those loitering in line but by switchboard staff monitoring the calls. Worst of all were the blokes who may or may not
have had a drink before getting on the phone to their wives. The
very last thing a wife, who might have had a tough day at work and
home, needed to hear was her soldier husband sounding cheerful
and possibly inebriated. Arguments broke out more often than you

would expect. Many were the times you could hear embarrassed men trying to calm wives who were overwhelmed at home. To add another complication, rumours of guys who had been 'playing up' soon got around in the tight SAS community back home. If these rumours—which were almost always untrue—reached the wife while the husband was in Afghanistan, there were more embarrassing scenes.

'Sydney' Bill Duckham was particularly prone to these upsetting calls. He always came back from conversations with his wife looking like he'd been shrunken by the heat of her anger. We felt sorry for him, because he was one of the people who really had done nothing to deserve it.

After he left us in the workshop, Hawkeye settled in to wait for his turn to call, squatting in the dirt and leaning against the wire of the compound's retaining walls. He could clearly hear Sydney just around the corner copping an earful from his wife. 'You haven't rung in three weeks! . . . Where have you been? . . . You fucken arsehole! . . . Over there enjoying yourself while I'm stuck here! . . . I know there are women over there! . . . You're on the piss all the time! . . . You don't care about me or the kids! . . . I'm gonna fuck off and take everything!!'

This wasn't an empty threat. We all knew of blokes returning to an empty house. According to Hawkeye, poor Sydney was just taking it, responding politely and with grace.

'I am sorry you feel that way . . . I am not enjoying myself like that . . . I haven't rung because I've been out on patrol for twenty days . . . There are no women here . . . I am just here with the blokes . . . Look, I have to go.' As he hung up, his wife could still be heard: 'Yeah, that's right, just fuck off, I won't be here when you get back and neither will the kids!'

He got up out of the dirt, lit a cigarette and walked past Hawkeye. He winked, shot him a big cheesy smile and said, 'Women, eh. Can't live with 'em, can't live with 'em!'

When Hawkeye got through to his wife, he said gently, 'Hi, love, how have you been?'

'Not too bad, but the kids are playing up.' Crying and screaming kids could be heard in the background. For Hawkeye, fighting AQ fanatics had just become the furthest thing from his mind.

―――

The younger single guys had better ways of protecting their privacy. The Americans were setting up an internet connection on the base—this was only a handful of years after the internet arrived—and Junior got extremely excited when he heard it was ready.

I followed him across to the far side of the phones, near the hut for the signallers, or communication providers, who were known as 'chooks' ever since Vietnam, when their Morse code tapping was likened to chickens pecking—although another explanation for the nickname was that in Vietnam their communications post was in a chicken coop. A tent was set aside, with three terminals partitioned from each other by scrim curtains.

'Wow, little wank booths,' I said, drawing on my vast experience of what the internet was used for. 'Better make sure there's a good supply of tissues.'

All sorts of strange stress-relief activities were going on. We even made the odd replica 'Wanking Machine' for a bit of fun, made legendary by the Australian film about the Vietnam War, *The Odd Angry Shot*. The Wanking Machine is a shoebox with a hole at one end, filled with feathers that can be rotated to tickle the male member. As a devotee of that film, I would create a number of Wanking Machines over the years to present to distinguished persons, including Major General Jim Molan, who received it in good humour.

When I suggested that masturbation was the purpose of the internet, Junior looked insulted. Being younger, he had apparently discovered more uses for the web.

'You're an old fart, Harry. The internet means you can talk to the wife, friends and family by email, check the footy scores and do your banking.'

'Yeah, sure thing, Junior, rhymes with wanking. Here, show me how to set up a new email address, mate, and keep your hand off my thigh!'

———

With the dangers outside the wire and the unusual stresses inside, we all had to find our own ways to release the pressure. You could lose your head out on a patrol, or you could lose your mind in the base. Either way, this combat life was a long way from healthy.

For stress relief, one of the other SAS troops on this deployment adopted a monkey they bought from a local market. Attached by a chain, their monkey accompanied them on a long-range vehicle patrol, roaming over their car. They grew very attached to him until he bit 'One-Up' Burnside, the operator who cared for and loved him for all those weeks. ('One-Up' was so called because he was always one-upping everyone else: whatever they had done, he'd done better. He was also nicknamed 'Elevenerife', as in, if you'd been to Tenerife, he'd been to Elevenerife.) A doctor found out the monkey had bitten and scratched a few of the team, so there was a chance of rabies. The crew were pretty unhappy when their monkey was taken from them and flown to Germany for testing. One day at Bagram, One-Up was told that there was good news and bad news about the monkey.

'What's the good news?' One-Up asked.

'He's been cleared of all disease.'

'Great, when's he due back here?'

'Er, that's the bad news. They had to cut off his head to test his brain.'

The story spread quickly as an example of military 'intelligence'.

Without a monkey to distract us, our team relied on cricket. Back home, ever since I'd been a kid, my place to turn for stress relief had been the great game. I don't mean competitive cricket for clubs or schools, the formal eleven-a-side game with proper equipment and rules. I mean spontaneous backyard cricket. When I was growing up, my father, my two younger brothers and I would break out a game of cricket anywhere and everywhere. If it wasn't in our backyard, it was inside the hallway or the lounge room with a nerf ball and a plastic bat. At the dinner table, we improvised cricket games with a ruler for a bat and a crumpled-up piece of paper for a ball, and the fielders sat on either side of the table. We always had a bat and a ball in the car with us, and if we had to stop anywhere for five minutes, that was time enough to set up a game.

The great thing about this classic cricket upbringing was the social side. My father was in the military, which meant we did a lot of moving around to new houses with new neighbours in unfamiliar parts of Australia. Street and backyard cricket were our ways of making new friends. The beauty of street cricket is that if you bring out a bat and ball, regardless of skill or sex, it's easy for anyone to join in. Street games attract kids, simple as that. You start a game, and shy kids don't need to ask, they just join in, and soon you're offering them a turn to bat. From then on, they're 'in'. Mandatory street cricket rules like 'can't get out first ball' and 'one hand, one bounce' catches build empathy for weaker players, as do conventions that make sure everyone gets a bat in a certain order, nobody misses out and nobody hogs the strike.

When I first arrived in Afghanistan in 2002, we played a few games at the Bagram Air Base, among the workshops and air strips inside the wire. A first bat, which we had liberated from an air base, had gone missing on a trip when we went out to Asadabad to assist the US Special Operations Forces. Upon arriving there, it became apparent that we weren't going to be doing as many foot patrols as we were originally asked to provide. Our job was going to be overnight patrols, dropping in and out, with most of our time spent on the base going quietly nuts. That was my trigger to act.

We had an interpreter at the compound who went by the universal name of 'John'. He was a ripping bloke and we all liked him. Joe 'Rowdy' Sloan and I got John talking cricket, which he loved, and one day Rowdy asked him, 'Hey, John, is there any chance you can get us a cricket bat?'

John wobbled his head as if to mean no, or yes. 'The only place you can get a cricket bat is across the border in Pakistan. But that is not going to be easy. You've got to imagine, this is over into the federated states of the north-west. It's the most dangerous area on the planet right now.'

I didn't take this literally as a negative, but as a starting point of negotiations. Anything could be done for a price. My mates and I cobbled together US$100, which was a lot of money in Afghan currency. I paid John and he vanished. For the next three days, when he didn't reappear, we thought, 'That's the end of that. The prick's liberated our money from us.' Either that or he had been caught by the bad guys, who might have chosen to 'liberate' his head from his body.

John had received a fair amount of badmouthing by the time he resurfaced—with a rolled-up carpet, which he proudly presented to us.

'Nice carpet, John,' one of the boys said.

John proceeded to unfurl the carpet and pull out an object that was a cricket bat, no doubt about that. A most unusual-looking sun-damaged, warped implement, it had obviously been sitting in a shop window somewhere in Pakistan since 1996. It was a standard no-name cheap bat with an enormous sticker on the face, covering more than half the blade. The sticker was faded back then and hasn't changed much since. In different shades of sun-damaged blue, this sticker had the photo and name of the Pakistani cricketer Shahid Afridi, with the slogan '37 Ball 100'. On the back of the bat was another sticker showing Afridi, this time wearing a pair of aviator sunglasses.

Afridi was one of the more interesting characters in international cricket. His nickname was 'Boom Boom' for his big hitting. As a twenty-one-year-old, he made his debut for Pakistan against Sri Lanka in a one-day tournament in Kenya in 1996. In his very first innings for his country, he broke the world record for the fastest-ever century in a 50-over international, blitzing 100 runs off 37 balls. Today, nearly twenty-five years later, it is still the third-fastest century ever. It was the cricket equivalent of breaking 10 seconds for the 100-metre sprint—and Afridi did it in his first-ever innings for his country. He also equalled the world record for the most sixes in an innings that day, hitting the ball out of the park eleven times.

In the six years between then and my receiving this bat—and in the further thirteen years he represented Pakistan—Afridi's batting career never reached those heights again, though he did play in a winning team in a Twenty20 World Cup final and he even captained Pakistan from 2009 to 2011. He was a more than useful bowler, an eccentric 'fast leg-spinner', probably the most difficult bowling style of all, which only emphasised his natural talent. But he managed to get mixed up in all sorts of controversies through the years. The one I remember best is when he was caught changing the condition of a cricket ball—the illegal practice of 'ball tampering'—by putting it in his mouth and sinking his teeth into the leather. The problem was that the whole world saw him doing it on TV. Maybe he needed some work on his situational awareness. He was an appropriately unique cricketer for this unique bat.

'I've risked my life to get this bat for you,' John explained. He said he had crossed the border into Pakistan, passing through an area where cricket, along with anything western (photos, music and so on) had been banned by the Taliban. Afghan interpreters working for the US, such as John, were prized targets for the Taliban and AQ, and he had gone into their stronghold—the Federally Administered Tribal Area (FATA) of Pakistan, the most militant and extreme area in the region and the epicentre of Taliban and AQ support. US forces were conducting raids into this area but had not been able to establish a strong presence, as the terrain was very harsh and support for extreme Islam ran deep. Westerners, and our supporters, were in constant danger in that area, which was only a short distance from our Asadabad base. As cricket was frowned upon as a western entertainment, John had bought the rug to conceal the bat inside.

Having badmouthed him for three days, we now had a full appreciation of John's courage. We told him, 'Keep the carpet yourself, and the ten bucks fifty change too.' Given the job he did, a few extra dollars were the very least we could contribute.

We played cricket for hours in that base. The terrain lay in two steps, and we chose the lower one for our field. It measured about 40 by 20 metres. On one side were parked cars, and on the opposite side were rooms built up against the mud walls, which included the 'cookhouse' and an open area where the locals prepared their food, which was very tasty but a bit iffy hygiene-wise. On a third side were gardens and farm animals. There were toilets in the corners of the compound, from which the Afghanis collected human faeces to fertilise their crops.

In my capacity as curator, I stepped out a pitch thirteen large paces long and placed rubbish bins at each end. The ground was all dirt, so we swept the pitch on a good length to make it as even as we could. The ball still tended to jump around a bit. John had also brought back some rubber balls in a tube made of the mesh that oranges come in. On the question of ball maintenance, some guys wanted to tape it on one side to make it swing, but Rowdy and I, the cricket purists in the patrol, indeed in the entire regiment, ruled that the ball must be untaped.

Our routine was to play cricket in the late afternoon. Stand-to in the base was at 4.30 a.m., which historically was the most likely time for an attack. Sometimes you had been up during the night on piquet duty, for which shifts were two hours long, staggered to overlap with each other. After the high-alert period early in the morning, we received intelligence briefings from the night's activities and then conducted preparations for missions that sometimes eventuated but more often did not. By lunchtime it was very hot, and we would eat and sleep before getting up for afternoon downtime. That's when we played, in that lovely time of day when the shadows were lengthening, the sun was setting, and you could take the game into the evening.

Our team comprised our six patrol members: the Chief, Rowdy, Junior, Pigpen, Slick and me. The odd American would join the game, but very soon the Afghanis were drawn in, at first watching, then cheering, and inevitably picking up the bat or ball. At long-on was the cookhouse, with men working the pans and ovens making food for the locals and the Australians (the Americans stuck to their own food). In a highlight of that season, Rowdy drove the ball over long-on into the cookhouse, and we heard the pots and pans flying everywhere, closely followed by what sounded like Pashto expletives and then a burst of uproarious laughter from all of us, Australians and Afghanis, a joyous sound you *never* heard except during games of cricket.

The cookhouse guys turned out to be handy bowlers who could drop the ball onto a length. Some were useful with the bat, too. One of them, deadly serious, wanted to show us how much he loved his cricket. He marked out an exceptionally long run-up, pushed off the cookhouse and steamed in at Rowdy, letting rip a first-ball bouncer. Rowdy played an unconvincing pull shot that lobbed safely into a gap, and the cookhouse guy, encouraged, kept charging in off his long run, bowling Rowdy the odd bit of chin music.

John the interpreter was also a pretty good right-arm leg-spinner, dangerous on the unpredictable wicket. One memorable afternoon, he pitched a ball a metre outside Rowdy's off stump. Rowdy went for the big hit, but the ball jagged back in. The huge wrong'un clean-bowled him. Rowdy (who was never out, according to him) claimed it had hit a rock, though when we looked around the very clear mark the ball had made in the dirt, the culprit rock was hard to locate. 'I couldn't use me feet to get to the ball and smother the spin,' Rowdy went on with a new excuse. None of this gave us much confidence in Rowdy's self-declared 42.75 career batting average 'in all forms of the game', a figure proudly displayed next to his signature on the bat.

I hadn't realised how much happiness cricket would bring me and the other Australians. The Yanks were not really interested in dealing with the locals, all of whom they saw as potential assassins.

At one of the bases, where captured Al-Qaeda fighters were kept in makeshift cells next to the gym and spent their time whining and grizzling, the Americans went over to bang on their walls and tell them to shut the fuck up. The Americans had lost many soldiers to 'green-on-blue' incidents and were naturally sceptical of the locals, a frame of mind that, over the next ten years, would spread to us.

Back in the comparatively naïve days of 2002, however, we took the locals at face value and came with the attitude of innocent unless proven guilty. The Afghanis working in the compound were just Afghanis, not suspects. We played cricket for cricket's sake, and they joined in. There was always a lot of laughter when we and the Afghanis managed to take each other's wickets. It's hard to imagine what people outside the camp were thinking when they heard this yahooing. The Taliban had squashed not just sport, but the spirit of elation. In those games, laughter and joy were a momentary release from everything else around us, and from years of oppression in Afghan lives.

But that didn't mean cricket was a holiday from the war. All too often, when we were playing a game, a volley of rocket-propelled grenades (RPGs) would whizz over the top of the camp, putting paid to our match. The shower of bombs gave a new meaning to the phrase 'Rain stopped play'.

———

I became determined to take the Shahid Afridi bat on our next trip outside the wire. Any game of cricket, no matter where it was, felt like a little ideological battle we could win over the Taliban. One day at Bagram, we were following the Chief to a briefing for our next job. We carried our guns, pistols on our hips, and wore caps, T-shirts and shorts: usual relaxation attire for SAS operators, but out of whack with the more conventional army expectations of full uniform and body armour. But it was more than 40 degrees Celsius, and we had found that our chances of being hit by a mortar attack while in the Bagram base were unlikely to be affected by what we were wearing.

We chatted about the upcoming task.

'The Yanks are getting mortared every night down in Gardez,' the Chief said, 'so I think they want us to go down there to get up in the hills and look for the bad guys who are hitting them.'

'Yeah,' Hawkeye laughed, 'and deliver a few packages!' This was the lingo snipers used for taking out enemies. If a sniper had eliminated a threat, he might announce, 'Package delivered.'

'You're the postman, Hawkeye,' Slick said.

'We'll take down the sniper kit,' said the Chief, remaining on task, 'so have it ready, mate. And Harry, you better bring the cricket bat and ball—we might be there a while.'

'Ack that, mate,' I agreed.

We arrived at the combined HQ briefing room, staffed by Australian, US and British officers. The Chief had a gift for identifying an easily offended senior officer anywhere. He began: 'Hey, mate, we're looking for the ops centre briefing room.'

'And who are you?'

'I'm the Chief, and this is Slick, Hawkeye, Harry, Pigpen and Junior. Special Air Service Regiment Patrol Whiskey-1.'

'Well, I don't think they will see you dressed like that. You'd better go and do a better job of it, soldier, before you come in here.'

'Our uniforms are all being washed, mate,' the Chief said, 'because we just spent twenty days outside the wire while you were sitting in here sipping Gloria Jean's lattes.'

'You'd better drop the attitude, soldier,' said the officer, puffing up red in the face, 'before I have you disciplined.'

We were all smirking at each other as the Chief, normally very measured, snarled: 'Disciplined? Fucking disciplined? Has anyone told you we are fighting a war here, mate?'

'You special forces rock stars are all the same,' the officer said, flustered but sticking at his task. 'You go outside the wire and think your shit doesn't stink. You keep that lip up and I will have you charged, soldier.'

While the rest of us were laughing, I could see Hawkeye was working up his own outrage. He stepped up alongside the Chief, who, sensing Hawkeye was about to unleash one of his famous movie quotes upon the officer—'Well, you better make it murder, because I'm gonna knock your fucking head right off' (from the *Odd Angry Shot*)—physically restrained Hawkeye.

As the Chief did so, the ops room door opened and an American officer poked his head out.

'What is going on out here? I am trying to run a fucking war. Are you the SAS team?'

'Yes,' the Chief said in a small voice.

'You in charge of this lot? You come in and they can stay out here.'

'This "lot" and I come together,' the Chief said. 'We'll all come in for the brief.'

The American officer looked us up and down and understood that the Chief was a serious guy. 'Yeah okay,' he said, backing down. He almost—almost—looked like he was going to apologise. 'You Spec Ops guys always stick together. Come in, I don't have much time.'

As we filed in, Junior leaned towards the first officer and murmured, 'At what point of your careers are you dickheads taught to be arrogant arseholes, eh? It's you who should show some respect to soldiers like the Chief, you bloody idiot.'

We were given a task to travel to an isolated compound the US Special Operations Forces (USSOF) had taken over in Gardez. I smuggled the bat onto the helicopter in my gun bag, which I was now doing frequently. If we were with British crews, the bat would trigger cricket conversations. The American crews were more intrigued, and funnier. An American pilot once said, 'You guys are crazy! What's that thing, do you bash people with that?' He seriously thought I was bringing people to account with my cricket bat, as if it was some type of Indigenous-inspired warrior stick. Truth be told, that bat saw more action outside the wire than half of the ADF.

Gardez was a smaller compound than the one at Asadabad. It lay on one of the many rat lines for trafficking arms, money, people and drugs from Pakistan. Whereas our practice was to use compounds as temporary strongholds and then move on, the Americans had taken over the Gardez compound for months that would turn into years.

We were inserted at night by a 160th (USSOF air support unit) Chinook on one of the many roads radiating to the south of Gardez. The 160th 'Chook', in particular, was cool as cat shit, with its windows taken out, heavy machine guns, the pilots and crew all tooled up. Chinooks were built to fly low and fast, and often hit the treetops as they came in. They were up-armoured to withstand ground fire both in the body and the rotors. They are an amazing aircraft, so versatile they are also used as battlefield surgeries, and remain among the most highly regarded military flying machines on the planet. We swept in, landing on a road outside the Forward Operating Base in the middle of the night.

In those early days, Gardez was a typical SOF hangout. Bearded men in thongs and T-shirts spent the afternoons working out and listening to Nirvana and Stone Temple Pilots. The scene was quintessentially American—big pickup trucks with the tailgates down, a barbecue being sparked up, and operators throwing an NFL ball. On this mission, we bumped into a Navy SEAL who was sporting a T-shirt of The Externals, a band I had been in since the 1990s. He was a big fan and appeared stoked to meet me. He played a few tunes off our album *Sale*, just to cement how genuine he was. I had to travel to one of the most dangerous places on the planet to get some flattering feedback about our little rock band.

The typical Afghan mud-walled compound sat just outside the town of Gardez, which was run by men who were unsympathetic to our cause. Isolated on the stony plain, the compound came under repeated heavy attack from rockets, heavy machine guns and small arms. Some of the rockets landed in the cemetery next door, where the blasts would expose human bones to the dogs of war who would wander in, dig about and take the bones off to chew. These dogs wandered the battlefields in search of human bones and remains, as they had done since Homer's time.

Our job was to get out at night into the mountains surrounding the town to search for and disrupt the enemy teams launching these attacks. Over time it worked, but it was tough going. The US forces rarely left the base unless there was a big chance of getting a bad guy.

On one mission, we were heading out on an ambush task. We did our briefings during the day and loaded up in a 4WD for a four-hour drive, in a convoy of about ten cars carrying thirty people, plus some Afghan cars with local soldiers and interpreters, as was required by the Afghan government. The mission was to drive to a valley, park the cars and walk over a mountain into the next valley through which the suspect was anticipated to be travelling first thing the next morning.

As we were loading our large packs into the back of the 4WDs, a US SEAL said to me, 'Man, you guys are carrying too much shit.' He placed a daypack and a gun, a fraction of our personal cargo, into his car. Knowing that we would be overnighting above the snow line, I mumbled something I'd learned in my early days in the SAS: 'A fool and his sleeping bag are soon parted.'

We drove off-road (which has an altogether different meaning in Afghanistan from Australia), and lost a couple of cars to break-downs before we arrived at the base of the mountain. From there, it was a three-hour trek into the opposite valley, where we were to set the ambush.

At the insertion point, we each loaded up with our 40-kilogram packs filled with warm kit, medical stores, comms equipment, cooking stuff, extra ammunition, water, food, guns and explosives, plus a .50-calibre rifle (range 1000 metres) and a MAG58 machine gun (range 1500 metres). This trek would take us from around

2700 metres up through 3300 metres, above the snow line, and down to around 3000 metres on the other side. Timelines were tight, but being pack-fit from hours on the Ghani Stair-Master, we got into an early groove. The US guys couldn't keep up. As we peaked the summit, one of our blokes from another team, Scarface, carried not only one of the US soldiers' backpacks but also his M60 machine gun. The Afghan soldiers took nothing, and fairly scampered up to the top. When we got there, they were curled up on the rocks—above the snow line!—catching some zeds. They were tough bastards, wearing something similar to a pair of Julius Marlows for shoes, no socks, their standard dishdash with a couple of woollen blankets. It must have been minus 5 to 10 degrees Celsius, out of the wind. I remember this as the coldest night of my life—and I have had some cold ones high above the snow line. *That's exactly why we won't win anything here in this war—they're too tough for us.* CIA John's voice echoed in my head as I looked across the ridgeline at our Afghan guys peacefully snoozing. Here they were, resilient, tough as fuck, curled up in the snow, while we were carrying ridiculous amounts of kit, suffering from the cold and far from our comforts of internet and chocolate bars.

We eventually dragged everyone up the mountain and down the other side. We all lay on the ground a few hundred metres from the road that the target was apparently going to drive along, on some high ground with clear fields of fire. We Australians, as soon as we were in position in pairs, took turns at getting out of our sweaty clothes into some dry heavyweight warm clothing. I even had my sleeping bag ready to climb into, as we were on the windward side of the ambush and it was blowing well below zero.

The plan was that one of our blokes would disable the target's car with his .50-calibre rifle, using an anti-materiel round to compromise the engine block, and then a team would assault forward to kill or capture the bad guy, with the rest of us providing covering fire, as we expected his security detail to come out firing at us. Within minutes of the ambush being set, however, one of the US members became hypothermic. The medic assessed his condition as severe. Just then, a car fitting the description we were waiting for entered the valley. It stopped, turned around and left. The Afghan soldiers said it was likely some locals knew we were here and warned the target off.

So it was now—big anti-climax—an extraction mission. I took two men back over the ridgeline and mountain to where we had parked, retrieved the vehicles and drove for two hours to get around to the pick-up point, which was now in the middle of the proposed ambush site. By the time we arrived it was about 8 a.m. and warming up. I had been awake for nearly twenty-eight hours straight, driving for four hours through some of the gnarliest country Afghanistan has to offer, then three hours on the stairmaster, and now driving due east into a baking Afghan sun, to extract a guy with hypothermia after a cancelled mission.

Leaving aside the brutal bumps and crashes as I forced the car across the valley floor and onto the road proper, every few seconds I was dozing off, overwhelmed with exhaustion, the adrenaline having drained out of me with the cancellation of the mission. I can't remember ever being so tired, unable to keep playing the mental games I needed to play to stay awake. I felt like I was asleep more than awake for the last thirty minutes of the drive, only woken up when the car scraped or hit yet another large rock. We arrived at the pick-up point, where the American was stable but still needing extraction. Our team had set up a little camp and were making a brew on the hexamine stove while warming up old mate. Hawkeye handed me a cup of shitty ration-pack coffee, which I welcomed, and a cigarette.

'Fuck, Harry, you look terrible. So no change to the usual, eh!' He laughed.

'Get fucked.'

'Here you go, mate, well done, we've had a kip while we were waiting for you, so one of us will drive back. Fucked if I know how we'll go. Broad daylight through the bad lands, the ambushers are gonna be the ambushed for sure . . . Plus, old mate there,' he said, indicating the hypothermic American, 'he was sitting right beside me in the ambush. I wish he'd told me he was cold—I have a spare sleeping bag and hand heaters in my kit!' We burst out laughing. What else could you do?

I slept like a baby all the way back.

—————

The FOB at Gardez saw a few cricket games with the Shahid Afridi bat. Our 'cricket ground' was dirt again, a narrow strip with a row of Toyota Hiluxes fielding on the leg-side and a damaged Humvee on the off-side. There was no room straight, so we played against a wall, which doubled as automatic wicketkeeper. It was more like a driveway game at home.

We also had the odd game outside the wire on this deployment, though this was not without its dangers. We weren't comfortable chasing a cricket ball through mined countryside—that is, when we knew it was mined. After one particularly long day on a vehicle patrol near a place called Ghazni just up the road from Gardez, we set up our cars like a wagon circle in a John Wayne movie. Some locals came out to watch us from their compound. We assumed they were thinking nothing more than, *How unusual, a bunch of white fellas have pulled up in our fields.* Not so! Next morning, they told us we were smack bang in the middle of a field of mines left from the Russian war, some of which were devastating anti-tank mines. Kindly, they offered to show us a way out. I always preferred being on foot, given vehicles' vulnerability to mines and the deadly improvised explosive devices (IEDs) the enemy set up in ambushes, increasingly their favourite means of attack. You got to the point where walking on eggshells was more comfortable than driving over the top of them. Most of us took the attitude of, 'Bugger it, if I lose my foot, I lose my foot.' That was another example of the naïveté we took into that first year of the war. Over the coming decade, we would lose more than the occasional foot or limb to mines and IEDs.

While at Ghazni, we visited the British SAS in their safe house. A close mate of mine, the Chechen, who had been having a few issues with the local food, went straight to the shitter with explosive and aromatic results. Unfortunately, it was just on the other side of a curtain a few feet from where we were eating and drinking. Our eyes were watering. The locals were unfazed, but the Brits fell unusually silent. 'Who wants a game of cricket?' I asked, and found some eager takers, who couldn't get out of there fast enough. The game was a landmark, for being the first legitimate 'driveway' game of the campaign—it took place on the driveway to the house—and for being an international fixture between England and Australia, maybe the first between our countries in this war, definitely, I would argue, the first outside the wire.

Occasionally, we had little breakout games in the middle of nowhere. One process the militaries employed in Afghanistan when going into a new area was called Key Leadership Engagement (KLE), which meant ringing ahead and engaging with the local chieftain, who was usually a criminal living well in a lush compound. Our leadership would go in for a 'shura' to discuss how we could move around inside their area in exchange for protection or supplies. While waiting outside while the shura was taking place, we'd pull out the Shahid Afridi bat and try to strike up a game with the gangster's armed henchmen. Sometimes they were up for it, sometimes not. Innocent as this might sound, once a cricket game had started, it felt like a sanctuary. The game itself defused hostility. It was as if nobody was prepared to compromise the spirit of cricket with any ill-feeling, no matter how minor. Inside our momentary cricket bubble, we felt insulated from the war and threat. The game seemed to relax everyone, including the most surly and hateful among them, and us.

———

The Afridi bat saw more action when we got back to Bagram, where the atmosphere was a little more civilised. Cricket bridged all settings, from the villages way out in the regions to the main base in the capital city. At Bagram, cricket was just one of many distractions. While we were at the air base, the NFL Dallas Cowboys Cheerleaders visited. We drove to the top of the massive line-up of US and Coalition troops who were waiting to get photos and signatures, brazenly picked the Cowgirls up (liberated them) in our six-wheeler long-range patrol vehicle and took them to where our guys were waiting. We had about twenty minutes of photos with the women before returning them to the Americans, who were shaking their fists and shouting by this point. *Typical arrogant Aussie SAS*, I'm sure they thought, but I cherished it as one of our *Odd Angry Shot* moments. The women seemed to enjoy the theatre of it all, especially the celebrations that broke out when they were returned to their countrymen.

During our stay at Bagram, we liberated a few local pushbikes and rode out the front gate to a little Afghan bazaar outside, where we would shop for trinkets and rugs. This became my other passion: rugs! I would collect around twenty over my time, including an extremely valuable one gifted to me in 2011 in appreciation of work I did for some locals in Kabul.

One rare commodity we could get from the dodgy street merchants was alcohol. One time, we had just come back from a two-week patrol and were up for a few bevvies. But our usual source, the Australian postal system, had not delivered. We didn't want any party poopers at HQ to know; there was an official ban on alcohol, but it was an open secret. Because these nights off were so rare, and we had been working so hard, the hierarchy cut us some slack.

After a game of cricket, we jumped on some Chinese-made pushbikes, which we joked were probably the same ones Ho Chi

Minh had used to run the Vietnam insurgency. These bikes were the unsung workhorses of many a war, on both sides, and were commonly used by our foes in Afghanistan to smuggle contraband through crowded areas. One of the bikes we rode that day is now proudly on display in the SAS museum in Perth. We rode down to the front gate to meet with the street vendors, who would sell us a bottle of the dodgiest 'vodka' you could imagine. I am pretty sure the opaque milky liquid inside the (obviously compromised) bottles had Band-Aids, fingernails and pubic hairs floating around in it. After some hard patrolling, we weren't fussy.

We mixed our fuel (and I wouldn't rule out that it contained aviation fuel) with Coke, until it ran out, then lemonade, until it ran out, then Powerade, until it ran out, then powdered Gatorade mixed with water to finish off the night. In the morning, and indeed during the night, we discovered the meaning of 'blind' drunk: the local vodka turned our eyesight cloudy for a while. It was all harmless, noisy, but good fun and a great way to de-stress after tough nights outside the wire.

A crucial source of morale was old-fashioned mail. The internet and email were not yet reliable or ubiquitous, and we had limited time on the phone. So most of our contact with our loved ones was through snail mail. Someone would cry, 'MAIL!', and it would be like Christmas morning. To come home from the field to a bunk with letters and packages lying on it was one of the greatest gifts a soldier could receive from his family. A letter from the kids or my wife, Danielle, would regularly bring a tear to my eye, sometimes a full-on bout of crying. To not receive mail, on the other hand, was like a dagger to the heart. We would share if we had to, and sometimes we would readdress names if a person had not received any. Everyone took great joy in seeing what everyone else had, not least if there was (suspected) alcohol and treats. These all got stacked in one pile, on the principle of 'What is yours is all of ours'.

Then things would go quiet as we got to our letters. I remember looking around the team and seeing everyone reading at the same time. Letters from family—mums, dads, sisters, brothers, kids, cousins, aunties even . . . I would steal a glimpse of welling eyes, a nostalgic paralysis, a sentimental yearning. These were some of the most powerful moments in my life.

Next, as we all came out of our emotional corners, the chatter would start up spontaneously as we shared stories about family and friends. Team members would carefully place their mail, pictures of kids in school uniforms and school merit awards up on the shelf where our meagre treasures were stored. My son, Henry, had sent me a small Bob the Builder figurine, and I placed him over my bed so he was the last thing I looked at every night.

Finally, we would all come back to the moment and explore whatever 'treats' the mail had brought.

The Shahid Afridi bat brought as much morale as anything else we received. When it came time to return home, I decided to bring that bat with me. It had been a good friend. I had two assault bags, each 1200 centimetres long, 500 centimetres wide and 500 centimetres deep, and also a gun case that fit three different types of long guns. I was not a weapons specialist, so I only had one or maybe two guns, which left room for a cricket bat.

At the end of this first deployment, we flew home in an empty Qantas jumbo. We took our bags straight on and there was no check-in. We got the run of the plane: first or business class, a whole row of four seats to lie on in the back, or best of all, a bed made out of twenty pillows on the floor. We ran a raffle for the best seats. (Later in the war, when more ADF personnel were getting on these flights, I caught a couple of officers divvying up the tickets in order of rank, making sure they got better seats than soldiers who had spent six months living in dirt and eating hard rations. You couldn't take your eye off those bloody officers for one minute.) But on that first trip in 2002, when it was just us, it was fun. We played a bit of cricket on the tarmac before being called onto the 747. I had a business seat next to Slick, and we ordered about a dozen non-alcoholic 'near beers' each, pretending they were the real thing, which we were not permitted. We talked about whether this was it, our one and only chance to deploy on operations. Little could we know what the next decade held.

There was a brief quarantine check when we flew into Perth. I'm fairly sure the Shahid Afridi bat was made out of a questionable timber that would be banned in Australia, even if it now has a yellow Australian Quarantine Inspection Service sticker on its handle saying 'Passed by inspection'. I would end up leaving it in a trunk for almost ten years, which I am sure is a long enough quarantine. In those early days of the war, the quarantine and customs officers would greet us by saying, 'You guys are great, don't worry about inspections.' They were more interested in asking about our experiences than checking our kit. I liberated rugs, trinkets, photos, bricks from Usama's cave, all sorts of memorabilia.

But it's the Shahid Afridi cricket bat that takes pride of place.

BAT II

DRIVING GENERAL MOLAN

IRAQ, 2004/05

Living in a palace was not exactly what I expected when I'd joined the army. But there we were, in a plush villa in a quiet leafy Baghdad suburb called Karkh, or 'Riverside', on the west bank of the Tigris. Before we moved in, it was King Hussein of Jordan's holiday home. As far as living conditions were concerned, my second deployment couldn't have been any more different from my first. But then, it was a very different kind of job.

The palace had plenty of room for four Australian SAS operators and our boss for the assignment, Major General Jim Molan. Big kitchen, big-screen TV to watch the cricket, big rooms all round.

Not such a big job, in the scheme of things. 'Big Jim' Molan was the senior Australian officer attached to the Coalition command headquarters in Baghdad a year after President George W. Bush had decided that the war against terror needed to focus on Iraq, not Afghanistan. Something about getting revenge for something Saddam Hussein had done to Bush's dad in the nineties.

I couldn't help feeling cynical about the so-called 'pivot' to Iraq. When the focus of the Coalition's efforts shifted from Afghanistan in early 2003, a lot of us wondered why. We had the Taliban on the run, and every indication was that we were pushing them all the way back to northern Pakistan. Their leaders had no freedom of movement and those who were not killed or imprisoned were scurrying off to hide in Waziristan. Strategically, all that seemed to remain was to get Pakistan's help in boxing them into a very small area. Just when we were on the verge of routing them, the US president decided that the entire Coalition had to go off chasing Saddam Hussein in Iraq. When I left my first deployment in Afghanistan in 2002 we went via Kuwait, where we saw literally thousands of tanks, helicopters and other instruments of war lined up ready to go into Iraq. The Americans were still denying it publicly, going through what now appears was a sham process of trying to obtain United Nations' approval for an invasion on the basis that Saddam was stockpiling 'weapons of mass destruction'.

All but a tiny contingent of Australia's troops were pulled out of hunting down the really dangerous terrorists of Al-Qaeda and the Afghan Taliban, to be redeployed for 'regime change' in Iraq. As many predicted at the time, we would be back in Afghanistan before long, to finish the job against a reorganised and rejuvenated enemy, who arguably had been gifted with two years to rebuild while we were in Iraq.

I was not in Iraq for the military phase of the overthrow of Saddam Hussein in 2003, but I went as part of the team driving General Molan around in late 2004, which turned out to be one of the most dangerous periods to be in Baghdad.

Whatever my ideas about the strategy, I was shedding no tears over Saddam. He was a nasty piece of shit. It was widely known that he and his psychopathic sons Uday and Qusay had wild animals under lock and key at their palace near Baghdad International Airport. I had been through the torture chambers in the palace, where I had liberated a couple of marble tiles (which we now use as cheese platters at home). One day I was out on a balcony having a cigarette and a Coke with a US major, who was describing what the USSOF found when they entered the grounds. Apparently running free were lions, tigers and other wild animals the Americans were required to shoot. The rumours were that Uday Hussein would venture into Baghdad, randomly abduct women, take them back to the palace and rape, torture and murder them before feeding them to the animals. The major was entirely convinced that they had found human remains in the lion and tiger enclosures. We know that the Hussein regime used chemical weapons on civilians, and I was absolutely open to the suggestion that these depraved cretins did indeed carry out such acts. Good riddance to them, and I hope they are burning in Islamic hell.

My mates in that team were Matthew Locke, Jack 'Streaky' Bacon and Dave 'Unreal' O'Neill. Ours wasn't a combat role, but we did have a front-row seat to the unfolding counter-insurgency campaign that was continuing post-Saddam throughout Iraq, some-times, as in a corporate box at the cricket, right behind the bowler's arm. During the day, we would drive the general to the command centre and then sit in the battle update area watching video, maps and other aspects of planning and reporting. With our top-secret clearance, we saw a lot of the top American commanders such as James Mattis and David Petraeus. General Molan was running the Special Ops war at that point and provided the liaison between those actions and the leaders in Washington who gave permission to conduct these most sensitive operations. Almost every night, we were woken up and told to speed the good general across town to the Coalition HQ so that he could make serious decisions about launching Special Operations teams on 'time-sensitive targets' or drop bombs from the Coalition-dominated airspace, where the war was played out with surgical precision. Often he would need to take a conference call with the White House to discuss riskier or more sensitive operations. The targets must have been important enough to justify the risk in CDEs. We used to talk among ourselves about the weight of some of these decisions and their impact on Big Jim.

Our job gave us great insight. When we knew something was about to happen in Sadr City, a known stronghold of the Iraqi resistance, we would go back to our palace, take our cigarettes and scotch and Cokes to the roof, and watch the whole thing go down. Being on the west bank of the Tigris, we had a clear view into eastern Baghdad, where the American and British Special Operations Forces carried out their missions. I remember one cool evening, sitting with our group's 2IC, Sergeant Matt Locke, in our comfy chairs on top of the residence, sipping on our whiskey, watching the latest raid across the Tigris.

'Fuck, I wish that was us,' Lockey said. The Iraq missions being undertaken by the US/UK Joint Task Force were becoming the stuff of legend in SOF units.

'Got to be careful what you wish for.'

'Nah, this is bullshit, mate, sitting here watching others do the real job and us babysitting a general. This is an MP's job, not an SAS job,' he said.

'Yeah well, that's what you get when the politicians and high rankers are addicted to the SAS,' I said, warming to one of my favourite themes. 'We're being over-used, and it's not gunna change any time soon either. Still, I suppose a gig is a gig, eh . . . This is paying for my new house, and my new backyard cricket ground too!'

We watched little-birds and Black Hawk helicopters fly over our heads, cross the Tigris and head north-east towards Sadr City, hugging the rooftops for tactical cover.

'Speaking of cricket, I bet these are about the best seats you've ever had at a "sporting" event, mate?' Lockey said. 'Front row at the war, eh!'

He was right. I had to pinch myself. The Black Hawks appeared to hover no more than a kilometre from us. We saw some sparks and fireworks, before the helos swept back past us and disappeared. There was a faint sound of gunfire. We each lit a cigarette.

'What did George Orwell say about war and sport, Harry?' Lockey laughed.

'You know, you're far too smart to be a water operator,' I said, falling back on a standard subject of SAS sledging, the rivalry between two of our specialties, Water (known for their athleticism and aggression) and Freefall (known more for our unconventional, somewhat eccentric thinking). 'You could have been a good Freefaller,' I added, 'but you'd have to do something about the random nudity.' (Wateries had a penchant for getting their kit off in random situations, often stripping down to their swimmers for no reason in the middle of a drinking session.)

'Nah, you blokes are as soft as a pensioner's turd.'

'Just more compassionate, I reckon, and better looking.'

'Shut up, Harry, and pass me a Heineken.'

'That's what I like about you . . . nothing!'

We laughed, drank, smoked and watched the war.

'Turn up the volume,' Lockey said. 'I can hardly hear it!'

Though it was a strangely comfortable lifestyle we were living, the assignment was interesting in its way and General Molan respected us because we were no-nonsense in getting our jobs done. But sitting on top of a palace drinking scotch and Cokes and watching a war wasn't why I'd joined the SAS.

General Molan was one of the better officer types I worked with. One morning in Baghdad, the four of us and a couple of US colleagues were musing about the meaning of war while sitting around waiting for the general. We talked about the recent spike in suicide bombings, including two the day before across the road at the local bazaar and the Green Zone café, both of which we frequented.

'What the fuck is this all about?' I asked. 'This is just sick religious shit, no matter whether they are Muslims, Christians, Jews, it doesn't matter.'

'It's all about sex, Harry,' said one of the US blokes, borrowing from the newly released *Team America* movie. We laughed, but somehow it seemed close to the truth.

'How so?' Unreal asked.

'Simple, mate. Whether you are a businessman, a king, or a general, it's about your cock, and how big you can swing it: who it attracts, how many partners, and how much power it gives you. Money for the businessman equals potential to fuck. Power for the king equals potential to fuck.'

'What about the generals, then?' I asked, an eye out for General Molan.

We all laughed and agreed that none of us could imagine any general having sex.

Big Jim wasn't too bad for a general. In the car, he would sometimes take a breather and want to talk about matters other than the job. He'd turn to me and ask, 'What about you, Harry? What led to you joining the army? Where are you from?'

———

I think of myself as coming from all over Australia.

My dad joined the navy when he was fifteen years old, and he took our family on his transient life. I was born in Melbourne, just one stop on our endless circuit around the country.

Dad grew up near Chinchilla in Queensland, a few hundred kilometres north-west of Brisbane. He was second-generation Australian, part of a large Moffitt clan of horse riders, roustabouts and farm workers—good honest people, big Queenslanders with big hearts and an equally big legacy of drinking. Many of them are long gone, having drunk themselves to death.

Robert Gregory Moffitt was different. He wanted to escape what he saw as a one-way street towards an early end. At fifteen, inspired by his intellect and great sense of adventure, he said goodbye to his parents, Charlie and Olive, and left outback Queensland for the navy. He had a sister and three brothers, two of whom would follow him into the services.

After completing his apprenticeship as a carpenter, which would lead to a job as a hull technician on naval vessels, Dad was posted to Sydney, where he met Sandy Waight, a nurse. They fell in lust and that was it. Soon after meeting, they moved into a home together in Jannali, in Sydney, where I was conceived. They hurried up and got married when Mum found out she was pregnant. In their wedding photos, her fashionable empire-line dress is fitted at the top but flares under the bust, and can't quite conceal the little bulge that is me. After the wedding, Dad was posted to HMAS *Lonsdale* in Port Melbourne and worked at the Williamstown naval base. He was a shipwright and part-time diver in the navy, and we were living in Footscray in the western suburbs of Melbourne when I was born on 23 March 1968.

It was a sacrifice for Mum to be married to someone who had to up and move every couple of years, though she didn't lack a sense of adventure. She has been the single greatest inspiration and influence in my life: biologically, behaviourally, morally and emotionally. In my mind, she is a giant. When 'Sandy' is mentioned, she is usually associated with one of four words—compassion, determination, liveliness and humanity.

Born in Subiaco in Western Australia to Hilda and Albert Waight, Sandra Joy grew up around the foothills of Perth. Schooled in Catholic colleges, she challenged even the strictest nuns. She loved sports but found school boring, so she quickly moved into an apprenticeship as a tailor. Her family was, and remains, very tight. Her grandparents on Hilda's side, Marie and Ernst, had migrated to Australia from central Europe just prior to World War I. After landing in Fremantle they settled in the south-west, eventually joining the German community around Guildford, which was then a rural area in the outer-eastern foothills of Perth. After living in Europe, Perth must have been a mind-blowing place. Mum's family were humble and hard-working tradespeople, labourers and butchers with whom I have had a lot to do through my life. Shunning the horse-trotting family business, she and her sister Kathy headed for the east coast when Mum was sixteen, an incredibly brave thing for a girl to do in the early 1960s, but she was extremely independent and determined. She got a job as a trainee nurse, where her work ethic and skills as a clinician immediately caught the eye of a renal unit surgeon who hired her on the spot after she opportunistically jumped in to assist during an emergency operation. She spent the next few years working in acute nursing in the renal unit at Prince of Wales Hospital in Sydney, before meeting Dad.

Mum always spoke fondly of family. It was more important than anything to her. When I was older and we were with all of her siblings, Kathy, Maureen and Brian, they would play the piano and other instruments loudly into the night, just like the old days when they were renowned as a Kalamunda version of the Partridge

Family. When I later got into music, with bands of my own, I knew where I'd inherited this love from (I won't call it talent).

Mum later worked in palliative care and nursing homes, specialising in caring for the aged, finding nursing work wherever we moved. We were in awe of her as a human being. She was a capital-W Woman who took pride in contributing financially and working full-time. I never heard her complain about anything nor utter a word against anyone. Dinner was always ready, and if it wasn't on the table because she was working a night shift, it was in the fridge with written instructions. She was super-organised and arranged her shifts around her children's needs. We might miss her for a couple of breakfasts a week at most. She was the most organised human I've ever met and could kick back and have fun as well. She was the life of the party, whether with her peers, older people, or even with my teenaged friends. Everybody loved Sandy; my friends still mention her fondly today.

When I was born our family was living near Williamstown, not on the military base but in normal housing in Droop Street, Footscray. The navy didn't pay well for tradies, so Dad had to take a second job to make ends meet. My younger brothers, Robert and Paul, were born in the next few years, and our lives were pretty humble. You could say that we were poor, but I would never have known it as the house was always full of love, music and friends. Mum would always ensure we were immaculately, if thriftily, dressed for school and other outings. Pride in appearance was a high priority of hers, and something I have carried over. Our maternal grandmother, Hilda, was living with us for a time, and I remember everyone having to take turns in the bath to save on hot water. We moved numerous times between Sydney and Melbourne, from Jannali, Hurstville and Cronulla to Footscray, Hastings and Frankston, which was unsettling of course, but as kids, wherever we could play street cricket, we felt at home.

No sooner had the Moffitts arrived in a new suburb than Dad, Robert, Paul and I would break out a bat and ball on the street. Mum was never far away; I often caught her stealing a smile as she watched on. How happy she seemed when she was with her family.

Even when they were tiny, I used to get my brothers to throw me balls all afternoon so I could hit them around the backyard and over the fence. On one occasion, we decided to play with a real cricket ball, a newly received Christmas present. I smashed it straight through the kitchen window, where it made almost a perfect cricket-ball-sized hole. I blamed it on my brothers of course, even though they could hardly lift a bat.

I remember in Frankston, while I was fielding a ball in the flowerbed, a stack of bricks fell on my left foot, breaking my toe and removing the toenail, which has never grown back. As they dragged me off to the doctor's surgery, I was more worried about one of my brothers taking my turn to bat.

I was a bit of a bossy brother, it's fair to say. I remember once, back in Frankston, having collected a few bags of bottles and cans to return to the milk bar for money, I employed Robert and Paul to assist, for payment of course. On the way, Paul tripped and cut his arm quite badly on a broken soft drink bottle, and it was bleeding heavily. 'That looks pretty bad, Anth,' Robert said, 'we should head home and get Mum to fix him up.' Paul was crying. I summed up the situation, tied a plastic bag around his arm—I had read somewhere that is what you do—and continued to the shop, exchanged the bottles, spent half of the booty on cobbers and footy cards, and returned home with a now very pale younger brother in tow. I explained to Mum that it had happened on the way home, a lie which cost me quite a few more cobbers for my brothers than I had intended. But, as a threesome, we were tight.

When Dad was posted to Perth—which made Mum happier, being close to her family, though she still didn't have her dream of our own house—we moved into a navy suburb and got to know other navy kids and families, mainly via street and backyard cricket. Dad would prepare a pitch on the grass, or we would play on the driveway with 'Shaun Ball', a tennis ball we shaved to obtain swing. Once Robert bowled an express in-swinger (although the rest of us called him a chucker, which riled him up and made him bowl even faster) and I jammed my bat down hard, breaking that same left-foot toe again. The Moffitt brothers quickly became the kings of local street cricket. Some days there would be a dozen or more navy brats running around till all hours, not an adult within coo-ee, before we were called in for baths and dinner. I loved those days and am still very close friends with our neighbours, the Chances and the Blakes, and others from those times.

I was a twelve-year-old when Dad was invited to Garden Island in Sydney for the last tour of the HMAS *Melbourne*, Australia's first aircraft carrier, before it was put into dry dock and, as Dad put it, 'turned into razor blades'. Dad flew me over from Perth to see the decommissioning ceremony. It was the first time I'd seen grown men cry. The men who had worked on the HMAS *Melbourne* for the best years of their lives were now seeing it destroyed, and it broke them up. It moved me deeply to see these hard men so sentimentally attached to a navy ship. In my military career, I would come to know the same pride, and also the same heartache and sadness at seeing my unit being torn apart.

For the return trip to Perth, Dad bought a bargain XC Falcon to replace our family car, an EH Holden, and we drove across the Nullarbor in less than three days. We only stopped once to sleep, at Mundrabilla, just after crossing the border from South Australia into Western Australia. I marvelled at Dad's discipline in keeping on going. I loved hearing him talk about his career in the navy, which included a stint as a ship's diver clearing mines in Vietnam. On that long drive, he told me stories about how the divers tied ropes around each other, went under the boats and cleared the mines by hand in total darkness. Telling these stories, he was suddenly an excited young man again, and I felt privileged to hear him open up with an enthusiasm that lit a fire under my boyish imagination.

After almost thirty years in the navy, Dad moved into private enterprise, operating his own business, opening a fruit and vegie shop while working for BP refinery running one of the plants until he retired at fifty-five. By then, the family had gone through some changes. We'd moved to Rockingham, south of Perth, where Mum finally achieved her dream: a house of their own that they built together.

Not long after, when I was about sixteen, my brothers and I got the shock of our lives. We were mad keen on fishing, and one day our neighbours Joe and Murray took us out on their boat off Rockingham. Dad's nickname was 'Pickles', as people said he'd been pickled by spending so much time out in the salt water. On the boat, Joe and Murray told me that Pickles was moving out from our home. I was very confused. There had been no prior warning or sign of trouble. At the end of the day, I rushed home to be with Mum.

Dad leaving us, and later remarrying, was the first major moral challenge of my life. I had to try to reconcile this version of Dad with my happy memories of him as a good father, a hard worker who looked after all of us and gave us the opportunities that he had not been given.

As a single mother of three teenaged boys, Mum, typically, cracked on without showing us any sign of bitterness. Her pride and joy was her family, and she wouldn't let that be taken from her. If anything, the break-up increased her devotion to us boys. With Mum working hard in a nursing home, I had to step up and take more responsibility to look after my brothers. It helped that Mum was so well organised; I didn't have to do all that much. But to help out with money, I got a night job at a restaurant, where I went whenever Mum didn't have an evening shift.

Over time, I became more aware of the effect that Dad's leaving had on Mum. While she never stopped loving us, her spark had dimmed. She spent a lot of her nights sitting by herself, and there was nothing we could do to cheer her up. She aged quickly. She was still our beloved Mum, but she never recovered her sense of joy.

My parents' separation was the most consequential thing that happened to me growing up, but being entrenched in my own little world, I was equally traumatised at the time by some bullying I copped at school. One year in early high school, I had been selected as one of a small number of children in Western Australia to participate in an accelerated learning program. (I still think they might have got my results mixed up with someone else's!) The program was called the ITP—Intellectually Talented Pupils—and if that doesn't put a big red target on you in high school, nothing will.

I would be walking through the schoolyard when I'd hear, 'Hey, ITP, come over here!' Lunchtimes, PE classes and after school were the worst. I would be eating my immaculately prepared sandwiches—made by Mum with precision and love—and a group of bullies would rock up to start a familiar ritual. They slapped my lunch box out of my hands, often stamping on it and breaking it. The leader took one of the sandwiches, my favourite peanut butter and jam or Vegemite and honey, opened one half, snorted back the biggest golly he could muster from deep in his nasal passage, and spat into it. Then he and the group told me to eat it, or else they were going to bash me. I was much smaller than them, and some were shaving several years before me. In the early days—this was a new school, yet again, after another move—I was so scared, I would eat it. I pretended to do it with relish, just to make them see they couldn't break me. They found this very funny indeed. My obedience, instead of showing defiance as I hoped, only confirmed in their minds how weak I was.

It didn't end at lunch. During PE, they would wait until we were in the change rooms. When I was half changed, they forced me into a shower cubicle and whipped me with a wet towel. The ones who couldn't get their hands on the towel stepped in to kick and punch me. At the bus stop in front of the school, they pushed me around in front of the teachers, who turned a blind eye, which caused me to lose respect for many of them.

During school hours, the bullies demanded that I meet them in a neighbouring quarry after three o'clock. I spent all day afraid and anxious: I knew what was coming, as they kept reminding me. When the bell rang, sometimes I tried to run to my bus to escape them, only to suffer the consequences the following day, or later in the week. Eventually, I decided not to run away, but to front up at the quarry and face them. As it turned out, the quarry was never as bad as the fear leading up to it. They punched, kicked and ridiculed me, but over time, if I turned up to my bashings stoically, they started to lay off me and their other victims throughout the day.

It is not too unreasonable to say that I took the brunt of the bullying on behalf of the ITP group, though a couple of others suffered too. I saw myself as a bit of a protector of the ITP kids, though I resented this at times. I am not proud to confess that I would take out my frustrations on my group. On a bus trip home from Fremantle to Rockingham, I taunted my dear friend Raelene Wherlock until she grew very upset. I have always felt bad about this, and though we laugh about it now, I still feel it was a lowlight in my life, particularly as Raelene had been my first high school romance.

Why was I bullied? I racked my brains, then and in later years. It wasn't just that I was sent off on that 'smart kids' program, though that seemed to trigger it. I was a new kid, moving in with my ever-shifting family, so I didn't have a network of friends to protect or support me. I was a *Star Wars* buff, so maybe that marked me out as a weak nerd, though I was also picked in all the sporting teams, so they might have been irked by that. One of my best mates, Steve Coyle, says I was a bit of a ladies' man, and although I never rated myself highly in that regard, I did get bashed once for speaking to one of the bullies' girlfriends.

Years later, I met one of them playing pool in Perth's Ocean Beach Hotel.

'Tony Moffitt? Didn't we go to school together?'

'Yes, Johnny, we did.'

'Wow, you've really filled out,' he said nervously.

We spoke about schooldays. He remembered what he'd done to me, I could tell.

'So, you're in the SAS now, Tony? Wow, that's pretty cool. Want a beer, mate?'

'Mate' indeed. He bought me beers all night. Not a grudge holder, I forgave him as we played pool, but I never forgot.

The important thing about that whole episode, overlapping with my mum and dad separating, was not the cause but the effect. These setbacks didn't send me into my shell. I refused to buckle. Being bullied made me more resilient, and if it helped develop the hardness that later allowed me to cope with my military experiences, then maybe I should thank my tormentors. Some of them ended up in jail. Looking back forty years later, I can see that they shaped who I am today. As a father myself, I am more forgiving of schoolyard bullies, as I've come to understand that they might be struggling to come to terms with their own weaknesses. It's possible that I wouldn't have taken the paths I later chose, or attained the fortunate life I have now, without that experience of being bullied.

And the first of those significant steps was joining the army.

———

While driving General Molan around Iraq, we worked hard but also looked for an opportunity to uphold the SAS's dual reputation for competence and mischief. It's an unusual cultural hybrid, but necessary when you are switching from combat to more menial duties, as we were on that trip.

During one of my first nights at the palace, I went for a walk around the grounds to familiarise myself. I noticed that one of the buildings was open, with lights on, so I went in.

BOOM! Right in front of me was the biggest rug I had ever seen. On closer inspection, I realised it was of average quality, but at around 20 square metres, weighing more than 50 kilograms, it was a ripper. To add extra appeal, it was almost entirely cricket green. I instantly fantasised about playing a short game on it with my brothers and Dad, with Mum cooking dinner, playing Elvis in the background, content in her dream of a family and a home.

A worker came past to lock up and snapped me back to reality. The building was a one-bedroom holiday apartment, palatial in style, undergoing repairs from war damage. I made my apologies and left.

Sometime in the next few days, we were returning to the palace compound when I noticed that huge green rug beside a pile of rubble. Later that night, I grabbed one of the boys and said, 'I have a mission. We need to liberate a very important artefact. It is a two-man lift.'

When we got to the rubble, we debated whether the material was being thrown out or preserved for the restoration. We agreed that it was being thrown out, and would form part of a body of evidence that could eventually lead to winning the war, not only in Iraq, but against terrorism itself. The liberation of this rug could underpin world peace. It was indeed a two-man lift. I managed to get it sent home via the internal post, putting 'SAS, Campbell Barracks, Swanbourne, WA 6010', care of a mate who would pick it up for me. My wife described the colour as 'hideous mint green' and refused to have it in the house, so it spent twenty years on the floor of our carport, which doubled as a gym, with our car parked on it every night. I reckon the rug had far more enjoyment watching our young family grow up than it would have had lying in a tip in Baghdad.

We weren't completely isolated from the war surrounding us. At one point, the general began to focus his work on infrastructure protection: trying to make sure power stations, oil refineries, bridges and other important pieces of the Iraq economy didn't get disabled by insurgent attacks. He couldn't always rely on the information people were giving him in Baghdad, so this required driving or flying out into the desert to see for himself. He was very hands-on, which, in my experience, was unusual for a general.

We were never attacked, but I remember a number of hairy moments. Markets and other public gatherings were targeted by rockets and suicide bombings almost every hour. On one occasion, an American intelligence agency operative was sitting in his car across the Tigris River from us when he was shot in the back of the head in broad daylight. Another time, Matt Locke and I were sitting in a queue waiting at a car wash when two mortar rounds landed about 30 metres behind us. I looked at Lockey.

'What are we gunna do?' I asked.

'Stay here,' he replied, and we did. There was nothing else we could do.

Another tricky moment occurred when we were coming back from a meeting in northern Baghdad, in the bad lands controlled by the rebel cleric Muqtada al-Sadr. On our way home, we came to an underpass where the road, a six-lane freeway, went on to cross the Tigris River. The traffic had come to a standstill, blocked for the next few kilometres.

For us, this was a red flag. A typical insurgent move was to stop traffic, throw a bomb under a car, then walk away and dial a mobile number that set it off. Alternatively, they might set the explosion with a timer, or someone else would phone in to detonate it immediately. Our response was to never stop moving, come what may. We couldn't afford to become a sitting duck in a traffic jam. As a civilian up-armoured car, our Chevrolet Suburban was conspicuous. We tended to think that every pedestrian who looked at us while talking on a phone was reporting on us. We were so paranoid, any sign was enough. So when we saw the length of the traffic jam we were in, we jumped across the median strip and began haring down the wrong side of the freeway, where the traffic was flowing smoothly. It was like a video game, weaving at high speed between oncoming vehicles. We got through, shitting ourselves of course, and were elated when we arrived back at the palace.

———

On many levels, that deployment gave me an amazing insight into war. In the lead-up to Christmas, there seemed to be a bomb going off every other hour. There was an almost unbelievable bar shootout, when one drunk Coalition contractor pulled a gun on a man from a rival company and shot him dead. It shouldn't have been a surprise in the bizarre nightlife scene, where every drunk on a dancefloor might have a holstered gun swinging from his or her hip.

The most unsettling thing in a war of insurgency was the random killing. Around the end of 2004, we were returning on 'Route Irish' from the airport to the Green Zone, more on edge than usual as there had been a significant surge in attacks and deaths on the highway by vehicle-borne suicide bombers. As we crossed the flyover that led down into the first checkpoints, we noted a burnt-out wreck, one of many along the route. This one had been blasted through the side wall barrier of the overpass, and the car had been propelled 25 metres onto the road below. We found out that some British contractors, having just left the safety of the Green Zone, were heading to the airport and, as they came up the ramp onto the freeway overpass, a red Opel Estate moved up alongside them and detonated. All four contractors were trapped in their car as it caught fire. As the electronics were burned out, they couldn't unlock their electronic doors. Their comrades from a second car reportedly tried to shoot out the windows, but, being bulletproof, they were impregnable and the occupants burned alive. This kind of thing was hard to forget.

Our guards on the outside of the palace were ex-Gurkhas from Nepal, now working for a UK security company. The Gurkhas' military history and contribution to the Commonwealth holds almost mythical status. They must have about the highest ratio of

Victoria Crosses and have proved their bravery across multiple wars. They were renowned for being the first in and last out at Gallipoli, and they inspired the saying that 'If a man says he is not afraid of dying, he is either lying or he is a Gurkha.' But these guys were being paid about US$20 a day for the privilege of making sure we didn't die. Or, more to the point, trying not to get killed themselves, because they were far more in harm's way than we were. Suicide bombs went off outside the palace grounds at any hour of day or night, and once a rocket landed about 50 metres across the road.

The scandal was that the security companies employing them were pocketing a large percentage of the income, passing only a pittance to the Gurkhas themselves. For their sacrifice, the Gurkhas didn't get to share the palace's small luxuries with us. While we slept in bomb-proof rooms with walls too thick to measure, the Gurkhas had to drive to the other side of Baghdad, where they slept in tents—air-conditioned, of course! I struggled to reconcile this treatment with the Gurkhas' proud history.

One night, a rocket landed in their tent city, killing four and wounding fourteen, some of whom would die later from their wounds. The scared and traumatised Nepalese guards turned up for work the next day, and when we heard what had happened, we couldn't send them back to the bombed tents at the end of their shifts. They didn't have clearance to sleep in the palace rooms, but we made sure they were okay to spend the nights in security boxes around the residence, not ideal but a lot better than where they'd come from. These poor guys were gutted. I wrote a letter on their behalf to senior ADF officers, pointing out how important the Gurkhas were to General Molan's security, and informing them that we had set up donations of money and personal items to make up for the fact that their employer, GLOBAL, was slow in responding to the incident. It struck me that I could help their morale further by getting them involved in a game of cricket.

Cricket was never far from my mind. On the palace's giant TV screen, we were able to watch a vintage year for the Australian team, highlighted by their historic Test series win in India—the only one in the last fifty-plus years—and a home win over New Zealand, which featured the famous half-century scored by Glenn McGrath, one of Australia's greatest bowlers but not exactly the best batsman going around.

I hadn't taken the Shahid Afridi bat to Iraq, but I crafted a replacement. With all the hours we spent sitting in a car waiting for the general, I had to do something to fill my time. I didn't have a bat, and without a bat I couldn't set up a game with anyone . . . so I would make one!

While we were visiting a construction site in Baghdad, I carefully selected a piece of pine with a nice, tight symmetrical grain. I had several knives, which I'd bought either online from America or in the local market we dropped in on to buy pirated compact discs (on the days it wasn't being attacked by suicide bombers; once they even used disabled people as 'mules' to carry bombs in their backpacks and detonate them in the middle of the crowd). For the bat, I preferred to use a pocketknife and an old metal file borrowed from the horse farriers. In the long hours waiting in General Molan's car, I worked away on turning the chunk of pine into a bat. Using the pocketknife, I carved a bit of 'belly' into it, making it more than just a bat-shaped plank. It was a labour of love, taking ten to fifteen hours of carving to get it to where I wanted, but I was proud of it. The only worry was that the handle was a bit long and thin for the size and weight of the bat. I got some gaffer tape and ran ring after ring around the handle to thicken the grip. I was always worried it would snap, but it held up a treat.

We four SAS guys held our games on a lawn, the size of a large swimming pool, inside the palace grounds. They were genteel rather than boisterous games, with a well-kept hedge serving as automatic wicketkeeper. Not many SAS soldiers played cricket, which you could tell pretty quickly. They humoured me and my fanaticism by joining in. Matty Locke was a good rugby league player but a rubbish cricketer. He bowled like Gigantor, the giant Japanese robot, and was a terrible chucker. By his own admission he was the worst cricketer among us, but he was very curious about the game and generous enough to ask me a lot of questions and, more generous still, to wait around to hear my lengthy answers.

When the traumatised Nepalese security guards moved in, we invited them to play with us. My homemade bat was low quality even by their standards, but some of them were more than credible players. These games were definitely more compassionate than competitive. As I saw the smiles returning to their faces, I realised this was more than just a game for them.

Our Iraq deployment lasted a little over five months. This odd duration was not, in our opinion, a matter of chance. We reasoned that the army bean counters knew that if we stayed away for six months, we would receive mandatory extra leave and an additional payment on top of our campaign allowance, only a few thousand dollars but enough for them to put their brilliant minds to denying us. So these trips always managed to stop a week or two short of triggering the six-month bonus.

I didn't come back empty-handed, though. From that Iraq trip I brought home a university enrolment, a bat and a brick.

Since early in my life, I had been keen to study psychology. My high school marks just qualified me to get into a course, and now, in my mid-thirties, I finally registered with Edith Cowan University in Perth as an online student and commenced my studies from inside the palace in Baghdad. Seeing how the ex-Gurkhas responded to and recovered from such a horrific bombing added to my evolving passion for educating myself, which in turn inspired me to seek educational opportunities for other soldiers later in my career.

The handmade bat did make it home, but only just. In Iraq, we took it wherever we were driving, and if General Molan had to go inside a building for a long meeting and we were waiting outside, we started a game. We often drew the curious attention of American soldiers, some of whom were game enough to jump in and play a game of French cricket with us, although they were never too sure about how seriously to take our incessant and merciless sledging!

One day we were at the 'Salt and Pepper Tower', the building in eastern Baghdad across the Tigris where the Australian conventional military were based, guarding the temporary Australian embassy. Suddenly, while we were in the middle of our game, the general came out and we had to move quickly. The bat got left behind. Disaster was averted when someone found it later and made sure it was returned to me. I got it signed by, among others, Major General Molan and my patrol mates Matt Locke and Dave O'Neill, both of whom would soon lose their lives.

The brick was all about Matty Locke. One night not long after we arrived, we were driving into the Coalition Headquarters building where the general was working. At the front of the HQ building was a rotunda entrance, about 10 metres high, that had been hit by a blast. The explosion had knocked a brick tile off the façade of the building onto the roof of the rotunda. One particular brick fascinated us: against the laws of gravity, it was somehow hanging over the edge of the canopy, looking like it had to fall, yet not doing so. We couldn't believe some OH&S nut hadn't seen it and removed it.

'We should grab that before it falls down and kills someone,' I said to Matt. On our trip to Afghanistan in 2002, we had liberated a brick each from Usama Bin Laden's supposed hideout in the north. To have a Saddam Hussein brick as well would be a nice souvenir. (If I had a brick from the White House, I later joked, I'd have the whole Axis of Evil brick collection!) One night, after a shot of whiskey for inspiration, we decided to do a late-night run. We climbed up the side of the HQ building, planning to rope down onto the roof of the rotunda and grab the brick. But we didn't plan very well: we had nowhere to tie our rope to, so no protection if we slipped.

'I'll free climb, and you hold the rope,' said Matt. Common sense prevailed, however, and we decided not to risk it.

More blasts happened soon after. On our way to work one morning, we noticed that our brick had fallen into a garden bed. We dropped the general off at his job, then circled back to grab the brick. I took it home in my weapons trunk. Matt and I decided to cut it in half once we got home.

We never got around to it.

Matt went to Afghanistan in 2006 and 2007. On the first trip, he received the Medal for Gallantry, one of Australia's highest military honours. The next year, in Uruzgan Province, he was shot dead during a contact. After his funeral, I gave his son Keegan, who was school friends with my daughter, Georgia, the other half of the brick. He'll understand when I say that his father, who I loved like a brother, was one of the best men I ever knew but a terrible cricketer.

Although the handmade bat is unique and contains happy memories of those pleasant afternoon games in Baghdad, it brings me mixed feelings. Matt was one of our best soldiers, mature beyond his years, a natural leader who died before he could achieve his promise. So too Dave O'Neill, who would lose his life in 2007 alongside two other SAS soldiers in a car accident. I treasure their signatures all the more for this reminder of the thin membrane that separates life from death.

Dad puts on a backyard cricket masterclass in Hervey Bay, Queensland, circa 1978.

Boxing Day Test, circa 1983, Kalamunda, Western Australia. Paul Moffitt bowling his usual around the wicket gentle 'offies'.

Kapooka, New South Wales, 1986. A young, skinny, anxious Harry Moffitt on the final pack march to graduate Soldier Training. For the first time in my life I felt like I really belonged to something important, I felt competent.

In the middle of the central Northern Territory, at my Survival Instructors course, 1993. Towards the end I lost close to 10 kilograms. On a rare successful hunting trip I caught this python and a goanna, both cooked up a treat.

Operating out of Tarin Kowt (TK), Afghanistan, 2002. I'm handing out pencils and paper sent from the children in Georgia's and Henry's classes.

Central Afghanistan, 2002. National bus route on Highway 1—standing room only.

Central Afghanistan, 2002. On gun piquet during a routine stop to communicate back to HQ. A .50-calibre gun is mounted on top of the Land Rover Perentie long-range patrol vehicle (LRPV).

Bagram Air Base, Afghanistan, 2002. The Dallas Cowboys Cheerleaders humour us with a photo. We 'abducted' the cheer squad (with their consent) from the American troops.

A young Harry Moffitt with one of good-humoured Dallas Cowboys Cheerleaders. If we hadn't been Australian, I don't think we would have got away with it.

Operating out of Bagram Air Base, 2002. This is the 'jingle truck' we inserted into Gag Ghar on the Pakistan border. I am first on the left.

Bagram Air Base, 2002. The phone home in this photo was the most comfortable, as it had a chair. You sat in the dirt to use the other one.

Gardez, Afghanistan, 2002. Doing a rug viewing—we bought a few beauties. I am first on the left.

The entrance to the cave system used by Usama Bin Laden while he was recovering on the border of Afghanistan and Pakistan. The rubble at the cave entrance is a result of the bombing carried out by the United States.

Willagee (The G), Western Australia, circa 2003. This was taken just after we bought our first family home, sitting on the future Moffitt Cricket Ground, or 'MCG', on one of the rugs I bought in Afghanistan.

The streets of Baghdad, Iraq, 2004. Daily VBIEDs (vehicle-borne improvised explosive devices) and car bombs were commonplace.

Baghdad, 2004. Just as we were coming into the Baghdad International Airport entrance a car drove to the top of the line-up and detonated a VBIED right in front of us. It split our windscreen and damaged our vehicle. Those in front of us fared much worse.

Christmas 2004, Riverside Palace, Baghdad, Iraq. We are out the back of the palace where we looked after Major General Jim Molan. On the left, past the building corner, you can see the cricket pitch we used. Left to right: me, Jack 'Streaky' Bacon, Dave 'Unreal' O'Neill and Matt Locke.

Tarin Kowt, 2005. A game of cricket on the evening after the TK suicide bomb, played on the helo pad. Rowdy is at first slip sledging the batter.

Operating out of Tarin Kowt, 2005. Meeting with Afghan village leadership in the middle of the Khod Valley. The elders came out to discuss our presence in the valley and share their concerns about their resources and safety.

On shitter detail at a stopover at a US Special Forces base, 2005.

Operating out of Tarin Kowt, 2005. Just after this photo, we were attacked by rockets and headed off to 'advance to contact' and engage the enemy. Often, these contacts ended with no result, merely skirmishes.

Near Tarin Kowt, 2005. We held double-staggered piquet every night we were deployed. It provides the unblinking eye that is required on military operations.

An LRPV troop returning from a sniper task south of our position.

Final checks before a rehearsal parachute jump in Afghanistan, 2005.

LRPV patrol, 2005. While stopping for comms and vehicle maintenance, a game of cricket broke out, during which the bad guys insulted us by sledging us over the radio. We asked them to come down and play us, but they declined, citing that we would bomb them . . . which we probably would have.

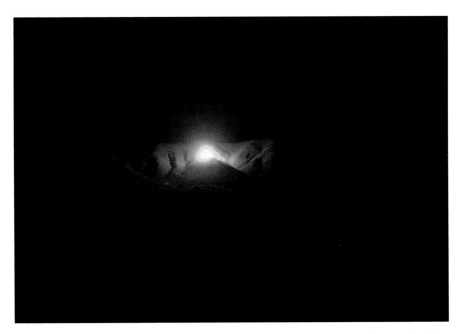

Bombing the cave systems—the inhabitants had been sledging us earlier in the day. I bet they wished they'd got one more game of cricket in.

Afghanistan, 2005. Nearly two months is a long time to be out in the desert, so quizzes, cricket and rock-throwing Olympics were popular ways to maintain morale.

Crossing a swelled Afghan river at the start of the ice melt in 2005. River crossings are nervous, as the vehicles are particularly vulnerable. This river west of TK was the scene of many contacts and ambush attempts by Taliban/Al-Qaeda forces, especially just before harvest when they would hide in the fields and lie in wait.

Negotiating the narrow lanes of an Afghan village during LRPV patrol. Ambushes would often await.

Resting during the day as we worked during the night. Afghanistan, 2005.

Gunshot holes in a backpack being worn by one of the lads. We had many near misses.

On the last week of LRPV patrol it started to get very cold and we were all beginning to fade a little in terms of morale and boredom.

BAT ‖‖

THE MISSING BAT

IRAQ, MARCH–APRIL 2005

A few months after the job with General Molan, our team was deployed as minders for an Australian political delegation visiting troops and commanders in Iraq. We were to design, plan and execute the visit as well as provide close protection and personal security.

We forward-deployed to Kuwait to meet the VIPs before going into country, to plan our visits inside Iraq, to check equipment and, while we were at it, to play a few games of cricket. It was my first job as an SAS team leader, taking charge of a fourteen-strong group. I organised for us to go to a firing range, about two hours' drive into the Kuwaiti desert, to practise our car and personal drills: rehearsing how we would respond if we were contacted by the enemy from the front, the rear and the sides of the vehicle; actions for when a car was disabled and we had to swap people between cars in contact;

as well as walking drills, shooting and other worst-case scenario preparations. We called these 'actions on' (for example, 'action on ambush', 'action on disabled', 'action on flat tyre') and we had dozens of them. We also had immediate actions (IAs) in urgent response to a situation. There is a myth that 'high-performance' people are inherently better under pressure. My experience is that high-performing people are just more disciplined in their preparation and training. They are brilliant at doing the boring basics and developing an attention to detail, which I was lucky enough to have learned from my parents. It's not rocket science: the more you rehearse for all contingencies, the more effectively you react. Additionally, preparation gives you a confidence in your ability to adapt when things go wrong, as they inevitably will.

Tragically, a respected colleague, Dave Nary, was killed later that year on the same range where we were practising, an accident with ongoing impacts upon those involved. Amid all the trauma of war, it is the memory of those mates who are killed far from home that stay with us and bring us closer. You become such a small tight unit, getting to know each other at remarkably deep levels, that losing mates leaves a deep regret inside.

The VIP party wanted to visit JTF 633, Australia's security detachment near Baghdad International Airport. They also wanted to visit the Australian embassy, which, operating with a skeleton staff, remained inexplicably in the 'Salt and Pepper Tower', across the Tigris from the Green Zone, needing a large contingent of regular forces providing security because whenever the staff left the building they were exposed to potential attack. On several occasions, including while I was there in 2004, the SecDet (Security

Detachment) vehicles were targeted in transit, often by explosively formed projectiles (EFPs), which could pierce armour plating and kill all occupants. Consequently, a new Australian embassy was being built inside the Green Zone opposite the Coalition HQ and next to the Ibn Sina Hospital, and the VIPs wanted to see that too, as well as several training outposts.

Our cricket matches on this deployment were fairly civilised. The mood was relaxed, as the insurgency had abated a little since my previous visit. We thought that Iraq would be the last of our potential fighting days, and once it was sorted we would all go home for another period of sustained peace. We played mostly in aircraft hangars, on roads and in the car parks of military bases. I didn't have much time to arrange matches; as team leader I was busy overseeing the activities of the deployment.

My appointment had put a few noses out of joint. I'd already been to Iraq, and some thought the jobs should be shared around more. I understood their feelings, but as this deployment was at very short notice, I was an obvious choice as I knew the streets and had a good rapport with the people in Iraq we would need to engage with. Still, the issue gave birth to a grudge or two. One mate, or former mate, stopped talking to me and has barely said a civil word to or about me since (though I did see him tapping his foot and watching from the audience when The Externals performed our last gig at the SAS barracks in 2012). Thankfully his was not an attitude that many others shared; almost everybody in the unit is invested in seeing their colleagues do well.

Anyway, being busy leading the group was my excuse for losing the bat.

———

It was because I was in a mad rush that I hadn't brought a bat from Australia. It wasn't a priority. When we were in Kuwait, after preparing our guns, ammunition, radios and body armour—which was so heavy it was more likely to cause than prevent injury—I caught sight of a Duncan Fearnley bat among the sporting equipment the Australian soldiers kept on the air base. Australian air bases all over the world invariably had a bat or three leaning in the corner of an office, with a number of balls at hand; indeed, tennis balls were often on the list of necessities requested from home, after photos, letters, food and alcohol.

I remarked to one of our guys, 'Hey, Trevor, we're going to need that bat for morale. Following around politicians and listening to their drivel has a morale-sucking effect and we will need to fight hard to maintain it!'

Trevor, who I'd known since joining the army as a teenager, laughed and said, 'Well, you're the psychologist, Harry.'

We liberated the Duncan Fearnley with the intention of returning it on our way back through Kuwait. Every intention. But then a war got in the way.

———

Rocket attacks were frequent but inaccurate. Your chances of being hit were very slim, unless you were not where the insurgents were aiming, in which case your chances went up considerably. On a visit to a hospital in the town of Balad, we were targeted by one of these attacks. We 'put down' the delegation in a secure concrete bunker where they wouldn't need the full contingent to look after them.

Knowing that if the rockets were being aimed our way we were most unlikely to be at risk, we grabbed the Duncan Fearnley from the car. It was hot, but I couldn't help myself. It wasn't long before soldiers around the base we'd stopped at were popping out of their tents and joining our game in a cleared area by a rocky car park. Military bases in the Middle East were usually carpeted with riverbed rocks or gravel to keep down the dust in summer and settle the snowy slush in winter. This was not conducive to quality off-drives or sneaky leg-glances, so we cleared the biggest rocks off a good length on our pitch. On this occasion, our US SEAL attachment Rosco was bowling, which meant no one had any idea where the ball might land—he was about as accurate as the insurgents with their rockets—so we had to clear a strip the size of a C-130 runway. When Rowdy was playing, by contrast, we had to make it a little more challenging, so we prepared a narrow strip of a pitch within the pitch, what we called a 'Brazilian' because it was thin, short and led to the juicy spot. No, we were not earning our money as comedians.

This day we were bowling into a strong desert wind and the ball and pitch were doing plenty. Not many batsmen could get a start, until about twenty minutes into the game one of the VIPs' aides came out of the bunker. For a moment, I thought he was going to ask us to shut up, stop or take the rocket attack seriously.

'What's up?' I asked, a little apprehensively.

'We can hear you from the other side of the tents,' he said.

'Oh, you want us to shut it down?'

'No,' he replied. 'The boss was just saying how it was great to hear some normalcy in such a dangerous place. Carry on!'

He lit a cigarette, and I joined him as we watched the boys arguing over a disputed leg-before-wicket call.

'First time to Iraq?' I asked.

'Nah, I was here last year before John Howard was re-elected. It's not that dangerous, really. We'd have to be very unlucky. And we have you guys.'

'Very unlucky, mate,' I agreed. 'Flying is more dangerous. In the SAS, our own helicopters have killed more of us than the Iraqis have. Anyway, the worst that can happen here at the base is an RPG or a few stray rounds.'

He looked a bit less confident.

'To be honest,' I went on, 'I'm more worried about bringing the other boys home than I am about myself. Some of these guys have been away from their families too much.'

'I wonder why we're using you SAS guys in here and not out there,' he said, motioning beyond the base.

'We wonder the same thing. The Yanks and Poms are fighting the real fight. We'd love to be in it. It's a little embarrassing, actually. You know what they call us here?'

'No, what?'

'Non-swimmers. We come to the beach with our towel and bathers, but don't get in the water.'

To show I wasn't too aggrieved by this situation, I laughed. He didn't. He was a little put out by what he no doubt saw as my unnecessary bravado. It wasn't lost on me that he would be spending hours talking with the VIPs and might pass on what I had said.

At least I hoped he would. Notwithstanding the amazing job the long-range desert troops had done in the early days of the Iraq invasion, much of our involvement by 2005 was minding visitors or following orders to make a political impression, and some of us were growing resentful about it.

'Non-swimmers, eh?' the aide replied with a stern face. 'What about those who have been injured and killed?'

'We're just a self-licking ice-cream here,' I continued. 'Almost all of our activity is self-serving. I spent last year with Jim Molan in town, and you see pretty quickly that we play a very small part here.'

'How many times have you been deployed, Harry?'

'This is my third,' I said. Three was a pretty big number in 2005, and I had no idea that it would soon become a pretty small number.

The political staffer had only heard the number, not the point I was trying to make. 'Three! Wow, you have been busy.'

This conversation was going nowhere, so I decided to try to draw something hopeful out of it. 'I hear talk of us going back into Afghan,' I said. 'Is that your intel?'

'Off the record?' He didn't wait for my assent. As I'd anticipated, he was all too keen to show how much inside knowledge he had. 'Yes, prep has already started for you guys to go in later this year. It might be you, so let's grab a ciggy some time then.'

I shook his hand warmly and that was that, back to the cricket. The game didn't go much longer, as another base 'rocket attack' alarm sounded and we had to rush to the bunkers to wait it out.

Over time, these small pitch- or war-side discussions would come to mean a lot to me. Listening to random strangers discuss the politics within the politics, you learned how war brings out the best and worst in mankind. War can be poetic but illiterate; stunningly beautiful, yet appallingly beyond imagination. It can be efficient and effective, but also the greatest waste of life and resources; humble and arrogant, sane and insane, fair and unfair, just and unjust, all at the same time. I was different from most operators, in that I didn't leave any assumptions about war in their safe place. In serious team meetings, I was often pulled up for asking 'Why?'

But for now, we had to organise the delegation into the cars and get them back to Baghdad. We flew back to Camp Victory at the airport, and radioed for the cars to come and meet us at the helipad. We ushered the VIPs towards their cars.

'I wouldn't mind walking back to the HQ,' one of the senior members of the delegation said. 'It's only a kilometre or so.'

The airport base was meant to be secure, and we were comfortable with his request, so a small detail walked with him while I and some others loaded up the car. A few minutes later, a rocket fired from outside Camp Victory landed, not too close but close enough for us to get serious.

Filthy Pierre, the driver, had been sitting alone in the car waiting for us. Moments before the rocket landed, Filthy, living up to his name, had ripped off the foulest of farts, and was enjoying the solitude and the smell, a widespread human habit that SAS soldiers are not above. He was known to have the ability to clear a western Queensland pub with one bottom-burp. He loved to claim credit not only for his stinkers but also those of others, if they were good ones. We referred to these as 'Jack-ollades', or stealing credit from others. (Someone was 'Jack' if they didn't pitch in to help do the hard work, or if they skipped a shout in a bar. Calling someone

Jack was a supreme insult in the SAS, short only of accusing them of 'lacking integrity', which would set bar stools flying.)

While Filthy was silently enjoying his farts, the rocket impacted. The other guys grabbed the senior VIP from his planned afternoon stroll and rushed him to the armoured vehicle, which was the correct drill. Far from feeling relieved at not being killed by the rocket, the VIP flew off the handle about the horrific smell.

Feeling he had to support the VIP, the detachment leader said sternly: 'Filthy, was that you, you pig?'

'Yeah, it's a fucking beauty, eh, sir?'

Not all soldiers are made for diplomacy, or for cricket.

We never got to finish our cricket game that day. During this deployment, the Australian team were playing a series in New Zealand, which I tracked on the internet. 'You're pretty obsessed with cricket,' one of my mates said after another long exposition from me about the game. 'Where did that come from?'

'Oh, a long way back,' I said. 'A long way back.'

———

Cricket had a lot to do with making me who I am.

The interest came from Dad. He was a natural sportsman who grew up playing cricket and rugby in his local leagues in western Queensland and continued playing when he moved away to join the navy. My two brothers and I inherited both Mum's and Dad's passion for sport—basketball and netball in Mum's case. I remember imbibing this passion while falling asleep in Dad's car waiting for him to finish up in a clubhouse after a game, long after my bedtime. Whatever was going on in there, I thought, had to be really important.

I loved sitting with Dad to watch the Australian Test team play. In summers, a Test match was always on. World Series Cricket arrived when I was nine, and Dad took me to one of the very first games at VFL Park in Waverley. I remember gazing in wonder at the shadows cast by the giant stadium lights on the cows in the paddocks as we approached through the countryside, seemingly in the middle of nowhere. As a kid, World Series Cricket and the way it was marketed were fantastic. You knew every player and imitated their bowling and batting styles. Our favourite, as it was for thousands of Australian kids, was trying to do Max 'Tangles' Walker's wrong-footed action.

Dad studied the game, and spoke of Doug Walters as if he was a great intellect. 'A thinking batsman,' Dad called him, 'a real cricket brain,' and I was as impressed by this as I was of the stories about Walters playing cards while waiting to bat or drinking copious amounts of beer. This deeper yarn-spinning fabric of sport got into me early, the sense that these players were complicated, complete individuals. It was a lucky time to be an Australian cricket fan.

Organised, eleven-a-side, 'proper' cricket wasn't really a part of my upbringing, however. We only tended to stay in one place for twelve or eighteen months, so it was hard to break into the cliques that inevitably formed around proper cricket teams. As a consequence, I've always rated myself a better backyard cricketer than most, while I'm only an average cricketer in organised formats. I can bowl into the wind, or maintain medium-pace accuracy under pressure, and I sometimes contribute some runs at number eight or nine in the batting order, but that's it. I lacked that last squeeze of lemon that makes a top player. My brothers were more talented. Paul, in particular, had all the skill in the world at numerous sports, and could have played at a high level, though all the moving we did and our humble beginnings eventually impacted on him, leading him to prioritise getting a good job and just playing his sport on weekends.

Street cricket also brought my Machiavellian mind to the fore, as it is a game with loose and adaptable rules I could turn to my advantage. This love of the ad hoc game, with so many more variables than in organised cricket, served me well on military deployments.

Dad would set up the rules of the game: the wickets might be painted on the trampoline, which became 'automatic wickie'. If you hit the fence on the full, you were out—Dad was a stickler for creating a game that forced you to hit the ball along the ground. It helped us become more cautious batsmen, and also limited the potential for broken windows. We dragged chairs out and placed them around the pitch as 'fielders'. All of us bowled leg-spin, cricket's great mystery art, including Dad, who claimed he could land the ball on a hankie. Maybe a tea towel. We specialised in the trickster side of wrist-spin and celebrated wildly when a perfect leg-break took a wicket. We started early on the sledging too. My old man, the ultimate sledger, never swore or made it personal, but his commentary, guffaws, false appeals and chatter between balls were all meant to mentally disintegrate you. We grew resilient to it. We gave it back too. 'Hey, Dad, can you put a hat on? The glare off your bald head is getting in my eyes,' we would say, pissing ourselves laughing no matter how many times we'd said it. He would rub his balding head and say, 'Don't worry, boys, one day this will all be yours!'

If you want an illustration of the unique character of street and backyard cricket—as opposed to real cricket—it was in our celebration of the 'chuck ball'. If a 'chuck ball' took a wicket, we went into a delirium, including the dismissed batsman. A 'chuck ball', in short, was a ball delivered by the left hand of a right-arm bowler. The bowler would approach the crease with his normal right-arm motion, and as his rear foot touched the crease, in the delivery action, he would surreptitiously transfer the ball from right hand to left, disguised by a swirl of elbows and forearms. The right arm would roll over as normal, while the left hand would sneakily chuck the ball at the batsman. If it was done perfectly, it was a magic ball, particularly lethal against accomplished batsmen who were watching for the ball to come out of the bowling hand. Though the dismissed batsmen always protested, many a non-Moffitt wicket was taken in this manner, and great was the Moffitts' joy.

Every summer Saturday or Sunday while I was growing up, we would play all day in the backyard. At one house, Dad put spotlights in the yard so we could play after dark, something I would emulate decades later at my 'MCG'. Finally, Mum would call us in for a shower and get us into our pyjamas . . . and then we'd play in the hallway as late as we could, batting and bowling on our knees with a miniature bat and a nerf ball, diving for one-handed screamers that left carpet burns on our elbows and knees.

Such flexible and negotiable rules, with three young boys who all went very hard at the ball, inevitably led to a dust-up or two. Robert,

Paul and I had massive controversies over umpiring decisions, and we sent cricket bats through doors a few times. We were also quite rough with each other, fighting and punching and breaking things over each other's heads through no greater controversy than a dodgy LBW decision. Due to cricket, we grew up into adults who could look after ourselves in a pub. Once in our early thirties, after a few too many grogs, Robert and I got into a scuffle with each other over a game of pool at the Serpentine Hotel in Western Australia. It was light-hearted at first, but then it started to get a little rough. Paul was there too, as was Dad. They say you should never try to break up a fight between brothers, because the first thing they'll do is turn on you. I'm not particularly proud of it, but when someone tried to intervene in our argument, the three of us banded together and punched our way out of the pub that night. Unfortunately, Dad got banned, which was no good as the Serpentine was his local.

I'm glad that the cricket I played in war zones never got as violent as it did in our backyard.

When we were moving out of Baghdad for the trip home, I asked the boys where the Duncan Fearnley bat was.

One of them had a stricken look on his face. 'Fuck, Harry. Sorry, I've let you down.'

The bat was left in a holding area at Kuwait or at Camp Victory.

It was the last time that a cricket bat was an afterthought on one of my deployments. From here on, a bat would be one of the first things I would pack, as now I understood the power of cricket for relaxing, for recovering from trauma, for gaining intelligence, for conducting reconnaissance, for building rapport with the locals or Coalition forces, or explicitly for security. I almost always carried a four-piece cricket ball too. It was easier than a football to carry and sure to spark a conversation with anyone, any time. I found it therapeutic to rub and shine a ball in my downtime, and flip it out of the back of my hand, practising leg-spin bowling.

As we took off from Kuwait, I was looking forward to some football with the Brentwood Bulldogs and then a full cricket season with the Applecross Cricket Club. It turned out I was being overly optimistic. A few months later, I would be on a long deployment. That political staffer's intel had been right. The war drums had started to beat in Afghanistan again, and the SAS, which had become one of the favourite units of both the American generals and Australian political and military leaders, would be first in again. We were in for a long war.

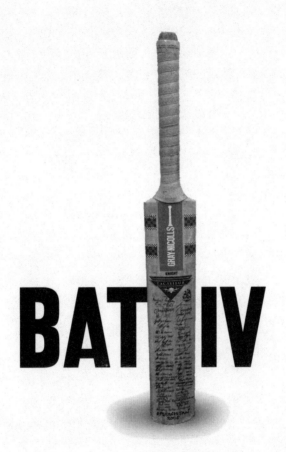

BAT IV

FIRST IN

AFGHANISTAN, 2005/06

We had been in country for a short time. What seemed like only hours before, I had been eating spaghetti bolognese on the floor in front of the TV, watching *The Simpsons* with my family. Now here I was, with my mates, buzzing around in the rudimentary huts at Tarin Kowt working on our cars and personal equipment. We were the first unit back on the ground for Operation Slipper (Slipper? I have often wondered what rocket scientist comes up with these names).

Few of us thought it had been a good idea to leave Afghanistan for two years. Our absence had all but handed back control of the porous 'agencies' and 'frontier' regions in the FATA, also known as Waziristan, overlapping the Pakistani border into which we had boxed them in 2002 and early 2003. Much of our effort in the first campaign, focused around the 'Parrot's Beak' of border territory, felt like it had been sacrificed. Now we were back, we were dealing with the threat in Afghanistan's central regions. While the US had overall coverage of the country and the UK was fighting insurgents and drug-traffickers in Helmand province to the east, we took over Tarin Kowt (TK), a base formerly occupied by the Dutch, in Uruzgan Province north of Kandahar.

The general thinking in Canberra was that TK was a sleepy settlement in the middle of nowhere, from which the Australian forces could set out to help build hospitals and schools and achieve other good works. The plan, as they say, lasted until the first punch was thrown. The portrait Canberra had received couldn't have been further from the truth, which was that Uruzgan was at the centre of criminal and insurgent rat lines between Waziristan and Helmand, one of the busiest and hottest areas of the Afghan conflict. We would joke about living 'in a shoebox on the Taliban Highway'. TK was a nexus of anti-Coalition operations, servicing Sangin and Lashkar Gah to our south-west, Kandahar to our south, Kabul to our north-east and Khost, Ghazni and Gardez to our east. We were not too sure who was advising the government. The ADF estimated our area of operations (AO) as about 1000 square kilometres. Since we covered all of the surrounding provinces, not just Uruzgan, our five teams were actually covering an area ten times larger than that. The SAS, in particular, was very busy from day one.

When we arrived in September 2005, we set about securing the base, which anyone and everyone could get into. It lay about two kilometres from the TK town centre, which was a relatively busy trading crossroads, much larger than a village, with a well-established local police, military and political presence. One of the first structures erected in the camp, after the B Huts for accommodation and headquarters, was a maxi-tower, made of six stacked shipping containers. This provided a 360-degree vista of the base and its surrounds down to the airstrip. Many of us questioned the logic of the maxi-tower, which was now the biggest aiming point and target for rocket attacks from miles around. However, the tower did provide a 24/7 piquet, an unblinking eye to provide overwatch as we set about erecting walls around the camp to make it secure.

While the camp was being built with local assistance, our troops were readying to set out on our first vehicle patrols. There would be six cars per patrol, with three to four people per car. Our aim was to get out into our AO and engage with either the locals or the bad guys. As it turned out, we rarely engaged one without the other being present.

We headed west through Deh Ravod and north to the Khod Valley, places I would return to many times over the next seven years. On one vehicle patrol, the longest I have ever been involved in, we drove for more than seven weeks. We spent a lot of time in the Khod Valley, where our routine was to pull back into the middle of the valley during the day, before advancing in the evenings to the villages on the edge of the valley floor, often into 'contact' with enemy forces.

Our job initially was to reconnoitre areas around Uruzgan and Daykundi provinces, many of which were more than 100 kilometres away, which meant driving some of the most dangerous roads in the world. Given enemy movements and IEDs, these reconnaissance exercises could be painfully slow.

Soon after arriving in TK, we were in our huts one day when a large explosion rattled the walls. It came from the nearby town centre, and as our security perimeter was still being built we all stood-to, getting ourselves armed and taking up positions to watch the perimeter. Was this the beginning of an attack? It seemed unlikely given that there was no small arms fire before or after the blast and it was the middle of the day. But, that said, sporadic rocket attacks on the base had been increasing. We continued guarding the perimeter, expecting information to filter through.

It was then that a medic from our very basic surgical facility ran up to the huts and asked for as many PAFAs (Paramedical Advanced First Aiders) as were available to help the influx of civilians who had been seriously injured in a blast. A couple of hundred locals, mostly men and boys, had gathered in an enclosure to gamble on dog fighting, a popular but gruesome pastime (others included tossing goat carcasses from horseback, a kind of twisted form of 'goat polo'). A suicide bomber ran into the dense gathering and 'cracked off', blowing himself to smithereens and killing and seriously injuring dozens of locals.

By the time I arrived at the double-sized tent that served as a surgical outpost, several locals were there with injuries ranging from lacerations and bleeding to traumatic amputations and severe head wounds. Though I had served in Baghdad during the campaign's most intense period of IEDs and suicide bombings, this was the most confronting situation I had been exposed to. Making it even worse was that many children were among the dozens of dead and dying. It was carnage.

As I approached the tent, another busload drove straight through the front gate unchecked, which was a concern, as one of the suicide bombers' methods was to set off a first explosion, wait for a response, and then attack the point of response, known as a 'honeypot' tactic. The numbers of people and buses flowing into the camp heightened the threat. I went to meet the arriving bus. Inside, blood was running down the footwells and stairs and out through the door. I began checking the locals as they stepped off. Many were carrying children or screaming for me to come on board to help with a loved one. It was so packed, they even had seriously injured people lashed to the bus roof. The women's shrill howling is a sound I have never forgotten.

Meanwhile, families of the injured were also descending on the camp. Fears of a second attack were sky-high. It was chaos, with people screaming and crying and demanding that we tend to their wounded. There were now about sixty people milling around the medical aid post, of whom thirty to forty were injured, some grievously. The local guards were shouting and waving their arms, trying to gain control, while our blokes formed an ad hoc triage in front of the tent, responding to whichever injury appeared to be worst.

It was then that I witnessed a display of leadership that will stay with me forever. Our doctor emerged from the tent, bloodied and steely, and set about establishing order. As I looked up from the young boy I was assessing—he had massive head wounds and would not survive—I vividly remember the doctor standing at the opening of the tent, absorbing the situation methodically and deliberately, taking a full moment to think about what he was seeing. Torn and twisted bodies were being tended to. We were overwhelmed, both in manning and resources. As I looked into the doc's eyes, I could see that he knew it too. This moment was truly surreal, like something from a Kubrick film. The doc seemed to move in slow motion, surrounded by a whir of chaos.

Assessing that we could not save everyone, he grabbed me.

'That one, that one and that one . . . over there,' he said. 'You there . . . get a container down here ASAP and start putting the dead in body bags, and place them in the container.' Then he turned to someone else and said, 'You—I want you to get the interpreters and have all of the non-casualties move back over there onto the hard-standing. I don't want another fucking bomb going off.'

Having seized control, he set up another rudimentary triage, dividing people into the dead, the untreatable, the serious and the non-serious. These were decisions based concretely in his training, but his leadership transcended training. He was calm and comfortable, almost at home, in the situation. I became his runner for the triage, helping to move the dead and untreatable so that the medics could work. I went to the perimeter and helped secure us from attack. I was the doc's tool in bringing the chaos back to a more manageable state.

I spent the last of this long, long day with a young boy, about fourteen years old, who died of his head injuries. This saddened me deeply as I thought of my daughter and son.

A few hours later, more Coalition forces arrived and I was no longer required. I sought out our doctor to shake his hand. I didn't need to say anything to him. The man and his actions will stay with me always. Being involved in this kind of action was why I became a soldier in the first place.

That evening, needing to unwind, we played a game of cricket.

———

I dreamt of becoming a lot of things—a cricketer, a footballer, even an architect—but when I look back, I was only ever going to be a soldier. Fish don't know they're in water. You don't understand the impact of your upbringing until you're looking back. When it comes to my destiny in life, I guess it was written.

On my paternal side, military service arguably goes back into the late thirteenth century, when my Scottish ancestors, named Moffat, reputedly fought under old mate Braveheart, William Wallace, when he took on the Poms in the First War of Scottish Independence. It was my great-grandfather David Moffitt, who served with the Royal Marines in World War I, who my father most talked about. On my mother's side, I was inspired by stories about her cousin John McMaster, who served with the SAS until a parachute accident brought his service to an end in the early 1980s. Nearer to my own experience, Dad's navy career normalised the military life for us, and he used to take my brothers and me to naval open days so that we could go on the ships where he worked. He had brothers in the army and the air force. When they got together, which was rare, their conversations had a military flavour that appealed to me.

As a young kid, I loved playing armies with the neighbours. We would break up into teams and play war games in the streets, jumping fences into a series of backyards. When I reflect back on it, I see that I always had a sense for tactical movement. These quasi-military games were a big part of our life, particularly in the navy villages where all the kids had this one thing in common.

During one of Dad's postings in Sydney, when I was in year four or five, I went into the Boys' Brigade. This was my only childhood experience of anything like cadets, which was not offered at the schools I attended, and we were never anywhere long enough to get into things like Scouts or the Australian Air League. Instead, sport dominated my radar: football, cricket and basketball. Dad was away so much, in Vietnam until the mid-seventies, that Mum was the dominant parent and our lives were shaped more by being cash-strapped than by being military.

Dad was a proud navy guy. His bar room was festooned with plaques and photos from the HMAS *Sydney* and HMAS *Melbourne*. There were uniforms, patches, boots, belts and other military para-phernalia around. You wouldn't get away with it today, but Dad had liberated and brought home all sorts of things from firing ranges, including defused training grenades and the odd live bullet, which I carried around in my little bag of prized trinkets.

Being a shipwright in the navy licensed him to tinker creatively, whether at work or at home. Our barbecue was partly made from the tail shaft of a crayfish vessel that had washed up at the back of Garden Island, the navy base in Perth. I helped him drag it up into a trailer and take it home. He built it into his barbecue and called it the HMAS *FOUR-X*.

I always marched with him on Anzac Day in his navy contingent. That said, while very proud of being a military person, he wasn't a flag-waving capital-P patriot, and nor were we a war-loving family. There were no Aussie flags around the house or up a pole. Dad was too philosophical and technically smart, very well read for a guy who left school at thirteen, to swallow pro-war propaganda or nationalism. I think his views were strongly shaped by his experiences in Vietnam; he spoke sadly of dropping off fit, vibrant, confident young men only to pick them up later as wrecks of human beings. Seeing that first-hand was something he never forgot.

Dad's pride in the navy was more along the lines of it being a good place to work, where you could achieve useful results and make solid friendships. Even though we moved around often, the navy was our steady community. Under his influence, I considered joining the navy during my high school years, going to the recruitment office at one stage, but it was always the army I was more interested in.

There was an inflection point in my life in my early teens when I met a guy called Martin Studdert, the brother-in-law of a good friend of mine, Geoff Bryndzej. When I was in year eight I walked into Geoff's house and there was a photo on the mantelpiece of this soldier with medals and in dress uniform, a captivating image. I said, 'Fuck, who's that?'

'My brother-in-law Martin,' he said. 'He serves in the SAS Regiment. They're right here in Perth, up at Swanbourne.' This set my mind on fire. I hadn't been in Western Australia long, and although I knew the SAS existed, I had no idea their headquarters were so close. I felt a real connection with Martin when I met him. I showed him my interest in world events, and liked to think he could see a glimmer of potential in me.

The seed of my interest in the SAS had been planted when, as a twelve-year-old, I'd sat mesmerised watching the TV coverage of an incident when six terrorists stormed the Iranian embassy at Prince's Gate in London and held twenty-six civilians hostage for a week in 1980. The siege held the world's attention, as nobody knew whether the British government would give in to the terrorists' demands to have some of their mates released from prisons in Iran, or if the people in the embassy would survive. After a week, the terrorists killed one of their hostages and threw him out of the building. And then it happened: the British SAS burst onto our television screens and front pages and we saw them doing their work. I was transfixed by the dramatic photos of these black-masked avengers breaking into the embassy. They ended up freeing the remaining hostages and killing all but one of the terrorists. Those Prince's Gate images welded themselves onto my brain. I had little idea what was going on from a political or martial response perspective. All I knew was that I wanted to do that!

Prince's Gate was the first time Special Ops was vivid in people's lounge rooms. The events were later dramatised in the film *Who Dares Wins*, adding to the mystique of the Special Air Service. I read that, at the end of the siege, when the British Prime Minister Margaret Thatcher went into the holding area the SAS had set up as a base for their operation to congratulate them, a great victorious cheer broke out. Reading about it gave me goosebumps.

I became obsessed with Cold War flashpoints, and read about the Entebbe and Munich incidents, where Special Operations soldiers also managed to defuse hostage-taking situations. I read and re-read a book called *The Rescuers: The world's top anti-terrorist units* (by Leroy Thompson), and another called *Fields of Fire* (by James Webb), which switched my young mind on to world politics and current conflicts. The week before the Iranian embassy siege, US President Jimmy Carter sent Special Operations Forces into the US embassy in Tehran in a failed attempt to rescue fifty-two Americans; Operation Eagle Claw, as it was called, resulted in eight American servicemen dying. I vividly remember Carter's successor, Ronald Reagan, addressing the TV cameras about fighting alongside the Mujahideen in Afghanistan to kick out the Russians. Politics, and the critical role of Special Forces in settling disputes, became a personal interest of mine. My schoolwork suffered as a result. I loved our English teacher, Mr Bill Beatty, but *Waiting for Godot* and *Watership Down* just could not match it with the raid on Entebbe, the SAS operations in Northern Ireland, Gibraltar and the Falklands, or the daring escapades of GSG-9 (the German Special Forces unit) in the Lufthansa Flight 181 raid.

It was hard to stay focused on school. I was in the middle of year twelve when the devastating and disruptive break-up of my parents' marriage occurred. I was shuttling between the family home in Rockingham and my auntie's place in Perth to do my exams, and I didn't do so well in my finals.

After finishing year twelve, my plans were in the air. Dad was encouraging me to apply for the Royal Military College at Duntroon, in Canberra, and I sat the selection test for officers. But, by nature, I was quite disruptive and entrepreneurial, not an officer type of personality at all. Martin Studdert answered my questions about the Australian SAS—essentially, what I had to do to get in. Martin was a Signals Corps captain posted to 152 Signals

Squadron, the SAS's communications unit. 'If you want a good long career in the unit,' he said, 'you'll want to go in as an OR, or "Other Rank"—as a normal soldier. Being an officer isn't where you want to go.' Martin really understood my personality, and guided me to the right pathway.

I had—and still have—a defiant streak that wouldn't make me a good army officer. It's not to the point where I'm not a team player, but I tend to question and show resistance towards hierarchical systems. It's fair to say that I have a bit of a chip on my shoulder, which goes back to where I came from, and it's always battled within me. During my career in the SAS, I would occasionally be asked if I wanted to take 'a trip to the dark side', or become an officer; by then I knew myself well enough to say no.

Martin's information meant not going to Duntroon but instead joining the regular army. I didn't mind the idea, and fate would step in. Towards the end of year twelve, I was working part-time as a waiter in the River Room at the Perth Sheraton. Alan Bond and all the bigwigs of the 1980s mining boom ate there, and I'd silver-tongued my way into the job that summer. But I was too cocky by half. One night after work, a few of us had some beers and Bundy and Cokes by the side of the pool, which was completely against the rules for staff. The security guy, who we nicknamed Rodney Rocket for his ability to be in ten different places in the hotel at once, caught us and sent me to the maître d', Mel, who was quite polite about firing me. 'You shouldn't have gone out to the pool,' Mel said. 'We're going to have to let you go.'

The army recruitment office was practically across St Georges Terrace from the hotel. If it had been open that day, I would have walked straight in. As it turned out, it was a Sunday. The following day, I joined the army.

It was ridiculously easy to sign up. Naval guys walked around with smokes in their mouths and tried to talk you into joining the navy. I avoided them and sought out the army people. I did the psych and basic testing, and that was pretty much it. In those days, if you had a heartbeat and could do a few push-ups, and were free of serious medical conditions, you were in. It seemed so simple and right, as if getting sacked from the Sheraton had been part of a higher plan.

When I got home and told Mum, she was upset at losing me so soon after Dad had left. I was the eldest, and had helped her to keep it together during the separation. But I really wanted to do this, and I reassured her that Robert and Paul would still be with her. I don't like to think I ran away from home. I'd dreamt about joining the military and the time had come. In life, there is never a good moment to make these tough decisions.

We flew to Adelaide to pick up some more recruits, and then continued to Melbourne for the five-hour bus trip up to Kapooka. They put the movie *Stripes* on the video player. As soon as we hit Kapooka, I absolutely loved it. I felt like there was a calling; I felt competent and confident as a soldier. It was exactly what I needed. And whether it was coincidental or not, the facial acne I'd battled for years suddenly cleared up while I was there. I took it as a sign: I felt more purposeful and less anxious as a person.

I didn't know anyone else joining the army, though my brother Robert would do so three years later. When you're eighteen, it's hard to throw yourself into a group of strangers, and many people

I knew based on their post-school decisions on what their friends were doing. But my friends in Perth were unsurprised by my choice. I was well known for my love of risk, adventure and shenanigans. The question was whether the army could provide enough of it.

There was all manner of people at Kapooka, but I managed to fall in with a good group of committed young soldiers who got on well with each other. I was in 11 Platoon, Bravo Company—a good omen, as my lucky number was 11 and I wore 11 for junior footy, while in cricket I have batted number 11 more often than not! We slept four to a room, and my closest mates were from that first room—Michael 'Macca' McMillan, a readymade infantryman from western Queensland, and Constantine Constantaris, or 'Con', a tough kid from Melbourne. Both, like me, had designs on the SAS. The fourth member of our room was Grant Main, a laconic South Australian. Michael, in particular, was a very squared-away bloke. He and I shared a bed space and a passion for what was ahead of us, and I was lucky to have him as my partner during the training. Our room inspections were very tight and I loved the discipline and would have done anything for the men in charge of us. During our three months at Kapooka, locker inspections were a regular flashpoint, because Con insisted on keeping a photograph of Elvis Presley taped to his door (my mother would have forgiven a picture of Elvis taking precedence over one of Con's own mum). At inspections, Con would argue with the corporal: 'You can have all the rest of the space, but this little bit I'm keeping for me.' Our room got punished severely because of Con, but we were happy to wear it as a team.

I was mad for the training and had the makings of a good soldier. We had to do three chin-ups whenever we walked under the chin-up bar on our way to the mess, and I would do ten, not to show off but because I had my pathway in mind: I was determined to be one of the elite who made it into the SAS. I was always among the first to have my weapon clean and ready for inspection. I was put in positions of responsibility more often than not for drill or navigation or on bush exercises.

For the first time in an institutional setting, I wasn't a trouble-maker. I had quite a healthy relationship with the platoon staff—the corporals, sergeants and lieutenants—who appreciated my sense of humour. Indeed, I think they enjoyed coming into our room down the end of the hallway, as ours was about the most squared-away. At 0530 every morning, the duty corporal would walk into the hallway and whisper, 'Hallway Eleven!' upon which all of the recruits, with clean-shaven heads, would leap from our beds in our green army boxer shorts and white T-shirts, the top sheet from our bed slung over our right shoulder, to stand against the wall at rigid attention. At 0525, Michael would already be sitting on his made bed with his sheet over his shoulder, eager to be first into the hallway. He woke the rest of us up so we'd all be ready. Few other rooms were as prepared as us. Most guys would still be half-asleep, standing in the hallway at attention, as were the erections they had woken with. As they tried to rearrange their tackle, the corporal would yell, 'Don't MOVE!'

I said to Michael out of the corner of my mouth, 'Fuck, mate, here I was thinking you just wanted to make our room look like it was squared away by being the first out, but I realise you just wanted to avoid everyone seeing how small your dick is.' We all, including Michael, burst out laughing.

Quick with a response, he said, 'Moff, I was only looking after you. Does yours come in men's size?'

I liked to think I helped people at Kapooka, though I didn't always live up to my own standards. Blanket-bashing and other forms of hazing were still commonplace, and occasionally encouraged. Our bastardisation was not as bad as what Dad had told me of his. He went to Nirimba, the notorious naval apprentice school where physical abuse was so bad that some of it resulted in suicides. Once, in the middle of the night, Dad was hung from a tree inside a sea-bag which they filled with water, leaving only just enough room for him to purse his lips above the waterline and breathe. On a freezing cold Nirimba night, he was left to hang for hours. Most of the thuggery, committed by senior apprentices on juniors, was tolerated by the instructors. It was a deep systemic culture. Once apprentices joined their ships, it continued, though a little less physical. Apprentices were known as MOBIs—Most Objectionable Bastards Imaginable.

A herd mentality was encouraged throughout the military, and I was not above getting pulled along with it. The formula for punishment was to hold the entire barracks accountable for one person's mistake—even honest mistakes or just falling short, which no one meant to do. It occasionally turned eighteen-year-olds, all of us frankly shitting ourselves, against each other. If the punishment was cruel, the internal barracks politics it created were crueller. The tough guys would slap the weaker guys around and say, 'We're sick of doing extra PT [physical training] because of you.' I saw it happening, and, perhaps relieved at not, for once, being the target of bullying, made myself complicit by not saying anything.

By the end of our three months, we were put into 'The Funnel', what I called the army's method for determining where to send us. Everyone sat an aptitude test, and our results dictated the technical level of the skills and corps we were assigned to. In those days, we had little choice, which was devastating for those who were sold a dream at the recruiting office of becoming an aircraft mechanic or a diver. My heart was set on joining the infantry, because Martin Studdert had told me that was the proven pathway for SAS entry. But I sabotaged my own plans by doing too well in the tests.

From memory, the top three employment categories were aviation, engineering and signals. Within signals, the top echelon was cipher: code writing and code breaking and so on.

When they announced the results of our assessment, they said, 'All those going to infantry, step forward.'

I stepped forward.

'Moffitt—what do you think you're doing? You're going to Sigs Corps!'

I was gutted. Our whole room went to infantry with 1RAR, which was my intention. But instead, I found myself packed off to the School of Signals, aka School of Typing and Morse Code! There were no guns, and I would be surrounded by people typing. Being in a typing pool in Watsonia, a suburb of Melbourne, one of two blokes in a class of thirty women, was definitely not where I saw myself, though it did have its perks.

Typing was, and remains, a useful skill, and the SAS's business was based on sending and receiving Morse code around the world, which was the only way to communicate globally in pre-satellite communications days. But it wasn't the start I was looking for, and when I was sent from Watsonia to Townsville's Signal 103 Squadron, an operational deployment unit, and then into 1RAR's communications unit for three years, I was exactly where I wanted to be to set up my next step.

———

In the early days of our deployment to the Tarin Kowt district, we recce'd an area just outside the camp to test and set our weapons, lasers and optics ready for combat. One of the themes of our training was 'Be Brilliant at the Basics'. A senior operator, a very good mate of mine, drove around the range to clear it of personnel and livestock, a courageous or dumb effort given it had not been cleared of mines. He deemed it safe and said the line of fire would not impact the farming compounds scattered through the valley as they were outside the 'trace', the area soldiers could fire into, in this case about 2000 metres in front as well as a few hundred on each side.

While we were shooting, a small team of Australian regular soldiers came up to the firing point to share the range.

'Who's in charge here?' the young officer leading their group asked loudly, his tone conveying a familiar contempt for Special Operations Forces. He seemed tense and edgy. My mate who had cleared the range welcomed him and tried to explain the layout—left and right of arc, weapons and ammo, radio and medical proce-dures—all important information as the range had none of the conventional safety signage and flags required back home, and, given there was community and public land down there, it was potentially critical information. But the inexperienced leader, on his first deployment, wouldn't let my mate get a word in.

'Yeah, mate, got it, I know, got it, yeah got it, I've run a heap of ranges before, it's not rocket science . . .'

Obviously struggling to control his emotional state, his awareness was poor because he wasn't listening. This was not lost on some of his soldiers, who shrugged in silent apology to us as he led them over to the right flank. We laughed and continued racing Coke cans down the range with our pistols. When we eventually left, we indicated to the young leader that the range was now his.

'Yeah, got it, I know,' he interrupted us, before barking orders at his men, many of whom were more experienced than he was.

Later that day, in passing, we asked him, 'How did you go up there, mate?', mostly to set him up for a sledge, but to our surprise he responded, 'Great, no worries. Good range, I especially liked the gallery shoot at the mock village.'

'Gallery shoot? Mock village? What the fuck, there is no gallery or village up there, mate!'

His eyes went as round as dinner plates.

The young officer had ended up engaging a compound 50 to 60 degrees off the firing line, well outside the range area. It turned out to be a local family home complete with gas cooker, barking dogs and many obvious signs of life. By extreme fluke, no one was hurt. The most disappointing thing was that at no stage during the after-action review did he stand accountable for his actions. He attempted to shift responsibility to the loose, unkempt and undisciplined SAS soldier who had instructed him and 'failed' to give him 'authorised' Range Standing Orders or a Range Brief. His leadership was in stark contrast to the doc's; opposing ends of a mental spectrum I have since used to evaluate leaders.

What happened at that range was a small incident that high-lighted a larger issue that would emerge over the coming years and deployments. The disposition and strategic objectives of SOF were largely incompatible with those of the conventional forces. The 5-Eyes Special Operations Forces community to which we belonged, with our Canadian, New Zealand, UK and US counterparts, was almost entirely focused on targeting the anti-Coalition command, those high value targets (HVTs) and their subordinates, who were running the insurgency. Back in 2002 and 2003, we had worked exclusively alongside those and related units, to very good effect. But now, bedded down with a growing conventional Australian military presence, our strengths and capability were in danger of being dulled. I do not wish to sound negative about Australia's conventional army, which is among the best in the world pound for pound, especially our front-line infantry who, inexplicably, had not been among the first units deployed to Afghanistan. Over my next five deployments to Afghanistan, Australian SOF, under Australian Army command, I believe were placed in unnecessarily vulnerable situations based on what I believed to be, at times, a poor appreciation of how we could best be employed.

To be fair, we didn't give them much reason to love us. Conventional military have always had tensions with Special Operations Forces, characterised by our long hair, beards, baseball caps, civilianised clothing and apparent disdain for hierarchy.

Often, we were lambasted for modifying issued gear, or even buying new equipment online when the issued stuff was inadequate. For example, many of us wore boots more akin to running shoes (and sometimes actual running shoes) rather than the issued boots, which were terrible. We bought our own boots because they were better suited to the mountains of Afghanistan, which didn't stop a decree coming down to cease wearing them on pain of being sent home. Rather than asking why we preferred this footwear, and how this might be useful for the rest of our fighting force, they saw us as arrogant and insubordinate. Eventually, the ADF adopted more sensible footwear and attire. To be honest, a certain degree of arrogance or 'humble swagger' was required to be an SAS operator, what the unit's founding father, David Stirling, called 'daring'—which is not to say we didn't occasionally get it wrong.

If you are standing on the edge of the ramp of a C-130 Hercules, at 5000 metres above the earth, at night, with someone strapped to your front, and you are leading a parachute team out the back into the mountains of Afghanistan, I believe you need to have convinced your team that the mission is achievable. You need supreme belief that you will pull it off, self-confidence above the ordinary. If you have just completed six hours of combat, fighting and killing, experiencing the trauma of war, and then have to come home to your cot, chat to the kids on the phone, and then, hardest of all, get a good sleep because you will have to go and do it again in eight hours' time, the ability to switch off and suspend your emotions is essential. To fight an enemy who plays by no rules at all, who kills innocent women and children at will and scatters headless corpses along the roadside, you must find a way to fight on the very edges of your moral virtues, the law and rules of engagement, without crossing the line. This requires almost a kind of cold empathy with the enemy. As a psychologist, I now realise that this constant transitioning between the many mindsets one must be able to navigate can come across as arrogance at times. It has taken time for the realisation to take hold that we must support our soldiers with the training and cognitive tools they need to navigate this complex psychological terrain because eventually they need to return to society. I have long thought we've let our soldiers down in not providing such training, for example for the moral dilemmas that they often face for the first time on the battlefield. I remember a quote I learned in a class I took many years before, from a US Special Forces soldier, Peter Dillon: 'Proficiency comes from practice. Yet too often the reality is that for ethical decision-making, practice starts on the battlefield.'

———

Between missions, we were going a bit stir-crazy. We were sitting around the wooden huts at Tarin Kowt on a typical Afghan winter's morning with blue skies and a warm sun punching through the freezing air. The enormous snow-capped mountains were a constant reminder of how high we were, around 2000 metres above sea level. When the sun came out, the locals would surface from their mud houses and squat along the walls in the bright light, grateful for any warmth. We mostly only saw men and boys. The women and girls were probably getting breakfast ready; in any case, in most provinces they were seldom allowed into sight.

If we didn't have cricket, I felt, we would drive ourselves mad waiting for the next rocket attack. You join up for action, but the reality was days of tedium, missions being prepared and then cancelled at the last moment, with the occasional risk of instant death. It wasn't conducive to sustainable long-term mental health. Whatever flooded into those long gaps in time was up to us, and my choice was cricket.

The bat I took on that trip was a Gray-Nicolls Excalibur, the first bat in my collection that I had been using at the Applecross Cricket Club. I'd even made a few runs with it, a rarity for me, including my highest score for the club at the 'Royal and Ancient' Shirley Strickland Reserve, or 'Stricko' as we called it. The highlight of my 74 was being sledged, and then dropped, by another SAS guy on the opposing team. Armed with these good memories, the Gray-Nicolls went into my assault bag and came to Afghanistan, where it was present during a number of contacts in the Khod Valley as well as on the base in Tarin Kowt.

Those first games in Afghanistan in 2002 had been a bit of fun, and the ones in Iraq were primarily to kill time. On this tour, the games meant more to me and I began to look after the bats better. I was beginning to think I could keep them as souvenirs for my man den, or 'war room', back home. After some of the improvised and questionable-quality bats I'd used on previous trips, it was good to be playing the full range of combat-zone cricket with a genuine implement.

It was then that I decided it would be a good story to tell that each bat had been out on a mission with us. On our long-range vehicle patrols out of Tarin Kowt in 2005, lasting up to five weeks at a time, it could get very boring. Morale was most important, so I was always devising games to keep our spirits up. It wasn't always cricket either. We played the Rock Olympics, which had two events: one was to compete to throw a 15-kilogram rock the furthest, and the other was to be able to hold a 30–40-kilogram rock above your head for the longest time. In both events, Khod Valley records were repeatedly smashed. Another event was a pop quiz lasting hours, that, because the questioner could make up twenty questions to which they alone knew the answers, resulted in many a controversy. Chip Bradman, being ex-navy, would get up everyone's nose by asking questions like, 'What is the diameter of a piston flange on a frigate diesel engine?' Rowdy's response was always to ask, whenever his turn as quizmaster came, 'Why is my arse itchy?'

Variations of cricket were, of course, my go-to distraction. On short breaks, if we didn't have enough time for a proper game, we would set up slips catching practice, where the group would stand in a semicircle around the batsman, who would hit them hard catches. We turned this, too, into a competition, where the 'King of the Slips' stood in a certain position and had to keep holding his chances until he dropped one and was succeeded by the next contender, and likewise for relegation to the other end of the queue.

When we had time, we set up a game in the middle of a 'harbour' (a circle of cars, or a secure compound with tight security all round). These games were very ad hoc with basic rules and no scoring, and nothing was written down, only remembered by the players and spread by word of mouth, thereby allowing all kinds of bullshit to emerge. Umpiring was by consensus and equipment was highly valued. Slogging and expansive shots could get you barred from cricket for the rest of the patrol, as there was no chasing after balls outside the harbour. The bowling was strictly spin only, or off two paces, as most blokes couldn't spin their way off a dancefloor. Tea breaks were not scheduled, as their timing was usually decided by the arrival of a firefight or a rocket attack.

The pitches in the Khod Valley were universally bowler-friendly, and an uncommon number of hat-tricks were taken. This was actually a pretty good effort by some of the cricketers involved, who were hard-pressed to land three successive balls on the pitch but could then allow the rocks and boulders to do their work. It's safe to say that not many 'backyard tons' were scored.

Often, while we were playing these games, Taliban or Al-Qaeda fighters were watching from the hills, talking about us to each other on their radios. For some reason they were less interested in shooting at us than in badmouthing our cricket technique.

'Hey, Harry!' our interpreter yelled one afternoon as I beat the edge of Streaky Bacon's bat yet again, then appealed to an imaginary umpire for the theatre. 'They reckon you are a bit of an average bowler!'

'What?'

The terp was listening, via a Motorola radio, to their communications, which they conducted on ordinary Motorolas they bought online.

'The bad guys!' the terp called out. 'They are watching from the hills up there and reckon you are shit cricketers!'

'Is that fucken right? Let me speak to these pricks.'

I stormed over to where the troop commander was. He was smirking, always a little bemused at how cricket made me more animated than fighting the Taliban.

'Can you speak to them?' I demanded. 'Tell them to come down out of the hills for a game. I'll show 'em who can play cricket.'

The interpreter talked in Pashto over the radio, and likely surprised the enemy with the invitation.

'Tell 'em whoever loses has to leave the valley,' I said.

To nobody's surprise, they declined. The back and forth deteriorated to asking them to send down their toughest soldier to fight ours and to settle our dispute the old-fashioned way. They declined again, saying we would call the planes to bomb them if they came down, which strangely, in my mind, suggested they were vaguely considering playing us. In all honesty, we would have bombed them. In fact, later that night, we ended up in a firefight with them and called in air support to bomb a cave that many of them ran into. They should have got one last game in.

Of the many memorable cricket games on that trip, one stands out. It was the evening after the 2005 suicide bomb attack on the dogfight that I have recounted. In the aftermath of the explosion, there was a fatigue among us that I had not experienced before. Fear, adrenaline, stress, shock, horror, trauma: everyone processes it differently but it ends up with a common exhaustion, low mood and deep reflection. The boys needed to let out the tension. 'Who wants a hit?' I asked.

The pitch, on the semi-bitumen apron of a helicopter landing zone, was the best in TK, and we would often play there between patrols. A broom was brought in and the pitch was cleared of debris and rock. A bin was found to be the stumps, and pace bowling was allowed. We had good quality tennis balls and umpires, and even set up a scorecard. I organised cold Gatorade and some 'bung-hole' (tinned fruitcake found in ration packs, so hard that if you ran out of bullets you might throw it at the enemy with similar effects—it was called this because it caused constipation . . . it bunged up your hole) for tea. It was the nearest we could get to a real cricket match.

The Chechen came steaming in to Rowdy, an accomplished turf cricketer and normally a quiet and measured man who, too easily, contracted white line fever over any game of cricket. The Chechen had a unique stuttering and skipping run-up with a double-hop bowling action that bamboozled even the most experienced batsmen, and this time he was frustrating Rowdy, beating the bat on several occasions and catching the edge once. The catch was dropped at second slip, by me, though it was flying low and at searing pace . . . Finally, and clearly frustrated, Rowdy advanced down the pitch to drive the Chechen over his head and missed, the ball crashing into what would have been middle stump of the bin. The reaction around the field, all caught on video, was jubilation. Rowdy, who gave no quarter and was good on the lip, was silenced. This 'other ball of the century' is still celebrated today. After what we had seen during the day, it was the perfect, if momentary, antidote.

———

I had started saving my bats for a personal collection, sensing that they were objects with deeper resonance. Sometimes a ball found its way into my memorabilia, such as, at the end of that deployment, a 'Shaun Ball' that we'd played with in a game in the Khod Valley. Streaky Bacon smeared a shot through cover and the ball went under a vehicle parked on the edge of a cliff above a wadi. We thought we'd never see it again. About five nights later, I was driving behind Streaky's car, we were wearing NVGs, and this ball popped out from underneath his vehicle. I thought, *Hang on, is that Shaun Ball?* It had been wedged under the running gear and driven hundreds of kilometres around Afghanistan. And now, like me, after plenty of wear and tear, it is back in Australia.

By the time we finished our 2005 deployment, most of us were exhausted and a little frustrated, knowing how many of the gains of 2002 and 2003 had been given away. This frustration and fatigue spilled over when, as part of our end-of-deployment 'march out', we were required to undergo psych debriefs prior to our return to Australia. After such a long and arduous deployment, I was called into a room that was obviously a spare admin office, not a psychologist's workspace.

I sat in front of a very young female psychologist who looked as if she was fresh out of university. I don't think I am being sexist when I observe that it was odd to choose a virtual trainee, non-combatant, young woman to debrief a group of SAS operators, weary and desperate to get home after a long deployment. Whatever her professional skills, did they expect this kind of cohort to be really open and honest with such an interviewer? Like the office, and with no disrespect to the psychologist herself, it smacked of not having been thought through. I make no comment on her ability, and am sure she was an excellent psychologist. It's just that the decision-makers should have understood the power of credibility and buy-in among those being interviewed.

She asked me questions about the trauma and psychological stressors I had experienced.

'How are you sleeping?' she asked.

How was I sleeping? I was not sleeping. When I managed to drift into unconsciousness, I was soon woken by bad dreams.

'Fine,' I said.

'How are you feeling generally?'

How was I feeling generally? I was constantly lethargic and tired, I suffered from significant homesickness, and by the end of the trip I felt down a lot of the time. My back was in constant pain, and I felt guilty because Danielle had been left doing all the work in raising our children in a new house that, for good measure, we were in the process of rebuilding. And just a few days earlier, the army had notified me that I had been overpaid, and they were going to draw back large sums from my upcoming pay packets.

'Good,' I said.

'Would you like to talk about anything you've seen?'

I had changed a tyre in the middle of an ambush with bullets tinking in the rocks and against the car, completely at the mercy of fate. I had provided covering fire for a group of mates who were being peppered by rockets, grenades and rounds. I had been close to the biggest battle Australian troops had been in since Long Tan in Vietnam, where only the non-explosion of an enemy RPG in our guys' lead car had prevented a small massacre of SAS soldiers. I had placed children into body bags. I couldn't shake the smell of dead bodies that seemed to be everywhere and forced me to relive the worst experiences. I had seen headless bodies left on the roadside by a murderous band of rapists and criminals. I had tried to comfort defenceless people who had just seen their families wiped out in front of their eyes. That young boy I had been caring for after the suicide bomb attack visited me in my sleep. Even after I came home, when the rest of it had settled down, I still saw him while I was swimming laps at the pool, or while I was driving to the shops, playing with my kids, watching television, batting in the nets. *Bang*, there he was. I would feel sadness, guilt, and occasionally depression and anxiety. I would see a psychologist regularly to deal with it. I would only really get over it when he told me that my feelings were normal and it wasn't within my control where that boy was when the suicide bomber detonated; in fact that the boy was lucky to have had me there in his final moments and that he was visiting me to thank me, not to bring me sadness; and that he wouldn't want me to be depressed, and that I should welcome him and indeed look forward to telling him how I was going now. These imaginary conversations would change a number of things for me, and eventually I would smile and feel glad when I saw him, to remember that in his last moments he received care and compassion.

But when I sat there for my debrief, this was still a long way into my future.

'No,' I said.

There was no incentive to tell the truth. In fact, the incentive was to lie. If I said what I really thought, I would be psychologically downgraded. I would be designated unfit to deploy, as the next deployment would be within a short time of my return home. No matter how bad I felt, I knew I would recover and be raring to go again. Also, I couldn't tell the truth because my mates would know about it and I would carry the stigma of being 'mentally fragile'. And lastly, admitting to feeling this way might turn me into a 'pin cushion' for scientists and psychologists to probe and study for their PhD and Master's research into PTSD. No thanks.

As a psychology student myself, I wasn't going to denigrate the seriousness of these debriefs, but it was wrong place, wrong time, wrong chemistry. I said as little as possible and got out of there, boxes ticked.

But there was always an avenue for the larrikin SAS operator to have a last bit of fun. One of my mates, after establishing that he felt totally fine, was asked if there was anything else he wanted to talk about at the end of his interview. Aware of who was coming in next, he said, 'Well, I am a little worried about my mate who you're about to see.'

The psychologist, immediately interested after so many brick walls, replied eagerly, 'Yes, tell me more?'

'Well, the other day I found him drunk, naked and crying in the showers, clasping a handmade rug he'd only just bought. I am a little concerned. I feel bad for telling you.'

'No, not at all, I am glad you mentioned it. Thank you!'

Subsequently, the next bloke spent two hours defending himself, trying to convince the psych that he was really okay, wasn't drinking, and had no handmade rug, in the shower or out of it. It was a bit naughty to lead the psychologist on, but the laughs we got out of it were the best medicine. It had been a long and bloody tour.

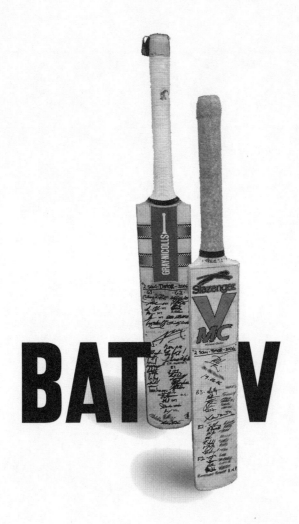

DILI ON FIRE

TIMOR-LESTE, 2006

'You have come here to kill me, haven't you, Harry?'

'No, Alfredo, we're just keeping an eye on you. Mate, you've caused a whole bunch of trouble down in Dili. And, hey, that bottle of wine isn't a microphone! Any danger of a top-up?'

From the moment I met Alfredo Reinado, I liked him. There is a danger that my memory is altering him, and because we spent a lot of time with him in his mountain hideout at Maubisse in the highlands of Timor-Leste, I am suffering from a kind of Stockholm syndrome. He was an articulate, charming and handsome man, something of a Promethean figure who was turned into a rebel by his passionate love for how his country used to be. I thought he was a good bloke, though many will disagree. I knew that he had a chequered past, yet our personalities—particularly our shared scepticism about authorities concealing their political agendas— were in sync. I warmed to him immediately, as he did to me.

Within a couple of years of our encounters, after he signed a cricket bat for me at the end of one of our frequent games at his hideout, Alfredo Reinado was, just as he had foretold, a dead man.

———

The Timor-Leste deployment kicked off with the urgency that you expect in the life of an SAS soldier but very rarely eventuates. I was sitting on the floor at home, eating Coco Pops with my kids, when I got a text asking that I come to work immediately. Inside twenty-four hours, we were on our way.

There had been gossip within the regiment that we might be needed in Dili, the capital of the island nation that had won independence from Indonesia in 2002. Australia had played a mixed role over the years, supporting the country with a peacekeeping force during its fight to de-couple from Indonesia, but also claiming income from the oil and gas fields in the Timor Sea, and infamously spying on the Timorese government during negotiations over the oil treaty in 2004. The independence leader Xanana Gusmão was named president of Timor-Leste in 2002, but he and the country's government were under constant threat and occasionally needed Australian military protection.

We forward-launched to Darwin, thinking we would be briefed and sent straight into Dili, which we were told was on fire. We were aware that there had been many deaths in skirmishes between rebel soldiers, youth gangs and police. It was complicated, but we were needed to restore order on the streets that very night. Over the next four or five days, however, the Australian government seemed to waver, not releasing us for the task, and we trained with Black Hawk helicopters outside Darwin in an increasingly agitated, impatient frame of mind. This being my first operational foray as a team commander, I was champing at the bit.

While we were stuck on RAAF Base Darwin, I organised some cricket games with a shitty old Gray-Nicolls bat I had taken from the spares bin at Applecross and chucked into my bag. We played on a concrete helo pad with a rubbish bin as our stumps. Hercules aircraft and helicopters were flying around us, and senior hierarchy would wander by, shooting us disdainful looks, no doubt thinking, *Those SAS pricks with their long hair and sunglasses and hats on backwards, yahooing over their cricket match.* No one ever comes up to say it to your face, they just mutter under their breath, their body language giving their thoughts away.

We planned for an Emergency Action (EA), which meant moving at as little as thirty minutes' notice onto helicopters and inserting straight into the airfield at Dili. We had also war-gamed a number of Deliberate Actions (DAs), which aimed at securing Australian personnel and interests, such as the embassy. This time, because so little was known about the situation on the ground other than that people were being killed and gang violence was escalating out of control, it was an EA, which meant we had to improvise when we got there.

It was one of the longest EAs ever, with twelve of us crammed into a helicopter the size of a small minibus, on high alert, loaded and wearing all our kit, for a sweltering, ball-busting four-hour flight. Everyone was sweating like pigs and highly stressed by the time we approached Dili. As it turned out, there was so much cloud and rain over the city that we couldn't land, and instead we were dropped at a town called Suai, on the opposite side of the island from Dili, where we camped in literally a pile of pig manure. By the time we entered Dili the next day, we weren't even the first in; because we'd taken so long, the SAS team who were meant to follow us got in ahead. It was a bit embarrassing, and an inauspicious start to the mission.

Soon, however, we were organised. The plan was for SAS patrols to base out of the airport, which had been taken over by Australian military forces, and conduct patrols from there to make sense of what was going on around the city. We would report intelligence back to the army, who would send in regular units to carry out patrols, establish order, liaise with the local government, and eventually hand security back to the Timor-Leste military police so that the upcoming elections could take place.

When we arrived, there was no law and order, as the police and local army had fractured, mostly along familial and regional lines, and dispersed. We drove the length and breadth of the city to assess the disorder. Pouring into the capital were displaced people, rioters, looters, criminals and thousands more who were terrified of a repeat of the kind of massacres that had taken place during the 1975 genocide and subsequent Indonesian rule. Among all of this humanity, there were only a handful of Australian soldiers: two SAS patrols, on the streets. The Australian conventional forces had arrived at the air and sea ports but were not allowed to leave. Some SAS operators were deployed to guard key people such as

President Gusmão, Prime Minister Mari Alkatiri and Foreign Minister José Ramos-Horta, while others went to the parliament to keep an eye on comings and goings and to try to figure out what would happen next.

At times like this, all the planning in the world was for naught. We had to go into reactive mode and deal intuitively with what we were seeing. This is where we found out if our selection processes had picked the right people for the mission, who could adapt to those moments and take charge.

At one point, we had to get through all the burning, bashing and looting to attend an intelligence briefing in a building at the sea POD (point of deployment). Not far from the gate, an SAS team was handing out blankets and food to thousands of displaced people. The guys were so overwhelmed at the back of the truck that they had to push women, children and young men to keep them back.

'You need a hand?' I asked one of the blokes.

'What do you think, mate?' he responded as he shoved away a young woman trying to get to the tents and food.

'We've only got a minute,' I said as we jumped out to organise the people into some kind of line. Through keyholes in the crowd I thought I could see armed men loitering. Nothing focuses the mind quite like scanning a crowd for someone with a gun.

We handed out biscuits, tents, blankets and other aid supplies from the back of the truck to the masses. Not a shot was fired, but it was one of the most tense situations I was ever involved in; we knew that one loose gunshot could set off a stampede and kill hundreds. If panic or violence broke out, there were too few of us to be able to do a single thing about it. Knowing there was a huge

Australian conventional military force holding fast within the seaport a block away was bewildering. Without a coherent plan to deal with the breakout of mayhem, all we could do was stay cool and keep our fingers crossed. As Groucho Marx said, in adapting Kipling's poem *If*, 'If you keep your head while all about you are losing theirs, you will be the tallest person in the room.'

I indicated the gates of the port, behind which armed Australian personnel were standing.

'What are those pricks doing?' I asked one of the boys.

'We asked for some help earlier, but they are under orders by old mate there.' He motioned to a very young and overwhelmed-looking officer inside the gate.

Once some local police had been corralled to help with the crowd management, I went up to the gate.

'Any danger of you pricks giving us a hand? There are armed locals out here.'

'We are under strict orders to maintain the security of the gate,' the navy guard said, clearly uncomfortable with a duty that was not normally their job. 'If we open the gate, they might all rush in.'

'Yeah righto, whatever,' I said. 'Can you let us in?'

'I don't have authorisation to do that.'

'You fucking what? Whose side are you on, mate?'

'You need permission.'

'From who? This is fucking ridiculous. Who's running this rock show?'

The guard nodded towards the very young officer.

'Okay, well let's speak to him then!'

The officer seemed very reluctant to talk to me, and demanded to know who I was. I told him I was there for a meeting with the headquarters battle captain.

Flustered, he made a call.

'Glad to see they breed you guys so tough,' I said to the guard. 'You wouldn't want to have to deal with these women and children out here.'

The guard leaned in close to me and lamented, 'I wish I could help, mate, seriously. This is fucking mental.' I could see that they shared my frustration; they wanted to get out, but policy or risk management from higher up was preventing them.

After his phone call, the officer let our team in grudgingly, and his men slammed the gate shut after us before going back to their stations.

We went through the port and were met by an army major. The first thing I asked him was whether he could authorise the guards to go outside the gate and help our blokes.

'I'll let them know inside,' he said. 'The navy are in charge here, so everything has to go through them. Anyway, come in, we need to get this brief done so you can start your journey up into the hills.'

As he led me up to the second floor of the building, he outlined what was going on.

'You're probably aware that Alfredo Reinado has been coming down out of the mountains and causing trouble. Well, it seems a lot of people, including some pretty powerful types here, want him dead, mostly because he's popular and they might owe him and his blokes a few bucks in back pay. It's all a bit complex and seems to have come to a head. We need to get someone up to find him before the pollies' goons get to him and start a civil war.'

'It all seems strange to me,' I said. 'I thought they were on the same side?'

'No chance, mate, the entire executive is in-fighting. Money, power, the usual. Here, sit down and I'll grab the intel officer.'

We sat on the floor and grabbed some water bottles from a well-stocked pile. It struck me how we take these advantages for granted: metres away from some of the poorest people on earth, we had all we needed and more.

'Fuck, they go all right here, eh?' Stuey 'Two-Up' said as he crammed a bunch of chocolate bars into his pouch.

A young male civilian who introduced himself as Tom came to grab us for the meeting. 'I don't have long and I need to get you on your way,' he said as the team got up to follow him, none of us quite sure what we were doing.

'Er, there will only be room for two of you,' Tom said. 'The others can stay and collect chocolate, eh? Just in here, Harry.'

He led me and Stuey to a door with a toilet sign.

'Yeah, sorry, guys,' Tom said. 'It's not the best meeting room, but it is the most secure place we have for now.'

The three of us crushed into a storeroom just inside the toilets and began the meeting. It was turning into a comedy skit. Tom muttered about listening devices being everywhere. He tried to open his file and write notes on his clipboard as he briefed us on the job. This was made particularly difficult not only by our proximity to each other—we were literally chest to chest, nose to nose, and Stuey and I were in full body armour—but because I needed to keep opening the door to let light in so we could see Tom's pictures. I couldn't help thinking about Agent 13 in the *Get Smart* series.

'Um, Tom, why don't we just go into the toilet proper?' I asked. 'I'm not sure this is necessary.'

We completed the meeting in the slightly larger washbasin area, where Tom took out his maps and documents. He wasn't that bad really, just excitable, like a smart uni student suddenly thrown into the biggest adrenaline rush of his life. But there was no need for such secrecy; anyone listening in wouldn't have had a clue what he was on about, I'm sure. We certainly didn't.

Afterwards, as we walked back down the stairs, Stuey asked, 'Did you get any of that, Harry?'

'Not a thing. We'll work it out. Was that you that farted in there?'

'Nope.'

'Must have been me then.'

We laughed, and acknowledged that we had enough information to go on. This was common in such complex environments. Our intelligence agencies and military hierarchy are high-level professionals who design, plan and execute with precision and decisiveness, but in my experience these qualities are rare at the bureaucratic and staff officer level. It is often left to the sergeants and corporals, and the junior officers, to get the job done. If we got it right, we would hear nothing back; if we got it wrong, it would all be our fault. We knew the truth of the saying that success has a thousand fathers and failure is an orphan.

Mostly by good fortune, those first days in Dili passed without serious incident. The conventional forces were let out of the seaport and we were released to do our jobs. For our team, that meant heading up to Maubisse and looking after Reinado, to keep him in check and transport him to and from Dili for negotiations.

Reinado already had deep links with Australia, outside what was happening politically. As a boy, he had been taken by the Indonesian military during East Timor's 1975 struggle for independence from Portugal, and he lived in Indonesia until he escaped, in a rowboat, to Australia in 1995 when he was twenty-seven years old. He worked in Australian shipyards for four years, developing a love for boats and the sea, before his country invited him back to work in the military, after it voted for liberation from Indonesian rule in 1999. When Timor-Leste gained independence, finally, in 2002, Reinado was given a commander's position in the two-boat navy. He was in and out of the military and the police after that, constantly clashing with authority, throughout it all travelling to and from Australia to be trained by our army. His family also moved to Australia to live.

The Timor-Leste military was divided between several factions, some loyal to the government, others to individual politicians. In early 2006, some 600 soldiers deserted in protest at being overlooked for promotions due to what they believed was ethnic discrimination. Reinado was the highest-ranking officer to join them. After a number of skirmishes with forces loyal to the government, he fled into the mountains around Maubisse, a town in the hills 70 kilometres south of Dili, where he and his supporters holed up in a lovely old Portuguese colonial building called the 'Pousada de Maubisse' perched on a knoll overlooking the idyllic mountain village. This was where we found him.

It was reported that SAS soldiers had to hunt Reinado down, but he wasn't hard to locate, and the object of the exercise wasn't to detain him so much as to ensure his security while he entered peace negotiations on behalf of the rebels.

It was impossible to travel far without coming across reminders of the Indonesian occupation, especially roadside memorials to various atrocities. We visited the memorial in Balibo, where five Australian journalists were murdered in 1975, and went to the 'Kissing Wall' or 'Kissing House', where the Indonesians were alleged to have made Timorese women kiss the wall, often leaving lipstick or blood from their lips, before raping and killing them.

When we had to stop for the night, we would camp on the side of the road, maybe break out the Gray-Nicolls and have a game while cooking dinner or setting up a communications exchange via high-frequency and satellite radio, before settling in for an all-night piquet, taking turns to sleep. Sometimes we even had a spot of beach cricket or a bodysurf.

I can't say our improvised cricket games captured the hearts of the locals, who were too scared and tense to participate. Our job was reactive, trying to help and calm people who feared their country was on the brink of disintegration. Again. We spent a bit of time in a town called Maliana near the border with Indonesian West Timor, a known smuggling crossroads near where contacts between Indonesian and Australian soldiers in 1999 occurred.

We did have one memorable experience of getting a bit closer to the people in Bobonaro, the hilly province of which Maliana was the main town. In the Bobonaro villages, people were living in grass huts without electricity or running water. We had a look around a village where one of the Indonesian-speaking members of the team, Mick 'Windmill' Miller, and I went to the chief's hut and asked what, if anything, he needed from us.

On the left-hand side as we entered the hut was a shelf with two Polaroids on display. I did a double-take.

'That's my mate!' I cried.

Windmill took a close look at the Polaroid with me. There was nobody in the world who could be mistaken for Hawkeye, who had been part of the Australian forces in the area in 1999.

This coincidence broke the ice with the chief, who replied to my claim that Hawkeye was the world's ugliest man by saying that Hawkeye and his mates were friendly and helpful. Seven years later, they still loved him and talked about him. It's true that Australian soldiers are good at caring for local people and genuinely wanting to help them, and it was gratifying to see that we wouldn't be quickly forgotten. I took another look at the photo of my mate. Whatever his good works, there was no disputing he was as ugly as a hatful of arseholes.

——

At Reinado's house in Maubisse, we came upon a unique scene. There was only one way in, a road winding around the knoll in the middle of the town, atop which was the mansion he used as his headquarters. He invited us to eat and drink with him on the veranda, enjoying the cool of the evening after dinner. The people up there loved him. He certainly did not command an army of thousands, or hundreds for that matter, and he was protected only by a small squad of henchmen. The highlanders saw him as a representative of 'the people', a man who would stand up and fight for them if necessary. The official leadership of the country was deeply compromised, and most of the people we spoke to had had a gutful of the prime minister, Mari Alkatiri. He was a polarising figure, as a Muslim in a Catholic country, suspected of benefiting personally from the Timor Gap oil deals, rumoured to be tied up in the sandalwood smuggling trade, and widely perceived as having risen to influence as a puppet of the Portuguese government. Around this time Alkatiri's claims to the prime ministership were under pressure from Ramos-Horta, but both men had become symbols of the country's many social and financial problems. Even the revered Gusmão appeared to have lost favour in some parts of the country, and many of us who met him at that time observed that he was tired and in poor health, chain-smoking and putting away more than a couple of scotches a night. The nation was at war with itself, and larger powers were meddling in the background, including Australia, interested in one thing—oil.

I might be accused of having listened to too much of Reinado's side of the story, but it still upsets me how various Australian governments had knowingly looked the other way since 1975 while the Indonesian Defence Force committed some of the most heinous war crimes of the twentieth century. More morally disconcerting still, as an Australian soldier, was to learn that we did so knowing that Britain and the United States were arming and training those very Indonesian forces who carried out the genocide. My father had often talked about the injustice, so I wasn't just getting it from Reinado. In fact, long before our deployment, I had written a song called 'East East' for The Externals' album *Sale*, describing the horrors Indonesia visited upon East Timor. The chorus went:

Oh no, not me, it happened right in front of me
It's not wise, to loosen your disguise
Oh no not you, what the fuck is happening to you
East Timorese

Our recent visit to Balibo confirmed the reality of Australia's complicity; it was not a story the charismatic Reinado was inventing to win our sympathies.

He invited us most nights to dinner with him in the main house. We were sleeping down the hill in the workers' huts where we'd set up radios to communicate back to HQ. The huts afforded us some security in case Reinado's goons tried anything, though I was increasingly confident that they wouldn't, as we had ingratiated ourselves with them quite skilfully. We still slept with our guns and kept a permanent piquet, the SAS's practice of being 'unblinking' 24/7, which enhanced our safety but didn't make for a great night's rest.

One particular night, Reinado and I were sharing a bottle or two of red wine and talking on the veranda. His charm, intelligence and passion flowed most of all when he talked about his family. We were both family men, and the pain of spending so much time away from them, as reluctantly absent husbands and fathers, was our common ground. We talked about our passion for sport and remembered when we could just go fishing. He told me of his dream to lead the Timorese Navy and one day retire as a fisherman, living on the coast with his family. Even at this time, however, Reinado seemed to know that he would never return to that life. He had gone too far; his fate was sealed. In fact, his bouts of paranoia would seep into the conversation and overwhelm those more wistful moments. After a few more drinks, and a few more, Reinado would get going on his conviction that the government had victimised him and his men, and that they were owed a great deal of money. He became bitter as he criticised politicians with their snouts in the trough while his men and their families went without. He had seen his nation ruined by corruption and drug-trafficking and was frustrated. Over time, I began to sense that his paranoia was winning the battle over his optimism. He obviously was not sleeping, and judging by the amount he was drinking and the duration of his daily hangovers, it was likely he was slipping into alcoholism.

He was, foremost, a military man. Having been trained by the Australian Army, Reinado was as fascinated as anyone by the SAS. 'So,' he would ask me more than once during these lengthy, soul-searching, intimate conversations, 'tell me again how you got into this?'

———

The first real SAS soldier I saw in the wild put the final hook in me.

It was mid-1989 and I was a twenty-one-year-old Signals Corp corporal and detachment commander working with 1RAR, the First Royal Australian Regiment, based in Townsville. We were out bush having finished a part of the 'Kangaroo '89' exercise, and at the end of it I asked to be dropped off at a service station in Charters Towers. I loved being out on those exercises so much, I would wait for the next group going out and jump in with them. That way I could stay out in the bush, away from the barracks, for weeks on end.

Towards the end of that exercise, I came into the bush camp for a shower and a hot meal. I was sitting in the dirt by the field kitchen with hot rations and coffee when this bloke materialised out of nowhere wearing US jungle cams, SAS attire from the Vietnam era. He was bearded, with strictly non-regulation long hair, and on his feet were runners rather than the boots everyone else had to wear. He didn't look unkempt so much as casual-cool. Most army guys have a certain submissiveness in the way they carry themselves, like they are used to doing what they are told. This guy was very different. Confident as Ricky Ponting unfurling a pull shot, he strolled over to the field kitchen, conducted an assessment of what they had on offer, and then disappeared again. I lost track of him until suddenly he reappeared with four milk crates, which he placed carefully in a circle off to one side.

The next thing I knew, three of his mates had appeared, smiling and laughing, all with that same self-assured no-shit look about them. They had extra food—spearmint-flavoured milk, hot pies, stuff we didn't have—and they'd set up their crates with cushions to sit on and an upturned box as a table. I was agog, thinking, *How good's that? I've got to get into that. They're resourceful, they're smart, they won't sit in the dirt like us . . . In fact, why are we sitting in the dirt?* There was a mini revolution going on in my head, perhaps it had been for a long time.

Back in Townsville, I grew impatient. Some signallers in 1RAR had a bit to do with the SAS, and a couple of my mates had gone off to 152, the signals unit attached to the SAS regiment at Swanbourne in Perth. The SAS bandwagon came to Townsville later in 1989, and a couple of bearded blokes gave us a presentation in the local gym. I put in my application, passed the precursor tests, and, all going well, would be on the SAS selection course for my twenty-second birthday in March 1990.

I'm one of only two people I know who failed and passed selection on the same day. There's a story behind that.

To prepare, the first thing I had to do was put on weight. I had originally strategised about applying for SAS selection when I was twenty-three or twenty-four, but after discovering that I loved the jungle and had the attributes of a good jungle soldier—I was intuitive, good at navigation, and could move without making noise or leaving any sign—I had accelerated my timetable, perhaps, I would later conclude, out of over-confidence. But standing on the scales, seeing I was 75 kilograms wringing wet, I thought, *Fuck, I've got to put on 10 kilos*, not an easy task for a lean bloke like me. I managed to increase my weight to almost 85 kilos by the time of selection.

One thing that helped me put on weight was moving back to Western Australia to live with Mum and Dad—who had got together again for a short period—for my final preparations. Mum's excellent Hi Ti Min (beef and cabbage stir-fry—still my favourite) and steak and kidney pie were just the thing. The family dog, who I called 'Chetan Sharma' after the Indian Test fast bowler, kept me company as I did my final running and stomping in the hills around Roleystone. I spent a few nights alone, having been told to prepare for solitude. I prepared myself well physically. What I wasn't prepared for was how to become a man.

I can vividly remember almost every moment of selection. The three-week course was all about physical testing and survival. There were psychological and knowledge assessments as well, but if you couldn't handle the physical side of it, the cognitive stuff wouldn't matter. Three weeks of extremes pushed my body and mind into dark places I never knew existed. Physically I lost all of the 10 kilograms I'd added in preparation, and the average weight loss of many on the course was higher. Mentally I was whittled down by the lack of sleep and the brain-bending ambiguity of the tasks we were compelled to carry out. Not one minute was wasted, with all spare time spent doing runs, push-ups, squats, navigation or writing essays. By the time you got to bed, often after midnight, you slept instantly—only to be woken several times to do more physical, psychological and intellectual activities, and eventually having to rise into another day of physical and mental challenges. Groundhog day for the most part, the pressure was high and the pace relentless. Nothing was left to chance in assessing whether you were up to the job.

We were sent to some old asbestos-lined army huts at Northam, then down south to the Stirling Ranges, and finally to the rugged hills around Wellington Dam.

At the beginning of the course, an SAS corporal introduced himself. 'I've been in the SAS for ten years. I am not the hardest bloke in the unit, but I would be in the top three. I am so driven, I once ate a whole birthday cake before my mates could tell me there was a stripper inside. For the next twenty-four days you will grow to know and love me as Corporal Punishment. Now drop and give me fifty burpees.'

Once we were done, he told us what they were looking for. 'It will always seem that you're standing in the dark in the cold,' he began. 'We're not looking for stars. The frontrunners in this group will fall by the wayside. The ones up the back of the herd will fall away. What we want is the grey men, the inconspicuous ones in the middle. If we haven't noticed you and are wondering how you're doing, that probably means you're hitting the marks.'

That suited me down to the ground, being a bit of a 'grey man' by nature. I can hear my friends scoffing at this description, but in situations like these, I preferred to dissolve into the scenery. Throughout those three weeks I concentrated on passing, doing my bit, being authentically helpful, and hitting my marks without being noticed. It was hard, but I loved every bit of it. The harder the better. A peculiarly stressful aspect of the course was the 'failure' going on around you. Attrition rates were roughly 10 per cent per day, higher in the first week of the course. Your mate one day was gone the next. You were unlikely to get told to leave unless you had a physical injury and the doctor sent you home, or you clearly weren't up to it. People who left selection almost always did so at their own request. We started the course with one hundred and fifty applicants and ended up with around forty. But I never entertained a thought of withdrawing.

A difficult activity was called 'Rate Your Mates', where you had to rate the ten to fifteen blokes in your section from best to worst. You had no choice to opt out. It struck me as unnecessarily cruel, but I came out of it thinking it was a great exercise in informing instructors what was going on inside the course from the students' perspectives, and formed a balance against their assessments of us.

One of the interesting things I found out about myself was that as I was helping others, with equipment, learning or motivation, I actually drew strength from others 'failing'. The more people who left the course, the stronger it made me feel. I would come to study this phenomenon, being intrigued by the psychology of it all. Because selection was conducted under 'silent running', meaning that the instructors didn't give us any feedback along the way, sometimes the only feedback we got on our own performance was when someone else left the course. I didn't want anyone else to fail, but when they did, it alleviated some of my own self-doubt. If I was still there and the next guy wasn't, then I had to be going okay. It has a parallel in cricket, in the saying that nothing is better for a batsman's confidence than when his partner gets out.

There was only one part of selection where I truly doubted myself and thought, *I'm not going to pass.* In the early days, we had to pass a fitness test: push-ups, sit-ups, chin-ups, running and so on. I had been cracking out around twenty-five chin-ups in preparation, but on the day I could only muster fourteen, just two above the minimum level. I was pretty gutted and had to talk myself through the negativity and de-escalate the catastrophe. It was another new skill I was developing on the run—how to move past failure quickly. There was no one to teach me, so I soon realised it was up to me and me alone. Coping tools such as self-talk, personal reflection and reframing, dealing with problems entirely within myself, were skills I had unconsciously developed throughout my life, and they came to the fore in my time as an SAS operator, and helped me teach junior operators later in my career.

Selection breaks you down in four ways: the physical breakdown, sleep deprivation, food deprivation, and long, relentless tests of concentration. They throw foreign weapons at you to learn rapidly, assessing your ability to learn quickly and under pressure. Then you have the 'Happy Wanderer', a solo four-to-five-day navigation exercise in the Stirling Ranges. I felt confident the whole way through and it was my favourite part of selection. I was by myself, getting a full night's sleep, and eating three (ration pack) meals a day. While those who thrive on Happy Wanderer tend to pass the course, others who really suffer from the loneliness get found out and retire from selection during this part. On the Happy Wanderer I only got to four peaks in the Stirling Ranges, which freaked me out until I discovered that they were less interested in the number of peaks you hit than the distance you'd covered, and on this measure I passed. By the time I had finished the exercise, one candidate had fallen off a cliff and fractured his skull, and another had dropped a weapon off another cliff. It was not a walk in the proverbial national park.

I came to understand that we were being assessed on our character, interpersonal skills and decision-making. Hoping to maintain my grey-man status and not stand out, the hardest day for me was my birthday, when they made me stand in the middle of 100 aspirants and sing 'Happy Birthday' to myself. My 'cake' was a piece of bung-hole with lit green army matches in it. That wasn't the hard part. The hard part was that everyone else had to do one hundred push-ups while I kept singing 'Happy Birthday' over and over. I don't know if you've ever done one hundred push-ups, but it takes a while. I thought everyone was going to hate me. And some did, believe me.

The last three or four days of selection were taken up by 'Lucky Dip', a notorious team exercise where you have to carry heavy objects, such as a fully laden and inflated Zodiac boat, through the heavy forest around the Wellington Dam and Collie River area, and complete a number of tests on an average of two hours' sleep per night. The assessors were crawling all over you marking you; it was super tough. There were exhausted guys cheating or cutting corners on Lucky Dip, not realising they were being watched by senior SAS blokes.

They would spring surprises. Like giving you a pot of cooked chickens, rabbits and guinea-pigs, only they hadn't been gutted or skinned—they were boiled whole. Some declined to partake, which was not only fatal to their assessment, but silly, as the protein and nutrients were no-brainers. Personally, I chowed down. Guinea-pig is not all that bad; it tastes like chicken! Then you'd be told you had to share a soaking wet sleeping bag with another bloke. If it wasn't already wet, they would throw it into Collie River and give it back to you and say, 'Go to bed now.' Then they would wake you up half an hour later and task you to whittle a knife, fork, spoon and dish out of the wood in the forest for a meal that never turned up. Then back to bed, and up thirty minutes later to carry some ridiculously heavy load to the top of a hill. When you got there, a guy would say, 'What the fuck is that doing up here? It belongs down the bottom.' When you got to the bottom, another guy would bark, 'Didn't I tell you to carry that to the top?' It was sadistic, but it was a test, and I relished it. Whatever they did, they weren't going to break me.

Which didn't mean you couldn't get hurt. One day, while carrying water jerries weighing 100 kilograms with another guy, I slipped on a log and crushed my left testicle. One of the SAS staff, respectfully known as Big Duke, was standing on the log in front of me when it happened. I let out this little whimper. It was so fucking painful, I shed silent tears. I looked Big Duke in the eyes, this guy who would turn out to be one of the people I most respected in my life. He grinned, as if to ask, 'What are you gunna do? You're two days from the end of selection, you're not going to pack it in now.' I cracked on, but that testicle is still damaged. To this day, every time I feel pain down there or have to adjust it for comfort, I see Big Duke's shit-eating grin: 'What are you gunna do, Harry?'

By the end of the course, I thought I'd done well enough to get selected. On the last day, we forty survivors, exhausted but excited, were nervous about the verdict. Some were worried that it was curtains for them, as they had missed marks along the way, but most took comfort in having finished the course, and so they should. We were lined up in three ranks near our huts at Bindoon. We'd showered and packed our gear. We were all emaciated, with black rings under our eyes, many also bearing bandages, sports tape and stitches. The regimental wing sergeant major (WSM) stood out front and said, 'If I read out your name, you're in. Get into the bar and wait in there. If your name isn't called out, go to your hootch, grab your shit, and you're on the bus back to Perth.'

That was the full extent of the debrief, after all the heart and soul we had put in. Nowadays they have psychologists and a full regime of care, after years of learning how the disappointment affects guys who've put their lives and careers on hold for two or three years to prepare for this, only to miss being selected. It has a life-changing impact on many unsuccessful applicants.

We stood listening to the WSM reading the names out. I was beside one of my old mates from the Signals Corp, Andrew Constantinidis, who, six years later, would be among the eighteen soldiers to die when two Black Hawk helicopters went down near Townsville. During the selection course, Andy and I were thick as thieves. We'd reassured each other about how well placed we both were. We had passed the individual tests and felt we'd performed very well across the rest of the time. We were both larrikins, and a few of the staff seemed to enjoy that part of our humour. However, we knew there were no guarantees, as many 'definites' had been returned to their units in the past, usually without explanation.

The WSM continued through the list, alphabetically. Those whose names were called out moved off to the bar with a spring in their step. The others stood in stunned disbelief. He passed through 'C' without mention of Andy. As he moved towards 'M', my blood turned cold. What if this was all for nothing? It can't be! The past two years of my life spent training? All of my dreams since I saw that picture of Martin Studdert, all my hopes going back to the Prince's Gate siege. All of it wasted?

The names rolled through the 'M's. No Moffitt!

'That's it,' the WSM said. 'Catch you later.'

Andy and I, along with a few others, were dumbfounded. No, we were absolutely shattered. We almost hugged each other, but thought better of showing emotion in front of anyone else. We wandered back to the huts, where I broke into tears as the gravity of failure caught up with the effects of the last few weeks. I was inconsolable as I put my final items into my bag. Nobody noticed—the few guys around me were lost in their own devastation. Angry as much as upset, I cried, 'Fuck, this is not right, it's got to be wrong!' I had failed SAS selection. It was one of the most fraught moments of my life, not least because we were totally blindsided. I felt humiliated. What would everyone say back at home, back at the unit? How could I possibly hold my head up? Where did I go from here? I am not afraid to say, I just wanted to see Mum.

We had to wait ninety excruciating minutes before the buses came to take the unsuccessful applicants back to Perth to start putting their lives back together. As we drifted like ghosts out to the bus pick-up area, a voice squawked over the tannoy: 'Candidate 15, candidate 68, report to the WSM's office.'

Andy and I looked at each other. We knew it! They had fucked it up! When we got there, they said our paperwork had been mistakenly lost at 152 Signals Squadron. 'Someone has nominated you to be a signals specialist on your forms. Do you wish to serve as a signals specialist or as an operator?' (Actually, what he said was, 'Do you wanna be a chook cunt or a hard-hitting infantry soldier?') The answer was obvious. We would be operators, the real thing. As we left the WSM's office, having been through hell and heaven, Andy and I hugged each other in delight like teenaged bloody lovers. We ran out the front of the office to find Terry O'Farrell, a legendary figure in the unit, waiting for us.

'Do you two pricks want to be SAS soldiers?' he asked. 'Get in the fucken bar.'

If only the challenges ended with selection. My experience was that the eighteen months after selection, called the Reinforcement Cycle or 'Reo', was a great deal harder. Selection was about survival and passing tests, but Reo was where you felt the constant pressure to perform while climbing a steep learning curve. At the end of Reo was the prize—the SAS 'sandy' beret—but getting there was considerably tougher than I'd imagined.

During selection, my weight fell from 82 to 70 kilos. At my first shower after the course, while I was scrubbing my face I could feel the bones of my cheeks and the sides of my teeth through my skin. These days the new 'Reos' are given ten days to eat and sleep and recover from selection. Thirty years ago, you had a weekend off, during which you got on the piss with your new mates, and on the Monday you turned up at Bindoon for five days of living on rations and learning about heavy weapons and explosives. I wonder if we were in quite the best state of mind to be handling 1 or 2 kilos of explosives! Nowadays much more care is taken with the soldiers, and they are trained with much smaller ordnance.

The patrol course component of Reo was, I'd venture to say, the toughest course on the planet. It went for about six weeks, with long patrols in the Koombooloomba jungle near Tully in far north Queensland, the longest of which was ten days, carrying loads of around 50 kilograms in foliage so thick that sometimes you could progress as little as 500 metres in a whole ten-hour day. It had rained nearly every day for six straight weeks, and we were in the middle of a bog, living under hoochies and facing an unstoppable grinding pressure to perform. On Reo, there were benchmarks for every course and if you didn't meet them, you were given a show-cause and then let go. The stress was intense. It was a privilege to be instructed by some of the original 'Phantoms of the Jungle', SAS operators from the Vietnam War era, but this also elevated the standards and the fear of failing in front of them.

During Reo, we lost several people who couldn't keep up with the technical requirements such as paramedicine, antenna theory, communications and Morse code, parachuting, mechanics, mathematics, and the science of explosives, high-level navigation, the list went on. Several levels above basic soldiering, Reo was the toughest university on the planet. The homework and study were demanding. Sometimes it wasn't intellectual book work. On the paramedics' course, for instance, you slashed goats and sewed them back up, and you practised basic surgery and traumatic amputations. We practised on ourselves, putting each other on saline drips (a legitimate hangover cure), cutting out moles, and giving each other injections. There was a lot of fun to be had, but it's not really allowed anymore.

It bonded us as a cohort. Reo was a mixture of a continual baptism of fire and the longest footy trip ever. The suffering we shared was an experience that made us trust each other with our lives. I formed some bonds that are still ironclad today. What we all shared was a desperate desire to be SAS operators. The rough glamour of those men I had first seen at Townsville stayed with me. But it's a double-edged sword. Some in the rest of the armed forces can have a fair bit of contempt for what they see as SAS arrogance. You're on a flogging to nothing, so your coping mechanism is to turn into larrikins, taking the piss out of yourselves and your officers. We were lippy, confident, always cracking a gag when the chips were down. With the blend of intensity and humour, life could be like an extended version of *The Odd Angry Shot*.

The penultimate hurdle to passing Reo was 'Resistance To Interrogation' training, affectionately referred to as going in 'the bag'. Designed to give us an insight into the experience of interrogation, the stress was mostly psychological. With extreme sleep and food deprivation, uncomfortable seating positions, and isolation for many hours at a time, you were forced deep inside yourself. For many, this meant an occasional glimpse over the precipice into vivid hallucinations and delusions.

The night before it started, we had just come in from a ten-day patrol and were aching for a hot feed. We were told to pack up our hoochies and stretchers in the jungle camp, move to the mess, grab a feed and be on the road outside at 1700 to get on the trucks. We all knew it was a lie and something was afoot. We knew we were going in the bag. We ate a large and hearty meal that was unusually spicy, but we couldn't stop ourselves after a week-plus on hard rations. We lined up with packs, webbing and rifles and awaited the inevitable announcement that 'The trucks have broken down, we have to walk out', a very well-worn phrase in the unit. Given it was about 20 kilometres out, we knew they were just going to fuck us over so when we went in the bag we were truly exhausted.

We set off in patrols of five or six (some guys had withdrawn from the patrol course so we were down a few in numbers), and it wasn't long before the sting in the tail revealed itself. The chilli or spices in the last meal kicked in and just about everyone had to break track and sprint for a shit. The whole 20 kilometres of road was littered with men wearing packs sprinting off to drop their dacks. There were poo-tickets littering the road, as we didn't have time to bury anything, given that the instructors were shouting at us, 'Get your fucken arses back out and moving.' I don't think there was any environmental damage, given the very organic nature of our needs, though I still joke with mates that the chilli may have had a radioactive half-life.

It dehydrated some of the guys very quickly, and many, including me, were picked up by the ambulance. Eventually, we all made it to the trucks, exhausted after hours of shitting and stomping with our packs on this forced route march. It was standing room only on the back of the trucks, and being driven around for four more hours topped it off. By the time an 'enemy' group of terrorists opened up the trucks screaming, 'Get off, you infidels, you are all our hostages!' one of the boys replied, 'Thank fuck for that, Ahmed, the blokes that are apparently on our side have been trying to kill us for ten hours. Lead the way!'

We were taken off the truck and placed facedown in the dirt. My head was enclosed in a pillowcase and my hands were 'plasticuffed'. We were then frog-marched to a reception room and photographed, stripped naked and given an ID number. From there, we were real-located to a large holding facility and forced to sit cross-legged on shower mats, sprinkled with beach sand for extra discomfort. The next days and nights were characterised by the endless repetition of John Lennon's 'Give Peace a Chance'. I fucking hate that song. For a treat, they put on 'The Ballad of the Green Berets', made famous in the John Wayne movie, and for small pockets of time we would sleep.

At some point, an anonymous guard stuck a toothbrush in my hand and whispered, 'Look after it, don't give it to anyone.' This set off a continuous game of stealing and replacing toothbrushes. No sooner had a guard snatched your toothbrush, or inserted additional ones in your hands, than a voice would echo down the hall: 'Comrades! It seems we have a thief among us. One of your comrades has had his toothbrush stolen, and we all know how important oral hygiene is!' As if sitting naked in the dirt with a bag on your head was not important. 'So we will be coming around to check everyone's toothbrushes, and if we find the culprit there will be punishments.' Which meant reduced rations or time in the 'hole'. In the end, I just placed my toothbrush inside my pillowcase and when one was placed in my hand, I threw it. We were all going in the hole anyway at some stage.

Naked throughout, we were exposed to numerous interrogation methods, one of which was humiliation. Once I was man-handled into a tent and told to 'Wait'. There I sat cross-legged, wrists tightly bound, pillowcase on my head and toothbrush in my hand. A woman's voice told me my next interrogator was here. She removed my pillowcase and started questioning me: 'What's your name? Which unit are you from? What are you doing here?' I gave the trained response: name, rank, service number and date of birth. This continued for maybe thirty minutes, during which she grew increasingly tired and fed up with me. She ordered me to do sit-ups. Though I was seriously fatigued after six weeks of jungle training and the subsequent days of sleep and nutritional deprivation, my fitness held up and I churned through thirty reps. This only frustrated her further, and she continued her line of questioning with growing impatience.

As I was conducting sit-ups there in the dirt I looked down to my shrivelled, turtle-like penis (it was cold, what can I say?) and noticed a bug crawling across my 'meat and two veg'. Instinctively, I paused briefly mid-sit-up, pinched the bug in transit and threw it off to one side. Then I continued my sit-ups. My interrogator, who was standing over the top of me by now, was further enraged, as if the bug was her personal emissary and I had insulted it.

'What are you doing?' she screamed. 'Did I tell you to stop? I will tell you when to stop. And I will tell you when you can remove a bug from your dick!'

Her focus switched to the dirt beside me, where I had thrown the bug. She combed the dirt looking for it.

'Aha,' she said. She duly placed it back on my old fella, looking quite satisfied with herself.

'That's not the same bug!' I said.

And the bug didn't look too happy either. But I did manage to survive the interrogation process.

If it weren't for moments of humour, we'd have gone mad. And if such moments didn't present themselves in the form of a fortuitous bug, we had to create them. Our last course in Reo was paramedics, at the end of which we were inspected on a parade in Portsea, outside Melbourne, by the head of the medical corps. It was pretty serious with marching bands and formal dinners, an anniversary event, and we had to parade in our best uniforms. Some of my mates and I thought we'd have some fun. Before the big Friday ceremonial parade event, we reported in sick with the flu. We took off to the city and hired two gorilla suits and a rabbit suit. We went to the gym and changed into these suits, and as the general did the inspection with the military band playing, we sprinted onto into the parade ground, in front of a few hundred troops and onlookers, and pretended to rumble, fight and root each other. The whole place, including those on parade, burst out laughing. A major chased us into the sand dunes. One of us turned around to give him the finger, but the gorilla suit gloves wouldn't fold down, so he gave the major 'the hand'. We got back to the gym, dressed, put the suits away in the corner, and sat down pissing ourselves laughing. We thought we'd got away with it. When a sergeant major came in and asked if we'd seen any suspicious activity, we said, 'We don't know, three blokes came and went, we're just here to have a shower.'

We got away with that one. With all the pressure on us, pranks were a way of life. One night we broke into the officers' mess and glued their knives, forks and spoons, and some glasses, to the tables. We made sandwiches and left. To cover our escape, we set off the fire alarms and sprinted along the beach in front of the barracks, which seemed like a good idea at the time. Everyone came out in their pyjamas, including a few fellas who had been visiting the nurses' lines, and we just blended in. The old major who had it in for us gave us a long examination, noting we were in our stepping-out clobber. We said, 'Evening, sir, lovely night for it, eh?'

We were smart-arses, but it was great fun. The night before our final parade, we constructed an enormous 5-metre-by-5-metre template of a winged dagger, the SAS logo, laid it on the grass parade ground, sprayed some super-fast fertiliser to get the grass around it to grow, and created a spectacular bare patch in the shape of a dagger. The major had to see it from his office every day. That was a kind of pride-in-the-unit prank. Less so was when some of us sped a Holden Statesman De Ville into the middle of a physical training session, grabbed the instructor, wrestled him into the boot and 'kidnapped' him in handcuffs and hood before dumping him in front of the Sorrento police station.

Yes, that might have gone a bit far. The police found us and said, 'You can't do this, some old ladies saw it all and have rung us in a highly alarmed state. We have to punish you guys. We won't charge you, but you have to come clean the cells all weekend.' Towards the end of the punishment the on-duty policeman said, 'Go and get our coffee, bread and milk supply from the Safeway and then you can knock off.' The guys went and did so, throwing in a few treats for themselves on the police bill, and then went to the chemist next door to buy some Ford Pills which they crushed up and put into the cops' tins of International Roast. We found out later that it went right through the cop shop.

One thing that reinforced how lucky we were to have our opportunity was the experience of meeting imposters purporting to be former or even current SAS operators, often around Anzac Day. I remember playing pool upstairs at the Subiaco Hotel around 1991. Thommo—another SAS mate—and I had won the table and a couple of old fellas sporting medals came over to take their turn. Thommo and I were not wearing medals, firstly as it was not the done thing for operators out in public, and secondly . . . we didn't have any. We started the game and during some small talk about one of our opponents' medals he mentioned, from the corner of his mouth and in a low tone, that he was ex-Special Forces and had served in Vietnam with the SAS. Now, I know better than to cast aspersions, but when I mentioned the name of someone who had served in 3 Squadron in Vietnam and drew a blank look, I asked which squadron this guy served with. He said, '5 Squadron', which has never existed. We soon left. On another occasion in Brisbane, having just completed some training with the police tactical unit there, my colleague Tom and I were downstairs in Rosie's bar. I got talking to a fellow in his late teens. He was very keen to tell me how he had just made it into the military and was now being selected for service with the SAS.

'That's a fucking big call to make, mate,' I said. 'You can't just say that without any proof.'

As old mate reached for his wallet, I whispered to Tom, 'Check this bloke out.'

He opened his wallet to show a military ID, of sorts, and a hat badge available from any good military antique store.

'Wow, take a look at this,' I said to Tom. 'This bloke's with the SAS! Hey, mate, I know a bloke in the SAS. Frank Johnson, yeah, do you know him?'

The young fella was deep inside the fantasy now, and as I rattled off a few more names, he said, 'Yes, I know Peter Thompson!'

'Well, aren't you lucky, mate, cause he's right here.' I turned to Tom. 'Eh, Pete, this young fella says he knows you and served with you!'

The young fella took a moment to look around the circle of individuals crowding curiously around him, and realised that his worst nightmare was coming true. We could see it dawn on him as he turned and ran up the stairs. I often wonder what becomes of such people. We've all exaggerated at times, but this was a whole different level and bordered on some kind of delusional disorder.

———

Ever the grey man, I tried to slide into the middle of the bell curve in our group. But to stay there, I had to work harder than I ever had. It was like being captain of your local cricket club and suddenly finding yourself playing for Australia. Some of the other guys were born and bred to be SAS operators: super-smart country boys, resourceful, dedicated, efficient, and far superior to me. I never got a show-cause, but I was always under the pump to keep up. I suffered the full range of self-doubt and self-loathing, wondering what the fuck I'd got myself into. I felt that, at twenty-two, I was too immature to be among these guys. When I graduated out of Reo into my troop and received my beret, that immaturity was really evident. You were with hard older men, in an atmosphere that was at times like a prison yard. If you were 'shit', you were told so in no uncertain terms. I was a bit shit for a while. But all new guys were shit. It's a rule. You're shit until you do something that impresses someone, and I was one of the last to be able to do that.

The gym at the unit had a fight club in those days: not a boxing ring, just a bunch of mats in the middle of the basketball court. Because I'd been bullied as a kid, I had learned to defend myself. But as I looked across the ring at the forty-year-old man I was pitted against, I thought, *Oh, shit.* I was around 80 kilos and this guy was six foot six and must have weighed a dollar ten. He glared across the ring with a scarred face and an expression like a pit bull terrier. I was thinking, *We'll shake hands first.* Instead, he just stalked across the ring and king-hit me. I've still got a missing tooth from it. When I came to, he was standing over me saying, 'Welcome to the fucken real game, cunt.'

That was it—everything changed. Food tasted different, flowers smelled different, vistas looked different. People seemed different. Right then, I grew up. I'd thought getting into the SAS was a bit of a game. My first two years in the unit revealed a whole other level of brutality, based on performance, and not just physical. Psychologically and socially, there was no room for error. And it was primitive. You had to grow up quickly, as no one was coming to help you. Within a few years, I was so immersed in the tough physicality of that world, the confidence that grew in me through solidarity with my colleagues made up for my inherent self-doubt. If you were out on the grog and there was a problem, you felt sorry for anyone who picked on a regiment guy. I remember one night in front of the Cottesloe Beach Hotel, a bunch of patch-wearing bikers turned up, terrorising everyone. There was a fracas between them and some SAS guys, which the bouncers broke up. A biker said, 'Fuck off or I'll bring back a dozen cunts and we'll fuck you up.' Our guy said, 'No worries, Einstein, I should only need one other mate then.'

———

I liked to think that Alfredo Reinado relished hearing these stories and enjoyed the time we spent up at Maubisse. But I could see the isolation and boredom affecting Reinado, and didn't want it to set in among the team. As ever, the budding psychologist in me was always seeking something novel to break the monotony and pressure. Having the Gray-Nicolls cricket bat showed them that I had thought ahead. I saw daytime cricket games as a circuit-breaker for our guys, who were inevitably getting worn down by the conditions, spending weeks living in communities alongside very hungry and needy people.

We did some physical training with Reinado and his men, and invited them to join our cricket games. It has to be said that he was a terrible cricketer and sportsman. You know within seconds if someone has coordination or not, and he had none. In fact, I'd have to say there was no talent among any of his henchmen. Their game was soccer. They were mystified by this weird game.

Because bins were rare we used chairs as the wickets. We cleared the ground on a good length. Eventually we ran out of balls. We ordered replacements, but they were overly bouncy rubber balls. One of our guys, Stuey Two-Up, was a compulsive slogger. In Maubisse, as much as we tried to calm him down, he couldn't stop belting balls over the side of the hill into the jungle and that was the end of them.

Of course, this all took place in and around Reinado's relentless media interviews, a surreal scene that we capitalised upon through our games of cricket.

Reinado, this exotic, charismatic militia leader in his mountain hideaway, was reported to be one of the most interviewed pseudo-celebrities on the planet in 2006. He had CNN, ABC, BBC, and every other major news organisation lining up to sit in a small tent on this mountaintop outside the mansion to talk to him. Part of our job was to vet everyone who went through. With Reinado's paranoia, he suspected that some of them were spies from the government. He was always alleging that senior members of the government were in on crooked sandalwood deals and other corruption, and would have him killed before he could spill their secrets.

To vet the visitors, we set up a game of cricket. After they parked, they had to come through our game to gain access to Reinado. We could control the traffic by starting a new over and stopping people from coming through. During that pause, we took photos with hidden cameras and struck up conversations with them. If one of us was fielding at cover point, he could chat with the journalists and cameramen at the front of the queue to get a sense of their intent or suss out anyone who was just there to meet Reinado. It became a *Hogan's Heroes* type of situation, using the game to collect information covertly. We didn't plan it like that, it just evolved from one thing into another, as cricket always seemed to do.

———

I had two cricket bats in Timor-Leste. The first I had signed by Xanana Gusmão and, in late June, wanted to add the signature of Prime Minister Alkatiri, whose government was collapsing while we were in the country.

On the night of 25 June, we got word that his ministry were being sacked the next day. Many people believed he would leave the country for his safety. 'Fuck,' I said to one of my mates, 'I don't have his signature on the bat yet!'

We jumped in our car and headed to his house. When I arrived, I met another mate who told me Alkatiri was inside with his Cabinet holding a 'crisis' meeting. I grabbed my bat and headed in.

Alkatiri lived in relative luxury, as do most politicians in my experience, and the dining room was quite big. I entered to an intriguing sight. I expected to see a bunch of serious politicians plotting their strategies and planning exits and comebacks. Instead, I saw empty, upturned bottles of Johnnie Walker Red and about ten individuals in varying levels of drunkenness. The table was lit by candles. Alkatiri, at the head of the table, was very drunk.

'Sir, I am Harry Moffitt from the ADF, and I am a very keen cricketer. It is my habit to carry a bat wherever I go and to have my colleagues and other important people sign it. Would you do me the honour of signing here for me?'

'Harry!' he said cheerfully. We had met before in fact, and he was always friendly, but I hadn't been sure if he would remember me. He laughed merrily and looked about. 'Of course I will sign it,' he said, seemingly flattered by the recognition of his last vestiges of importance. I indicated for him to sign across the bat in the small neat size of the other signatures. But to no avail—he slashed his name obliquely across the middle. It was large and ugly, and I was a little annoyed. But I had it.

'Thank you, sir,' I said, and made myself scarce.

I left the room pretty disillusioned about the state of politics in Timor-Leste. We were risking our lives to protect a government whose senior ministers were carrying on like it was the last days of Rome.

Alkatiri's government did fall, and his sloppy signature forced me to get a second bat. I went to the 3RAR Q store at the airfield in Dili and liberated a polyarmour Slazenger bat, a Michael Clarke signature model. In our later weeks in Timor-Leste, we set up a gym at the air base and played cricket in the bulldust. The ball kept very low and the pitch got dustier the more we played. There was talk of pinning a tarp to the ground to give us an even surface, but we were too busy. During the hot middle of the day we also set up indoor cricket games in a big rec room, where we played throwdowns on the concrete floor. These games were characterised by some of the sharpest fielding I had ever seen. Indeed, many a diving catch was made in this hybrid of conventional and French cricket.

We probably stayed a bit longer in Dili than we needed. Towards the end of this deployment, we were getting in people's way, and the conventional army didn't want us around. After much gnashing of teeth, we left a small contingent behind and returned happily to Perth. After three months of the troubles, stability was achieved in Timor-Leste and the conditions were set for the elections.

A year later, the situation had changed and an SAS team attempted to eliminate Alfredo Reinado in a raid but failed, killing a couple of his henchmen. Alfredo escaped further into the hills. His hand was now forced, knowing that there was a 'bounty' on his head. I was always uncomfortable about the attempt. If someone gave the order to kill him, who was it and why? It did, and still does, feel a bit strange to me.

Of all the non-SAS signatures I have on my bats, my most valued is that of Alfredo Reinado. Spookily, it appears only centimetres from the signature of José Ramos-Horta.

In 2008, possibly consumed by paranoia and alcohol, Reinado came down out of the mountains and allegedly attempted to kill

Ramos-Horta in the driveway of his house. Reinado shot his rival several times in the torso, leaving him near death. Moments later, Reinado was shot and killed by Ramos-Horta's protection team. While I do not condone the assassination attempt, I sense that this was the end that Reinado had constructed in his mind some time earlier, as far back as when he had looked at me fatalistically and asked if I had come to kill him.

History has still to pass judgement on Alfredo Reinado. I intend to travel to Maubisse one day and have a glass of wine on the knoll overlooking the town. I suspect he will be well remembered there. He was right about one thing, that corruption and greed were ruining Timor-Leste, and perhaps in another reality he would have been able to unite his country.

THE EMERGENCY

TIMOR-LESTE, 2008

Between late 2006 and early 2008, I wasn't sent on any overseas deployments. This did not, however, allow me to spend much-needed time with Danielle and our kids; in fact, there was a constant round of exercises within Australia, some of which were challenging and enjoyable while others fed my tendency to cynicism about the hierarchy. Our unit's workload was relentless, and sometimes it felt like the military were trying deliberately to keep us away from our families, as if they didn't want us to relax into life as normal human beings. It might have been intended to make us better soldiers, but it also amplified marital and familial stressors, and hardened and dulled our emotions even further.

Having spent months away in Afghanistan and Timor-Leste, I returned home for a short leave break only to be sent straight back out for several weeks to support a conventional army exercise in Shoalwater Bay, on the Capricorn Coast in north Queensland. The thought of leaving my two young children, not to mention a wife who worked full-time, so that I could sit in the bush and be moved around the map by some general, was more than I could take. My mates felt a similar resistance, and we didn't take the best attitude on that exercise. We made campfires at night, carried shots of whiskey, and defiantly had a good time. At one stage we were supposed to find some pretend enemy camp. Instead, we stole a car and drove it through the training area to the enemy headquarters. We changed into civilian shirts and ate for an hour in the enemy mess, undetected. I even knocked on the door of the HQ tent and had a brew and a cigarette with the enemy battle captain—pretending we were Special Forces on their side. We then left the exercise area, lit a fire and sat around whingeing about how fucked the hierarchy were for making us do such stupid exercises when what we desperately needed was some rest at home before the next overseas trip.

Another problem between deployments was having to complete promotion courses that had little to do with our career trajectory. Nor did they add significantly to our skills. The SAS had developed an internal promotion and skills continuum that was directly related to our jobs, but because we were administered by 'Big Army', we were required to complete their promotion courses too. We appreciated that the regular army participants on these courses gained something out of our being there, but we were spending more than enough time away from our families. We wrote many letters to the ADF senior leadership, but nothing was done. I wrote more than ten letters and emails and not once did I receive a reply. My family, and mostly my children, were the ones who suffered.

Time away while I was in Australia was considerably harder than time away on deployment. As a parachute expert, I had to travel to complete regular training to keep currency. There were also courses in explosives, language, medical and call for fire (the procedures for calling in assistance from artillery or air bombardment), and then there were the unit courses, where we would instruct new people in the skills they would need to become SAS operators. Finally, there were specialised skills that the regular army lacked, so at any time they could call upon us to attend a course as a specialist, with no concern for our battle rhythm for the year. All up, we spent as much time away on exercises and courses as we did away at war.

I was also a survival instructor. Survival courses are tough. Not many people want to be on them. Even for the instructors there is little food, sleep is interrupted and it generally means walking long distances day after day. But I mustn't make this a big whinge, because I enjoyed the bush and those courses did provide many memorable moments. It was not as extreme as combat, of course, but you don't quickly forget the experience of lying in wait for a goat to capture, spending two hours on your back, rain pelting down on your face, when finally an unfortunate animal starts grazing on the grass over your face, giving you the chance to bash its skull in and slaughter it for food for your team. Nor do you forget fishing with handmade string and hook, not having eaten or drunk for so many days that you begin to hallucinate that your mother is paying you a visit with a cold glass of milk and a plate of toast with jam. I remember being so weak with hunger that my team and I chased after a cattle calf with our handmade spears, but our spears were so shithouse that our weak throws bounced off the calf, which did not even break stride as it bounded away.

One of the hardest skills was fire-lighting. Once we were in a cave on the Western Australian coast, trying for hours to get a fire going, but it was pouring with rain outside and we couldn't find any dry tinder. One poor guy, Robby 'Four-X' Sutcliffe, had been trying for hours to make fire. Everyone else on the course had achieved it, and the clock was ticking, with twenty-four hours remaining until the end of the exercise. Four-X was rubbing and stroking the sticks together, with busted blisters on his bleeding hands, as he tried over and over, increasingly desperate, until finally he got a little ember going. Triumph turned to despair when a single drop of sweat fell off the end of his nose and doused the ember. I have seen some disappointed individuals in my time, but this was right up there.

All these experiences, while not being in a war zone, added to that growing feeling that being at home was like being away and being away was like being at home. Being with your team was everything, and leaving them could feel like losing a limb. This was the hardest thing to cope with as a husband and father: even though I hated leaving my family, there was a part of me that was lost when I was not with the boys or out on the job.

―――――

The fight in which Alfredo Reinado lost his life and José Ramos-Horta was wounded took place on 11 February 2008. We were immediately sent as a reaction force to quell the inevitable unrest that would follow Reinado's death. Others would create trouble in his wake, and there was potential for a full-blown coup. Reinado's obvious successor was Gastão Salsinha, a less gregarious and more circumspect figure, who had seemed very suspicious of me and our presence in 2006.

Our job was to carry out a couple of raids on targets of interest, to signal to the destabilisers to think twice. As usual, the intelligence picture was fluid and often hopelessly inaccurate. Links between personalities within the power apparatus were complex politically, financially and familially; locals frequently used the opportunity to lie to us in order to trick us into interfering with their enemies. Reinado had likely been one of the more honest people we met: he was clear on what he wanted to do. He was committed and loyal to that, whereas a lot of others, including his own successors, had dubious intent.

We had our share of wild goose chases. One of our raids was purportedly on a militia leader, but when we raided the place, it turned out to be the home of a frontbench minister. Someone had misled us to piss off this important person.

Another day, we were planning to rope into a funeral that criminals and militia operatives were holding for one of their leaders. We knew where it was, and planned to cordon off the funeral party and arrest the people of interest. However, we concluded that it was culturally inappropriate and we weren't absolutely certain that the suspects would even be there. To make a mistake would risk alienating the local populace, so we called that one off.

We only played a handful of games of cricket on that trip, but they were unique. Because we were in Timor-Leste as a quick reaction force, we spent a lot of time sitting in our camp waiting for an intelligence feed. We would be in standby posture, milling around the cars, our guns on the seats and our body armour ready to put on, for an hour, for several hours, or for minutes. It was both tense and tedious at the same time. When I felt things going flat, I would take out the big Super Tusker bat I'd taken from Applecross.

I'd grabbed this bat out of the club's spares bin, which was hardly ever opened. It was a bat I had used in the nets out of pure nostalgia. It was more than ten years old and not much of a bat, but now that I was building a collection with a specific aim, I liked the novelty value. Not everyone can say 'Super Tusker' in a round of 'cricket bat brands' skolling games. The Symonds Super Tusker had been well known in the 1980s as the bat used by Allan Border and Mark Taylor, among other international stars. At our club, we tail-enders who didn't have our own bats liked to use it because it was heavy and if you managed to hit the ball, it stayed hit.

In the very first over of our first game in Timor-Leste, we lost the only cricket ball I'd brought from Australia, smashed out of the Super Tusker's sweet spot into the mosquito-infested jungle. I scrambled around in our gear to replace it, and came across some gaffer tape, which in the army was called '100 mile an hour tape', because that was how quickly it disappeared out of the Q store. If you went to any army house, you would find a few rolls of 'liberated' 100 m/h tape. It did literally everything. Along with spare batteries and hoochie cord, 100 m/h tape was about the most valuable commodity in the SAS. I scrunched up some paper, wrapped it several times in tape, even constructed a 'seam' out of some hoochie cord, and it weighed only a little less than a six-stitcher. We had a ball.

My most poignant memory of the cricket on that trip was how, unlike in 2006, the local kids got involved, fielding for us and chasing balls and laughing at our batting and bowling. The average age in our team was around thirty, and when Timorese kids played with us, I looked around the field at normally super-hard SAS human beings and saw them begin to relax, their toughness melting as they let themselves have a good time. When you were missing your own children as badly as we were, your instincts were crying out to grab the kids and hug or wrestle with them for some normal physical contact. It was complex, because a lot of us also carried guilt over the fact that when we were at home, we might be exhausted or concentrating on the next gig, juggling social, family and work obligations while also trying to relax with some 'me' time, and consequently were not always great parents. Playing cricket among the kids in Timor, all these sentiments came to the surface.

On the night when we mistakenly busted into the Cabinet minister's house in our body armour, carrying weapons in a threatening manner while clearing buildings, there were kids running around screaming in fear, traumatised by these stormtrooper-like men with big guns. Behind the mask, your heart went out to them. You wanted to get quickly to the part where you showed them that you were in control and you cared.

There was a standing policy of not interacting with the locals unless it was mission related. You were not meant to give them anything, or show them any favour. But these were kids! Sometimes you need to show a human face, particularly in the new paradigm of war fighting among the populace. There is a concept called the 'Krulak Three Block War' principle, named after US Marine General Charles Krulak. While it has its critics, it illustrates the complexity of the modern battlefield. It says that if you are engaged in a city, on one block you are fighting and killing, on the next block you are delivering humanitarian aid and patching people up, and on the third block you are engaging with key local leadership as a peacekeeper or diplomat. The model gave rise to the idea of the 'Strategic Corporal', meaning that rapidly evolving situations necessitate a devolution of leadership down to the corporal who is in charge of the smallest functional team. There is a perceived danger in giving this much control to the lower ranks, but in my observation this is how it plays out in reality anyway. I have heard senior officers joke, 'What do we need smart soldiers for?' But today's wars are for the most part run by the soldiers on the ground. We have to be hunters, humanitarians and diplomats, versatile and able to think on our feet, including knowing when to show simple kindness.

When I was in Timor-Leste, in many ways my most challenging deployment as a leader, we still had a way to go in the practice of kindness. Empathy, or humanity, instilled in me by my mother, was a key characteristic by which I judged SAS soldiers. The majority were, fortunately, high in emotional intelligence. While it was not one of the twelve characteristics assessed in selection and training,

I thought it typified the best operators, and also the best troops in general.

Soft diplomacy was a tricky matter, depending where we were. In Afghanistan, we would not generally hand out lollies and pencils and paper to the children. You could put a child in jeopardy if he had been favoured by you. You didn't engage with girls at all, because of religious laws and customs where women could be blamed for all interactions with men and infidels. We were briefed at length on that. But it wasn't hard and fast. Lollies (called 'shirini'), pencils and paper were prized by children, all the more so when the Taliban had taken them away. My children would collect pencils and paper from their classes and post them for us to distribute. Often we would drive through Afghan villages and throw lollies into a pile, then let the kids sort them out. In more progressive villages, we could discuss with elders in advance how to distribute lollies, pencils and paper to children.

In Dili, the customs were not so strict and the consequences not so severe. The kids engaged with everything we did on that second trip, especially our games of cricket, and they triggered the most powerful emotions. I missed Georgia and Henry so much, I was brought to tears and was constantly seeking an opening to call home. Now on my fifth deployment in as many years with the unit, I had to ask myself what this life was doing to me, what it was doing to my family, whether I was irresponsible for trying to combine fatherhood with being a soldier, and whether my family and I could ever recover from it.

———

During my deployments, I was now in the habit of writing 'death letters' to my family and myself. I outlined what I would like done at my funeral, I spoke of my love for Danielle and the kids, and in case it got too maudlin I would add in the big issues such as who got my footy card collection and reserves of Externals CDs, of which there were plenty. I usually wrote these letters the evening before we were going on a job where I thought we would get into a gunfight. I never felt like one of those soldiers who is lucky in war, though that has transpired. Instead, I always carried a sense of dread that I would fuck up and get in the wrong place at the wrong time, or not be aggressive enough, or make some critical error through being too forgiving of a potential foe.

The letters were mostly to soothe my own nerves through journalling and allow me to sleep for the few hours between finishing a planning session late at night and getting up before dawn. I wrote in bed or even at my desk, where I spent many nights before missions dozing, feet up. Sleep deprivation was normal, though it possibly amplified that deep nostalgia that urged me to pick up my pen.

Dear darling Danielle, Georgia, and Henry,

If you are reading this it is likely that I have been killed. I am sorry for the pain it is causing you and for dragging you all through all of this. You have been the most loving and understanding family a man could hope to have. I want you all to know that you consumed my thinking before I died and that I died facing the enemy. I want you to know that I am now at peace with my mum, in that place in your mind that you will hold for me. Take solace that I did not suffer and that I died knowing that you all

love me and care for me. Take care of Ned and the MCG. I love
you all deeply.
Your loving husband Anthony & father Dad XXXX

They meant everything to me.

————

Apart from my first 'true love' during high school, Raelene, I didn't
have any really serious girlfriends growing up. I was much more
interested in my sport and then my army life to have time for girls.

Not long after I joined the SAS, I was in O'Connor's Bar in
West Perth with some of my colleagues, having just finished a
close protection course, decked out in our best Roger David suits
and looking, we thought, pretty sharp. We got talking with some
girls, one of whom I was doing my best to impress. As it turned
out, she was not giving very encouraging signals, but her friend
was far more interesting. Danielle was studying social science at
university, and before long we were involved in a long and serious
conversation about some of the ideas she'd been developing.

During a pause, she asked, 'And what do you do, Harry?'

'Er . . . I'm a florist.'

To her sceptical look I added, 'I've got a shop in Melbourne, and
another one in Brisbane. I'm here in Perth because I'm looking at
opening a branch here.'

Everyone in the unit had a cover story, and this was mine.
It's not that we really needed one, but it was the done thing. We
thought a bit more of ourselves than we should have.

'A branch?' Danielle echoed, before asking me what kinds of flowers I specialised in. I had a few prepared answers, but she saw right through me. Looking at my hands, heavily calloused from five years in the army, she added, 'Your hands don't look like florist's hands.' Just my luck: she was an avid gardener.

It probably didn't take much to blow my cover, but I was impressed by her perceptiveness all the same. Once I told her what I really did, she wasn't particularly awestruck by that either. 'What's the SAS?' she asked. Which I liked even more. I was intrigued, maybe even smitten.

We had a conventional romance. I was really attracted to Danielle's intellectual curiosity and independence. She had her own mind, which inspired me to inquire into her areas of interest, such as social policy and equity in the Indigenous field. She had a strong social conscience and challenged me whenever I lapsed into regressive thinking, and I enjoyed those confrontations. And she enjoyed my after-midnight romantic visitations, throwing pebbles at her second-storey apartment window to wake her up.

Danielle was the eldest of four daughters in an archetypal Western Australian working-class family, tight with her parents, Joy and Fred, and sisters, and the brothers-in-law turned out to be good blokes too. They were the ready-made, expansive, generous, stable family that I'd been missing since my mum and dad's break-up. The contrast met a kind of craving I had. While my family was fractured, hers was strong.

We had a great first few years together. I was a VW Kombi enthusiast, and we drove across the Nullarbor in one; for me, bringing back fond memories of my trip across that desert with

Dad. In a couple of respects, it was even better: we drank a lot of wine and talked endlessly, occasionally pulling over on the roadside to sleep (or not sleep) while passing road trains tooted their horns. In time, Danielle became a teacher and I was establishing myself in the regiment. The early nineties were great, until it all went south in a hurry.

When I joined the SAS in 1990, there was little hope of an overseas deployment. The unit hadn't been in action since the Vietnam War, and for most of the decade after I joined, teams would only be sent away once, to Somalia in 1993. I didn't make the cut for that trip, and didn't expect to. I was working hard just to keep up and find my place in the regiment.

SAS soldiers were divided by three insertion skills. There were Water Operations, Vehicle Mounted, and Freefall Parachute, each with their own subcultures. The 'core' of the unit are quite like-minded people, but there are also some outliers and eccentrics, among whom I think I was seen. The Water guys—'Wateries', 'Bubble-blowers' or 'Crayfish' (body full of meat and head full of shit)—were hardened by a culture of long nights in the oceans around Australia, where they dived from submarines in the freezing southern waters. They saw themselves as the true elite of the regiment, and some of them thought they should comprise their own separate unit: direct action, big-hitting, strong hard men, which the majority of them were. They just weren't that smart.

The Vehicle Mounted operators—VM or 'Pie-eaters' (they were always stopping at roadhouses to eat pies)—were a much more laid-back group, country boys at heart who enjoyed camping with guns, 4WDing, and shooting things. Many of them ended up as snipers.

The Freefallers, known as 'soft' by the other insertions, tended to be a more liberal-thinking bunch. Not liberal as in politics, but liberal as in intellectually open-minded. In other words, there was more scope to be daring and think outside the box; we were more curious and tolerant, and by far the most intelligent! Therefore, we were mostly more suited to the special reconnaissance world, carrying out stealthy work rather than going in and taking out high-value targets in direct-action-type tasks. Freefall was really enjoyable and challenging and gave me all the fulfilment I was looking for. Initially I was a scout and comms man in my patrol, working under Big Duke. Whenever Big Duke spoke, we listened. We had some big personalities in the group and he managed them with a rare perceptiveness.

I was in the regiment for about two years before I really felt I belonged; 1992 and 1993 were enjoyable as the regiment accepted me, and maybe I finally accepted myself.

But in 1994, something shifted inside me. There was no prospect of my unit going anywhere, which saw some soldiers leave. Looking back, the effort I needed to put in to prove my competence and just keep up in the regiment burned me out. So I discharged from the military.

Compounding my decision to leave, my mum was diagnosed with breast cancer in her forties, and in 1994, she had a double mastectomy, part of a horrific year in which her health continued to worsen. It was unbearable to watch. The only good thing I can resurrect from this time is that Mum got to spend time with my baby daughter, Georgia, who was born in 1995. This gave her great comfort and I think some resilience to face her terrible reality.

Unfortunately the cancer had spread before they operated, and in 1995, at just forty-nine, she passed away. To think that I am now older than she ever got is something that knocks me for six. If anyone deserved a long and happy life, it was her. We, and she, were ripped off; it is that simple.

There is an old bloke's saying that 'you spend the first half of your life trying to be everything your father isn't; and the second half of your life trying to be half the man your father is'. If I am half the person my mother was, I will indeed be a good human.

I still get emotional today thinking about Mum. She was a saint, she really was, proof of the saying that the good die young.

After her death, I entered a slow decline to the lowest point of my life, which was increasingly in turmoil on many fronts: leaving the unit, Mum's death, the pressure of first-time fatherhood, and finally the breakdown of a carpentry business I started with my brother Robert as my post-defence job. The final straw was our home being burgled by thieves who stole all the jewellery my mother had bequeathed to her baby granddaughter. I was angry at the world. I had no reserves and was becoming impossible to live with. Danielle and I separated.

I had an emerging depression, was drinking a lot, and occasionally doing other drugs as well. If I had not been surfing, I'm not sure what I would have done. I knew I had reached the bottom when I found myself drunk, penniless, sitting behind a Cottesloe bakery at 4 a.m. waiting for the baker to bring the dud loaves out to the trash. As I rustled through the bin, I looked up to see a homeless man of around fifty. I glimpsed my own future. This was an inflection point.

Making that period truly catastrophic was the Black Hawk accident in 1996, when Andy Constantinidis, one of my closest military mates with whom I'd gone through the drama of failing-then-passing selection, was among eighteen deaths when two helicopters collided in a training accident near Townsville. It was a tragic day in the history of the SAS and the ADF, hundreds of years of experience lost in an instant. Just a year after Mum passed away, I went to many funerals and we all had a very hard time coming to terms with it, especially as some of us had flown the exact same mission profiles and, I believe, had come close to colliding with each other or at least had had concerns about it. My mates in the unit told me how horrendous the aftermath was. But there was still a place for black humour in communities such as ours. Not long after the accident, over a few memorial beers at the Gratwick Club (the 'Gratto') at the SAS's Campbell Barracks, one of the boys was telling a story about one of the deceased guys who was famous for having deep pockets and short arms. We suspected he always arrived to the pub late so he didn't have to get in a shout. 'Apparently after the helicopters crashed,' he said, 'he escaped. But then he realised he'd left his wallet on board and went back to get it.' We released our grief in uproarious laughter and fond remembrance. It was the type of thing we told each other to get through this, and other such times.

Danielle and I got back together but I was still lost for a while. I played in a band, I worked at an employment agency, I took a job as a postman at Cottesloe (career highlight—taking over the route of Test wrist-spinner Brad Hogg, who'd worked as a postie before bowling his way back into the Western Australian team), and I worked loading bread at Tip Top. I was a courier for a while. I worked with a builder, which provided better conditions and pay than the other jobs. By 2000, Danielle had qualified as a secondary school teacher and we decided to relocate to the UK, where she had a position in a school in Maidstone, Kent, while I was offered a job with the Kent County Constabulary as a tactical instructor. It sounds like I was adrift, and I was, but I don't regret those years. Fighting my way out of a deep hole, I learned a lot about myself and spent priceless time with my family. But there was always a restless, unreleased energy in me.

Music was also a big part of my new perspective and balance. I'd started The Externals in 1991 with two fellow SAS operators. We had many players in and out, but the band retained a connection to the regiment. I believe The Externals are the only original Special Operations Forces rock band in the world. None of us had a clue what we were doing; we just got drunk one night after a local punk show and agreed playing in a rock band didn't look that hard. We jammed and played a bit on the barracks, in Copeman Hall and at the Gratto, but we were shit, and that original line-up didn't last long. What you might call our fair dinkum line-up took shape when Rob Venville on guitar and Shane Toppin on drums, both qualified SAS operators, joined us. We now had a reasonable competency level and a list of covers.

Our first official show (we had played a couple of unofficial shows at piss-ups) was at the Swanbourne Hotel, in front of a pretty good crowd, supporting a thrash band called Thrombus. We were, it's fair to say, horrible. We worked out that playing covers was too hard. People expected a certain sound when you played popular songs, and many were quite complicated. I decided that if we did our own songs, kept them super simple (three chords max) and in the range in which I could sing (or yell), it was much easier. We had a breakthrough moment during one show at Swanbourne when my guitar strap snapped and my Ibanez fell to the stage, leaving me doing vocals only. I never played guitar live again, which was a big improvement. We gave up the covers, went original, and haven't looked back. Over the next twenty-plus years, we played hundreds of shows all over Australia, and always wondered why we weren't asked by the Defence Department to tour instead of some of the rubbish performers and bands they put on for the troops! We have so far put out six albums of original material and reached a pretty decent level, playing Big Days Out and alongside bands like The Prodigy, Powderfinger and Bad Religion. We modelled ourselves on Midnight Oil meets The Celibate Rifles meets Cosmic Psychos, if that makes any sense, which it probably doesn't. I've written the lion's share of the forty-plus songs we've recorded, and am (very) quietly proud of what we've done. We still play today and are recording at the time of writing this book.

After five years out of the unit, I was feeling more settled. I really enjoyed Georgia's early years, and in 1999, Henry was born. Danielle arranged to give birth in a local family birth centre, meaning I was able to catch him as he took his first breath. Henry was born fast and furious, setting the pace for most of his childhood. His birth was particularly memorable for me. He was born 'en caul', meaning in his amniotic sack. As he debuted into the world, he looked like a bank robber with pantyhose on his head. It was quite alarming as I didn't know what was wrong.

'Oh my God,' I whispered.

Danielle put her hand between her legs to feel Henry's head. It felt like a soft-shelled crab.

'What's wrong with it?' she asked, catching my infectious panic.

The midwife reached in and nicked the sac. It is said that people born 'en caul' are lucky in life, have an affinity with water and possess psychic gifts. None of these would describe Henry, though he does spend a long time in the shower.

Once we overcame that initial uncertainty, I went wild with joy. Danielle kept her wits about her more than I did and, typically, was back at work soon after. Things were increasingly solid between us as we committed to our life. It was 2001 when we moved to the UK, where the job with the police helped bring me out of my long funk. There was no longer a tension between what I was and what I wanted to be. Our nice little family was tight.

Working for the Kent Constabulary felt like a natural fit and was a job I enjoyed a great deal. I travelled around the county training police in unarmed defensive tactics, including how to use pepper spray, batons and (as a result of confrontations) first aid. Every week, sometimes every day, I was in a different village or town. Not hugely draining, the job brought me a bit of relief after my first stint in the SAS.

We were pretty free, though we were working hard to keep our heads above water. England was a fairly expensive place and we went across with nothing—I mean nothing. The first night we were there, our furniture not having arrived, the four of us slept wrapped up in the curtains from around the house that I had taken down to use as bedding and warmth.

I played some games for the Mote Park CC, based in Maidstone, a good sub-county level club that had hosted a few first-class Aussie cricketers. It had beautiful Tudoresque clubrooms and traditional sit-down teas where you had to remove your spikes and were served by staff. Village cricket was fantastic. I played on pitches with trees halfway to the boundary, and probably the most memorable was the Broomfield Cricket Club, which had a pub, the Oast, for a clubroom, overlooking Leeds Castle, a favourite holiday spot for King Henry VIII. The entire ground was on a hill, which made bowling a little difficult. Brilliant.

I could have had no idea what was coming next. But who in the world did?

During my time out, the SAS had only done one deployment, in 1999 to Timor. I hadn't left under bad circumstances, and when I was still in Australia I caught up for a regular beer with regiment guys. A lot of their talk was along the lines of, 'What are we going to do? When are we going to do something?' Their constant frustration was hard to hear, but gave me some comfort that I wasn't missing out on anything. The US Special Forces were doing stuff around the globe, but the Australians weren't allowed to go into their wars. It was embarrassing for the guys to feel like a bench team, because everyone in the Australian SAS had great pride in their capabilities and the confidence that, if tested, they would prove themselves. But there was no test. Quality individuals were leaving the unit for jobs in emergency services and the security industry.

In 2001, while I was in the UK, I was talking to Matt 'Stevo' Stevens, fellow founding member and bass player for The Externals and one of my closest mates at the unit.

'What are you up to?' he asked.

'Working with the Kent Constabulary, playing village cricket and drinking lukewarm piss. Apart from that, nothing much.'

'Ever thought about coming back?'

'Why would that be?'

'Storm clouds are brewing. A lot of guys have left. We need some of you back.'

Ever responsible, Stevo sowed a seed and over subsequent calls encouraged me to reach out to my great mentor, Big Duke, who was now the unit regimental sergeant major (RSM), for more information. Big Duke confirmed what Stevo had said, and put it plainly: 'We're looking to bring some guys back, Harry, and if you want a spot I can give you one.'

I hesitated. I was living just outside London and enjoying life. Georgia was six and Henry was two. But I guess those conversations put a new perspective on the five years I'd had in the SAS from 1990 to 1994. In my view, I'd been a struggler. But the fact that they were offering me a position back in the unit suggested that maybe I'd performed better than I'd given myself credit for. After all, they weren't asking everyone back. My self-confidence, which had been battered and bruised at the time I'd left, received a boost. I learned a valuable lesson about myself in those days, that the little commentator in my head was the imposter. We all have a commentator in our head—'Harry's in from the southern end, bowls on a good length and, oooooooh, just misses the outside edge and the top of off, nice delivery'—but mine is not always positive. My commentator's agenda during those years was to undermine me by telling me how shit I was. As a psychologist, I now know that many of us struggle with the imposter commentating on our lives. While the commentator cannot be silenced, I have learned to have regular harsh words with him and often put him back in his box.

On 11 September 2001, while I was training yet another group of constabulary in Kent, my good friend Mark 'Bungy' Williams called me inside as I was taking the team through their ASP baton drills outside on the concrete. I sensed the seriousness in his voice—we were hardly ever serious together—as we rushed to the TV room. The two World Trade Center towers were on fire. Bungy looked at me, I at him, and almost in unison we both said, 'Might be time to go back.' We had both left esteemed military organisations, me the SAS and he the Royal Marines. We watched the TV for a long while, wrapped up training for the day and headed back to Maidstone. He had mapped out his life outside the military, and was not keen to return. Danielle and I, on the other hand, were barely making a living in England, though we were just starting to get ahead and settle down. I knew, and I sensed Mark knew too, that I would get a call soon.

All of a sudden I had great purpose that scratched that restless itch. I started training in Maidstone where we lived, running through the hills of Tovil and Mill Pond to work every day carrying about 10 kilos, watching my time over the 5-kilometre course come down from thirty to less than twenty minutes in the freezing sleet and snow and driving rain of the English winter. I got under a pack and did some night navigation, map to ground, around the Kentish Downs where Pip of *Great Expectations* had rambled his way into my heart. I trekked in the snow with a backpack full of tinned food, working so hard that Danielle had to come and pick me up one time when I was close to suffering from exposure.

It was around January 2002 when I came back from the UK and focused on what might be my second selection. The drums of war were beating. Danielle stayed in Kent to finish her teaching contract and for Georgia to finish her school term. We'd all warmed to the idea of returning home, and I came back first with Henry before Danielle and Georgia followed a few months later. I hadn't been told whether I would or wouldn't need to do the selection course again, but, not wanting to leave anything to chance, I trained my arse off for four months. I was conflicted about my age—I was now thirty-three—but then again, the great Doug Walters had batted and bowled deep into his thirties. Not many people get a second chance in life. Leigh Matthews, one of the AFL greats and a hero of mine as a passionate Hawthorn Football Club supporter, said he was a 'better coach the second time around', which resonates with me profoundly. This was my chance to be a better operator the second time around.

Back in Perth, I stepped up my work in the gym and the pool. I set myself solo navigation courses (parking the car and walking out into the hills around Perth for two days without a compass, guided by nothing but a sketchy map), and did a lot of hard walking with 40 to 50 kilograms on my back. Pack walking sounds simple, but like burpees (my favourite and least-favourite exercise), pack walking is more about mental toughness than physical conditioning. On really hot days, I would do laps of a wasteland near my mother-in-law's property. I'm sure the locals thought I was crazy: fully clothed, a big military pack strapped on, carrying a steel bar while striding laps of this sandy dump in the eastern suburbs of Perth for hours on end. It was the middle of summer in Perth, and I was relishing the prospect of another 40-degree day to go out and punish myself. Perhaps I was a little crazy. But this was the mindset I had to forge. I had to not so much get fit, as get hard.

It was crazy, but I loved it. I wasn't going to fuck up my second chance. I was preparing to be an SAS operator, except this time I was preparing for war, which, as the Greek philosopher Heraclitus said, is the father of everything. It stops everything. It is humanity's greatest and worst expression. It is like a horror movie and like a ballet at the same time. It is profound.

They were right about storm clouds. A few months after I re-joined, it was on like Donkey Kong.

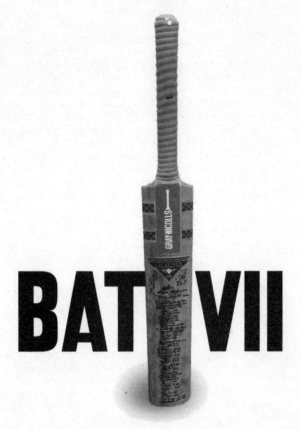

BAT VII

VALE SEAN

AFGHANISTAN, 2008

On the morning of 8 July 2008, a coin toss decided that it was going to be Sean McCarthy, not me, who died that day.

We were brushing our teeth around the car where we had parked in FOB Locke the previous evening, the first night of a planned long-range vehicle patrol in the Chora Valley. Sean and I had spent the previous day in the headquarters car of a six-vehicle convoy. Sean was an electronic warfare operator and specialist, a 'Bear' from 152 Signal Squadron, while my role was as a JTAC—a Joint Terminal Attack Controller—which meant I was responsible for directing aircraft to drop ordnance on enemy positions from heights ranging from helicopters at 50 metres to Intelligence Surveillance Reconnaissance (ISR) aircraft at 20,000 metres. With us in the car would be Willy 'Midsouth' Wade, our Troop Senior Sergeant, and our Afghan interpreter, Sammi Assad.

Each day of the patrol, Midsouth would be in the passenger seat of the vehicle and Sammi would ride in the tray, where there was a mounted .50-calibre machine gun. Sean and I would alternate between driving and operating the gun. We both preferred the gun to the wheel, and I had driven on the first day.

'Your turn to drive,' I said.

We had music going on our CD player. Sean, a cheerful, popular guy with a big ginger beard, a Kiwi by birth, took his toothbrush out of his mouth and said he couldn't drive, as he had to operate a particular item of signalling equipment.

'Come on,' I said, 'you can do that while you're driving. I could do that while I'm rooting!' We laughed a lot, Sean and I. We had grown close in our first weeks in country, as he was training for selection as an operator, and I joined him for stomps through the landscape.

As we both wanted to be on the gun, we agreed to toss a coin. It was a challenge coin, specifically manufactured with the unit's insignia on one side and the motto on the other. I flipped the coin into the riverbed dirt. Sean called. I lost, as it were. I had to drive. From a professional point of view, it was probably the best way to go, because Sean had to do a pretty serious signalling job, and we were about to drive through an extremely dangerous area.

I have had a lot of time to think about the toss of that coin. I can't escape the fantasy that if it had fallen the other way and Sean had driven, he would have made a different choice in the critical moment and both of us would have survived. Sometimes it keeps me awake all night.

But you think too much like that, you will send yourself out of your mind.

———

Not many people have had one near-death experience, let alone two.

My first one couldn't have been more different from what happened in Afghanistan in 2008, yet there was one common factor: the entry into a hidden level of consciousness. Time comes in a rush but also goes into slow motion; it's very hard to put this warping into words. Things of wildly varying importance go through your mind, but they are very clear. Something in your consciousness detaches you, and you become an observer of your own fate.

The other experience happened in the late 1990s, when I was out of the regiment. One grey lunchtime, I pulled into a car park overlooking one of the surf breaks along Thirteenth Beach, near Barwon Heads on the coast of Bass Strait, south-west of Melbourne. The clouds were darkening and a storm was rolling in, but—such is the surfer's compulsion—I only had eyes for the glassy head-high swell breaking perfectly over a shallow reef. Just two surfers were out, picking off as many waves as they wanted. Even though I wasn't experienced in that part of the world, the opportunity was irresistible. I suited up, walked down the limestone-scattered sand dunes, and paddled out to join them.

In the fifteen minutes between my car and the surf zone, conditions had changed. The wind turned onshore, so I was pushing out under one chopped-up wave after another. Out on the reef, the waves had deteriorated from the glassy lined-up hedges I'd spotted from the dunes. As I was paddling out, one of the two guys was coming back in. He said nothing, but I could see him thinking *WTF?* as this clueless out-of-towner headed out into the surf just as it was going down the toilet.

As I duckdived under what I thought was the last broken wave before I was out the back, I realised that the swell was bigger than I'd thought. I am only an average surfer, having taken it up as an adult, and was quickly out of my depth in larger waves, especially these long-period Southern Ocean swells that carried more heft than the tame beach breaks I was used to around Perth.

As I came up from under that last wave, the gravity of the situation hit home. The sky seemed very dark, even though it was the middle of the day. The wind had turned the sea into a washing machine. Currents and surface chop were fighting each other, making it very hard to gain any headway paddling. I pushed on, hoping to reach clean water. I distinctly remember thinking I should head back in, but I reckon there was a little bit of ego taking over. There were a few girls in the car park, no doubt (in my mind) watching, and one of the local surfers was still out there. I had to get at least one wave to prove whatever I had to prove to myself.

I tried to pick up an incoming wave, but the rain, spray and poor light all conspired to leave me inside the break. The wave was much bigger than I'd expected, and far from glassy. It hit me like a bus, the full force landing directly on me. My board got spat out and I was briefly pinned to the bottom. I grasped for my leg rope and started climbing up it to my board. I tried to stay calm. I was reasonably fit, so holding my breath was not too much of an issue. I had been in this position before and knew that as long as I was connected to my board I was okay. As I reached my tombstoning board, I broke through the surface into what felt like complete darkness. Just as I took a breath a second, bigger wave hit me. I inhaled not air but water, which caused me to cough out whatever little oxygen I had kept. I was rag-dolling again, under the second wave.

It was then that all calm deserted me. I was terrified. I was deep in the 'hurt locker'. My vision was twinkling at the peripheries and I could feel strong tingling sensations in my fingers. From my time in high-altitude parachute training, I knew what this was. I was trying to relax, but could not fight my automatic response to thrash towards the surface. My reptilian brain stem had taken over. Strangely, mixed into my awareness of the events was a slower-motion appreciation of what was happening. I thought about my mate who I was staying with. I wouldn't get back to make my bed before he got home, and he might be disappointed in me. I thought about Danielle, who was pregnant with Henry all the way back in Perth, and how I would never get to say how sorry I was for our separation, and how much I missed her. I even remember thinking about how I owed a workmate a few dollars for a punt we'd had during a lunch break at the Valley Inn that week. With these odd thoughts running through my mind, I fully accepted that I was about to die.

I found my board, but it was in the whitewash and I instinctively sucked in a lung full of water as a third wave poured over me. As the force ripped my board away, I could feel consciousness leaving me and a sleepy blackout state taking its place. My final feeling was of feeling ripped off, a little angry.

Coming back was literally like waking from a sleep. Without knowing how I had done it, I was sucking air into my body. There was a strong pain in my stomach and lungs, and I went into a coughing fit, my head just above the water. It was like my consciousness had given up, but my body had kept fighting. I located my board and my bearings. I was about a hundred metres down the beach and halfway in to the shore, in a trough between the waves. It was dark, chucking down with rain and a howling wind. However, despite the raging wind, my walk back to the car was warm and calm.

I climbed up the stairs to the car park, where one of the girls was waiting. 'Fuck, we thought you were dead! You didn't come up, we completely lost you. You are the luckiest person ever!'

I couldn't really respond. I climbed into my mate's Ford Laser, cranked up the heater and sat there for about an hour. I wanted to cry, but as the minutes passed the urge went away, as did the girls I had tried so hard to impress.

———

One of our principles in the regiment was 'Train hard, fight easy', meaning that we would push our training to the very edges of safety, including always using live ammunition, and stretch our capabilities to their limits, so that when the crunch came on the battlefield, we would not be facing challenges too far beyond what we had already experienced. While an average of one SAS operator has died per year since the unit's inception, only a tiny handful of those have been in combat. Training accidents and mishaps have cost us dearly, but, due to the rigours of that training, few have died during engagements with the enemy.

My fortieth year, 2008, was the best and worst of my life. It started with my most serious training injury. In April, having just won my first grand final for the Applecross Second XI on turf, I was at the naval base in Nowra, on the south coast of New South Wales, completing my Masters (Freefall) course. This intense seven-week course qualified you to instruct students and was pretty high level in the world of military freefall training. We completed about fifty jumps and many iterations of despatching a team, the foundation skill of the course.

To qualify properly, I had to lead a night jump from 6000 metres with equipment weighing about 40 kilograms strapped to my front while wearing an oxygen mask. Due to high winds at the Nowra base, the exercise was moved to Narrandera, in the Riverina region of New South Wales. We flew in a tiny CASA-C, conducting highly technical assessments and oxygen checks, which would have been done better and more safely in one of the Hercules that was more likely being used to fly around politicians and generals.

We chugged along in the back of the 'flying bus'. It was the size of a Mitsubishi minivan—deluxe, of course. When the time came to jump, we received a three-minute warning. I conducted the checks and we lined up on the ramp. To give you an idea of the room in the plane, the only way I could reach the rear ramp was to climb across the backs of the seats, as the narrow aisle was crammed with heavily laden SAS soldiers. Amid the freezing wind and, now that its ramp was down, the aircraft's deafening roar, I checked myself and my buddy, adjusted my NVGs and waited for the green light, so as to leap out at the head of the team. When the light came on, I left the aircraft and went into a freefall hold position, known as the 'frog' position, to observe the rest of the five-man team through my NVGs and see if anyone had a slow or bad opening. If that happened, I would not pull my handle until their canopy was visible and I was below them—the low man leads the team.

After I exited, through the last little moment of extreme exertion and arousal, I felt a little hypoxic, which was not uncommon after moving around in the back of the aircraft disrupting the seal around my mask. I watched the guys come out, one . . . two . . . three . . . four . . . and started a slow turn to the left away from the aircraft. I was travelling at 200 to 250 km/h, at night, watching the guys come out while trying to locate landmarks to get my bearings.

It was then that I lost sight of the last man. As I reached for my deployment handle, my equipment came loose on my right leg and I went into a ferocious flat spin. I had done about five hundred jumps before this and never had a malfunction. I felt like I was being launched off a giant hammer throw. The centrifugal forces were so strong, I was having trouble locating my handle. All I could think was that I needed to 'get the laundry' out, or get the parachute open so I could slow down and not be too cut off from the team, who would have been well and truly under canopy by now and forming up as they headed to the target. Someone was probably saying, 'Where the fuck is Harry?'

I finally found my handle and pulled. All of this probably happened in moments, but at the time it felt like forever.

As the rig disappeared off my back into the night sky, I braced myself for the shock of the chute opening. But there was none. I was spinning so fast that the chute was in full 'candlestick', which means it had twisted up from my flat spin like wrung washing. I was feet down, falling fast, with the entire parachute in a tight twist above me. Worst of all, as it opened it had ripped off my NVGs and communications earpiece.

I went straight into a separation drill, where you grab the risers (straps connecting you to the parachute) and try to kick your way out of the tangled mess. I could see what was going on from the good moon and the town lights of Narrandera below me. I checked my altitude: I was still about 10,000 feet, so I knew I had time. I kicked and kicked. Nothing happened. The tangle just followed me around.

I had to cut this rig away and pull out the reserve. As I checked my altitude again, I heard a little puff from the top of the chute. I couldn't see it, but I knew the sound of a chute trying to open. I kept kicking, and little by little it started to open . . . Eventually, at around 3000 feet, it did. I was in the saddle.

As the chute got fully open, my earpiece fell back down to me. I sent through a grid and direction to the others. One of the lads had taken control and was leading the team. I left them to it and said I would find a nice place as close to the target as I could.

It was pitch-black on the ground, I had no NVGs, and the lights from Narrandera were blinding me a little. At around 1500 feet, I started to get anxious. I had no idea of the wind direction or any obstacles. I caught a faint waft of cow shit. I tried to get my direction of travel, and figured out that the wind speed was quite high. I was headed for a downwind landing—bad news, as you always want to land into the wind. The difference can be between landing at an easy walking pace or faster than Usain Bolt, with all the attendant risks. I saw what looked like an open paddock and heard some mooing as if the cows were saying, 'Look at these stupid humans, what are they doing on the planet anyway?'

I was now on finals, a couple of hundred feet above the ground, descending into the warmer air. The smell of manure was strong. At about 100 feet, travelling at around 40 kilometres an hour, I braced for a brutal downwind landing.

On contact, I felt sharp pain ripping through my right knee and lower back. I hit the ground as hard as a fallen tree, and then got bounced and dragged for about 15 metres. The wind was knocked out of me as I crashed and rolled through the paddock scrub. Then . . . nothing. Silence. Except for a cow mooing. And the smell of the cow shit I had rolled through. I lay in the dark with serious pain in my lower back, through my left-hand side, and just above my right knee. I thought I had broken my femur, which could be extremely dangerous if I'd cut an artery. I reached down; my leg felt wrong.

I got on my radio, sent out a grid location, and told them I was injured. But the comms were bad and I wasn't sure they had heard me. I pulled out my mobile phone and rang the drop zone, telling my team I may have a broken femur. They said they would send the ambo immediately, but it would take at least forty minutes through a series of country roads and tracks to get to this paddock, and the nearest track stopped 500 metres away.

To assess my leg, I struggled to my feet, which was so painful I was fighting to hold back screams. I was not bleeding. I turned on my torch and noticed no discolouration or swelling in the leg. I put my whole weight on it, and realised that I had not broken it but most likely suffered a severe tear to my quadriceps and knee tissue. Maybe a ruptured ACL. I rang the team back and said I didn't think I'd broken my femur, which they were happy to hear.

After hanging up to preserve my battery, I lay back down, grabbed some water from my pack, tried to block out the pain in my leg and back, and thought about the consequences. I was supposed to be deploying to Afghanistan in a few months. This would surely put paid to that. The disappointment was as acute as the physical pain.

About twenty minutes later, my phone rang. It was an SAS mate in Perth.

'Harry! I just heard you had an accident?'

'Fuck me, doesn't news travel fast?'

'Yeah, so do you reckon you're gonna be right to deploy? 'Cos I'm on standby.'

Un-fucking-believable. Inside twenty minutes, the news had got back to Perth and the guy who was on reserve was on the phone to shore up his position on the next deployment. That is how keen we were.

As it turned out, I rehabbed my injuries in time for the trip. Someone else got injured, so my mate made it too.

———

Our 2008 deployment, a continuation of Operation Slipper, was meant to go from June to November. The SAS and the army were now in a regular battle rhythm of cycling troops in and out of Afghanistan. As I recovered from my injuries, we had a really good training build-up in South Australia, rehearsing scenarios for the exact kind of operations we expected, including freefall insertions. When we got to Tarin Kowt we went straight out for a vehicle patrol around the area of operations to meet with locals face to face and take in the atmospherics for our mission. Not too many forces did that, but we had always reaped great benefit, even allowing for the risks of going outside the base more often. Interacting with the locals was always challenging and our success depended largely on what family group we were speaking to. Some were keen to see an end to the Taliban and AQ tyranny, and would provide intelligence in exchange for food or other support. We had a ratings system for assessing the locals: in descending order of helpfulness, they were good-good, good-bad, bad-good and bad-bad. Come to think of it, we had the same ratings system for assessing our officers.

For our first main long-range vehicle patrol we went to an Afghan army outpost in the Chora Valley called FOB Locke, named after my good friend Matty Locke, who had been killed in the area. There was a whitewashed government building there called, half-jokingly, the White House. FOB Locke lay in the area, only 10 kilometres long by a few kilometres wide, where more Australians lost their lives and were wounded in action than anywhere since Vietnam. The reason for this, we gathered on our arrival, was the prolifera-tion of IEDs planted on roads and tracks. The Taliban had staged a successful recruitment drive, due largely to a failed harvest in the previous cold year. IEDs were a constant threat, and an SAS patrol had been hit by one, fortunately without any fatalities, just before our arrival.

We got the vehicles together and spent a week preparing for the patrol. The tension in the villages was several degrees higher than on my previous trips to Afghanistan. Unfriendly locals gathered in a building we nicknamed the Taliban Hotel, and sat glaring at us from the shade as we drove past.

Our first day out was very hot, and when we arrived at FOB Locke, we spent the afternoon setting up for a local night patrol. At last light we broke out a cricket game, which was a ripper. We played one of the longest uninterrupted games I can remember. It was magnificent.

The bat I'd taken was another Gray-Nicolls Excalibur, which Danielle had bought for me just before the trip. The pitch was made of riverbed rocks, which we cleaned up on a good length, after intense discussions and inspections. The sledging was predictable but always hilarious.

'Bowl him a hand grenade!'

'Watch out, Harry, it explodes off a good length here!'

'Mine-d your step, Harry!'

'Bat straight, ya bastard!' (A reference to Breaker Morant's famous last words.)

There was some good batting, as we couldn't blindly slog a ball into mine-infested country. Only spin and gentle seam bowling were possible. Tea was a cigarette and a coffee, or a cold soft drink (known as a 'goffa'). Rules were made up as we went, and the umpire doubled up as a fieldsman. It was our only serious game of cricket on that trip, and the most poignant of all the games I have ever played.

Sean wasn't interested in playing; he was not a fan of Test cricket, and I often promised to take him to a Test match and show him what he was missing.

'If you're not going to play, make yourself useful and take some pictures,' I said to him. We shared a love of photography; we sometimes laughed and agreed that when we were sixty, all we would have would be a pony of beer, a half-smoked rollie, a bunch of medals and some pictures of our time together.

Sean's photo of us playing cricket in the cool of the evening is the most iconic photo of the entire war, in my opinion. When I look at it, I see Tibby Cotter in the shadows of the Sphinx before he died at Beersheba in 1917, and also the famous game of cricket at Gallipoli. I'm batting, the field is set, and sitting against the compound wall on the on-side are about twenty Afghan national army soldiers, a couple of whom joined the game. Sammi is bowling from the northern end, a particularly sad image in light of what would happen to him the next day. The fine line between living and dying, which I see illustrated in that photo, resonates with me to this day.

———

As I was in the HQ element of that patrol, we were always held back, which was quite frustrating. Being a JTAC was a pretty big job, but I never liked it or thought I was particularly good at it. As a result, I wasn't looking forward to the patrol as much as others. That night, after cricket, we conducted foot patrols in the nearby farms and villages. Some of the guys came across a group of suspicious-looking men holding a shura, and managed to remain concealed even when the men broke from their meeting to take a piss virtually on our guys' heads.

I finished my work around midnight, caught some sleep and was up at four o'clock to get ready for our morning patrol. Sean, Sammi, Midsouth and I were milling around the car. Sean and I had had our coin toss, and we breathed in the fresh morning air. It was going to be another hot one.

We loaded up and drove a kilometre and a half south of the compound, while monitoring the bad guys on the radio. We knew we were going to get into a contact. There was lots of urgent chatter; we could almost predict when we were going to be hit. Our six cars drove 50 to 100 metres apart, taking turns in the lead, in a rehearsed choreography across the dasht. We didn't use roads when we didn't have to, and if we did we would send a minesweeper out in front. Where appropriate, we followed the tracks of the vehicle ahead. Not taking roads was meant to protect us from IEDs. Frequently we caught sight of little cairns of stones, fresh diggings in the earth, and plastic bags hanging from trees, all of which were possible indicators that a bomb had been planted nearby.

Early in the patrol, the lead car stopped at one of these signs and sent out engineers to find and disable IEDs if they were there. By slowing our progress, however, we were giving the enemy the chance to lay new traps ahead of us. Active IEDs aren't just planted and left to go off; usually the bad guys needed to get in and set them as our vehicles were approaching, or to get themselves into the surrounding mountains to activate the bomb at the critical moment by radio, phone or even a common garage door opener. To counteract this, we wanted to move as quickly as possible, so a decision was made to stop pausing at each suspicious sign, to leave the marked roads, and to move faster.

Ours was the fourth car in the convoy. As we came to the crest of a small hill, we had been strung out further than usual behind the three cars in front, due to the increased speed of travel. I could see a couple of the six-wheeled vehicles out to our right. At the top of the hill, Midsouth and I were guessing which way the vehicle immediately in front of us had turned. There were fresh wheel tracks leading both sides. Midsouth and I were the most experienced people in the troop and were certain that the fresher, deeper tracks were the ones leading to the left, and we should follow those. In hindsight, it was a fatal decision.

As I have said, I did not hear the explosion. I never found out if we went over an IED activated by a pressure plate under the sand, or if it was remotely detonated by someone watching from a distance.

I have no recollection of any noise, only that feeling of being in the air. My life was saved by the fact that I wasn't wearing a seatbelt and the high profile of those vehicles, which increased survivability in blasts. I recall being about 3 metres in the air, looking down at the seat and the steering wheel, and entering that peaceful, slow-motion, almost matter-of-fact state that I had momentarily gone into when I thought I was drowning at Thirteenth Beach. I saw my books, I saw Danielle and the kids, and I saw the Applecross

Cricket Club. And then, with an almighty thud, I landed on all fours, and life started up again.

I'd landed a couple of metres wide of the car, which had resettled on the ground. I found myself right across Sean, who had been flung from his position over the machine gun in the tray. I looked at his face. He was bleeding from the ears, nose and mouth. His eyes were closed and he looked at peace. My first thought was, *Sean's gone.*

Then I thought, *Ambush.*

My ears were ringing and my legs started to scream with shooting and burning pain. The blast had cut the vehicle in half. In shock, I behaved erratically. Certain we were about to be attacked by enemy with small arms and rockets, I became fixated on finding my weapon. It turned out to be 10 metres away and damaged by the blast. I crawled, dragging what I thought was left of my legs, to where a tyre had landed. I couldn't get up. I thought, *Fuck, I've lost my legs.* I couldn't bring myself to reach down and touch them. My back was aching, telling me I probably had shrapnel in it. I stopped crawling and saw my boot hanging to the side. I thought, *There's my foot and it's not attached to my leg.*

One of the guys from one of the other vehicles, 'Tiny' Waler, was rushing over. He could see I was breathing. Then he saw Sean, his close mate, and rushed over to him to start CPR.

Now I felt my legs. They were burned and bleeding, but still connected to me. The boot I'd seen, a laced-up shin-high boot, had been blown clear off my foot by the force of the blast, which had come up directly under Sean in the tray, travelling through to me and Midsouth in the cab. It had smashed my knees and shins into the front of the car as I went flying through the top.

Having crawled towards where I thought my gun was, I was about 20 metres away from the vehicle when my teammate 'Seadog' Waterman got to me.

'My back's fucked,' I said.

'How's Sean?' Seadog replied.

'He's fucked. He's dead.'

In the twelve years since, I have been over and over the events of that morning and my part in them thousands of times. With a great deal of talking and therapy and reconciliation, and other stages in the healing process, I have managed to forgive myself for all of my actions except this one. I deeply regret saying what I did while, a few metres away, members of my team were working to keep Sean alive. I was watching them working on him, wondering why, but also thinking, *What else can they do?* That's what they would be doing for me or anyone else. During their CPR, I watched as Sean regained a sort of consciousness for a few seconds. He sat up, grabbed the guy crouched over him, let out a semiconscious yell, and then passed out again. I will always be haunted by the possibility that Sean was awake enough to hear me saying that I'd given up on him. I don't think I can ever forgive myself.

Seadog told me I wasn't bleeding and seemed all right. He found me another gun and some water, and stayed with me.

'There's enough blokes helping Sean,' he said, and perched by my side, ready for an enemy ambush. 'I've seen enough death,' he added.

Medics were also treating Midsouth and Sammi. Midsouth fractured his arm and wrist, and had some shrapnel wounds, but was otherwise unhurt. Sammi, who had been sitting straddled over the side of the tray when we went over the bomb, had lost his right leg in the blast.

There were stray gunshots from nearby but, luckily for us, whoever set the IED was not capable of any major follow-up. The guys put down some smoke markers to show a helicopter where to come in, and carried Sammi aboard. I limped towards the helicopter, assisted by Billy-Lid, the troop commander, who was helping me off the field of battle like a football team trainer.

Behind us, Seadog shouted: 'Hey, Harry, don't forget your bat!'

He was running towards me with the Gray-Nicolls Excalibur that he had found near the vehicle. It had been stowed behind my seat. I used it as a crutch as I hobbled to the helicopter. Sean wasn't aboard: a final confirmation that he hadn't survived. Midsouth was treated at the scene and could continue on. I spent the flight with my cricket bat in one hand. With my other, I held Sammi's bloodied hand. We looked into each other's eyes and softly wept.

————

The doors of the helicopter were left open during the short flight back to Tarin Kowt. My ears must have been sensitised by the blast, and we had no protective headphones. The pain from the helicopter noise was excruciating. I ended up suffering a degree of permanent hearing loss from that flight.

But of course, my injuries were nothing in the scheme of things. In the base at Tarin Kowt, the doctors debrided and cleaned up my wounds, and iced my knees. Both of the meniscuses had been torn by my collision with the dash in the vehicle. They prioritised Sammi, getting him into emergency surgery. We were both flown to the larger hospital in Kandahar, where doctors fought to save Sammi's left leg and I had some shrapnel removed from my legs and scans on my back, hips and knees.

When I was in the Tarin Kowt medical facility, the camp sergeant major brought me a telephone so I could call Danielle. Modern warfare has some advantages over the past. The direct phone call was an army experiment after many poor partner notifications. In the past, vague or incorrect information had been sent home and occasionally, when someone came to knock at the door, wives refused to open it. I said to her, 'I've been in an accident.' To this day, she still refers to it as 'the accident', though there was nothing accidental about it. Influenced by the analgesics, to lighten her anxieties and show that I hadn't lost my sense of humour, I added, 'My meat and two veg are still intact.' I'm not sure if that clumsy attempt at levity made her feel any less worried.

After a few days at the French hospital in Kandahar, I returned to the base, feeling so guilty I didn't want to show my face. My patrol and others were still going out, and I was hopping around on crutches feeling like a useless piece of shit. I wanted to crawl into a hole. By taking that wrong turn on the top of that hill, I had killed a mate, and was directly responsible for Sammi's terrible injury—he later lost his leg. I wasn't sleeping, I felt humiliated and pathetic and cowardly; and then, realising that my inward-spiralling thoughts were all about me and my role, I felt a redoubled wave of shame.

A few days after I returned, Sean's funeral and ramp ceremony took place. I sat, legs bandaged, off to the side in a plastic chair feeling like a useless slob while my colleagues conducted the ceremony, carried Sean's casket and performed the rifle drill that accompanies military funerals. Once the ceremony finished, during which all I heard was the commentator in my head yelling, 'If you weren't such a fuck-up, Harry, he would still be alive! You killed him!', I hobbled on my crutches to the back of a patrol vehicle that would trail the car carrying the casket to the C-130, where he would be placed on the ramp. The cars drove slowly and respectfully to the rear of the aircraft, through the longest guard of honour you can imagine, about 400 metres of ADF members lining both sides of the road. It was one of the most punishing ordeals I have ever faced, but I felt like I deserved it. My inner commentator told me this was nothing. 'What about his family and friends, what are you gonna say to them, you weak cunt?'

All the way to the rear of the aircraft all I could think of was how every soldier, sailor, and airman and woman was looking at me and thinking, *You fucked up big time, Moffitt. You are a lemon. Hope you are happy with yourself.* I couldn't wait to get back to my bed, get my aching legs elevated, turn my face into the wall and put my earbuds in, with no music playing, and contemplate a way out of this.

Over the next days, being on the base amid so many courageous acts continuing around me, made it worse still. This was one of the heaviest periods of fighting for Australian troops in the entire war. A patrol was caught by an extremely intense ambush in a nearby valley. Mark Donaldson, one of those trapped in the valley, made it to safety at the other end only to realise that the patrol's Afghan interpreter was still lying in the field of fire, alive but badly wounded. Without a thought for his own safety, Donno ran back into the danger zone and somehow managed to drag the guy out. With that act—amid many other feats of bravery that day and others—Donno would become the first Australian soldier since the Vietnam War to receive a Victoria Cross. I was as admiring as everyone else of what he had done, but my feelings were poisoned by my guilt and compromised by my constant self-interrogation, all day and all night, of what I had done the day we lost Sean.

There was, and has since been, a lot of discussion about the turn we had taken at the top of that hill. The guys in the lead vehicle said they had seen a suspicious divot in the tracks, steered clear of it, and sent a radio message to the other cars to drive away from it. We never received any kind of clear message to that effect, but questions were still asked about whether we had not heard it, or had ignored it. There was also some chat about what a group of regular army guys, who arrived at the scene to remove our damaged vehicle, had said. One of the regs said to the medics who had been working on Sean, 'Why the fuck would you drive through there?' The regiment guys who overheard him had to restrain themselves from ironing him out. But that didn't stop the questions about why we had driven down that path. And as far as I was concerned, as the driver, it was all my fault and everyone was talking about me.

Within a week or so of my return to Tarin Kowt, I fell seriously ill with an infection that had got into my wounds and infiltrated a bone in my right leg. I suspect it came from the human faeces in the compost the Afghanis used for growing food. The medics gave me antibiotic tablets and then injections, but my leg blew up like a balloon, my nuts were swelling, and my foot couldn't fit into any shoe.

I look back on that infection as a gift, because it got me out of Afghanistan. I wasn't doing anyone, least of all myself, any good by hanging around. They sent me home on a Qantas jet, technically an invalid but also disabled by shame.

When we got to Darwin airport, I was still running a temperature and the swelling had not subsided. As luck had it, we were held up for more than an hour going through customs because my kit had been packed in a rush by my teammates, and a young regular army lieutenant at Darwin airport found an expended cartridge. This necessitated a laborious search through every item I had. That's the military for you. We had just come from a war zone, where I had been wounded and traumatised, and it never crossed their mind that they could just pick up an expended cartridge and forget about it. At the time, I felt like it was just another thing on that trip, no matter how big or how small, going wrong. I lost it and cooked off at them, which only made things worse.

They didn't worry about my cricket bat, which had travelled back in my gun bag.

———

That trip to Afghanistan was not about cricket, except for that fleeting moment when Sean photographed us and the Afghanis in the one game we had time for. But my recovery, without doubt, was helped by the great game.

Danielle and the kids met me at Perth airport, their faces solemn. Expecting to take me to the hospital, they were disappointed when, after a brief embrace, I was whisked off by army medics to Hollywood Hospital. Danielle came later with the kids and a couple of hot pizzas, the gap allowing time for me to be checked in and reducing the trauma for Georgia and Henry. After tearfully telling them I loved them and that I would be all right, I watched them leave with Danielle. After they had gone, the infectious diseases doctor, Clay Golledge, came to visit me. 'We don't know what to do with this infection, Harry. We see that you have had just about every antibiotic known to us and then some. We're going to try some pretty heavy stuff, but I have to say this is looking grim. I want you to know, if it gets much worse we will have to amputate your leg.'

That was a long night, the longest. I pondered what the fuck I would do with only one leg, in between bouts of vomiting and nausea brought on by the poison in my veins.

I was sent home with a PICC line still inserted, and a home nurse visited me each day. I could tell from her demeanour that she was concerned about my leg. My youngest brother, Paul, burst into tears the first time he saw me. The other aspect of my shame was having come home less than a month into a five-month deployment. I wasn't missing a limb, so why had I left my mates? Was I hurt enough to go home? Surely the infection would have got better in Afghanistan? In my twisted state of mind, the infection was just another sign of my failure.

In my first weeks back home, my weight fell to a near-skeletal 60 kilograms, more than 20 below my fighting weight. At Danielle's fortieth birthday party, one of her teaching colleagues I'd known for years walked right past me without acknowledgement. Greg had not recognised me. I was, if not quite suicidal, morbidly depressed. All I wanted was to sit in darkness in our bedroom and not come out. I had been writing in a journal for a long time, but my scribblings were now incoherent. I kept obsessing about that wrong turn I had made, and was fixated on the damage to my reputation within the unit. I reviewed my entire military career, second-guessing every decision I had made, every promotion I had gained, every task performance. I asked myself, over and over, *Am I really shithouse at what I do?*

I didn't know if I would be able to get back to work at all. Physically, my right leg had atrophied and became noticeably skinnier than the left. The infection and injuries eventually made it shorter too. No matter how hard I trained, I could not get it back to its normal size. Essentially I had to learn to walk again and build up muscles in both legs, as well as doing my cardio. I was forty years old now, and trying to get back up to elite fitness is extremely hard even for a younger man, let alone one hitting his first midlife crisis. But I was diligent and could rely on an underlying natural fitness. Having lost most of the muscle mass I'd put on since returning to the regiment, I obstinately built myself back up to around 80 kilos, a significant improvement on the low sixties I had fallen to during my infection.

Danielle tried her best, but those who are closest to you are often the most powerless in these situations. Georgia was only thirteen and Henry was nine, so for them it was frightening to see me in this state and it was Danielle's job to try to explain what was happening to me, and to love and protect them.

For Danielle, it was particularly challenging when she was going through my gear and found it soaked with blood, mine and others'. I walked into the laundry one day to find her sitting cross-legged on the floor, sifting through my clothes, the whole archaeology of my service in the fabric she was holding. There would be wear marks in the shoulder from the butt of my gun; or scribbles on my sleeves or legs—while on a raid, I would have to jot down important times and locations and other information, and my clothes were the handiest place—but most disturbing of all were the bloodstains.

One thing I really needed to do was get in touch with Sean's parents, David and Mary McCarthy. He had died a soldier's death, giving his life in defence of the country and values he loved, surrounded by his comrades in arms. I eventually spoke to them via email, but the opportunity didn't arise to meet them face to face, and to be honest I was finding excuses to avoid it. I kept rehearsing what I would say to Sean's mum in particular. 'Hi, Mrs McCarthy, I'm the guy who fucked up and caused your son's death, I'm sorry.' Nothing I could think of seemed right. I felt like such a coward merely for having left the battlefield with my arms and legs intact, to meet Sean's parents was a bridge too far. I would eventually meet them, and they were so gracious, so understanding, I wish I had had the fortitude to meet them earlier. They have been an integral part of my gradual progress towards making peace with it all. They were, and are, wonderful.

My recovery was enhanced by the unit's world-class physios and doctors, and I feel I was a good patient. And by engaging with the psychologists, I was able to reframe everything in my head. Eventually I grew to relish my rehab. It gave me goals to train and reach for. I loved the hours in the local walking pool with the elderly ladies, who I got to know on a first-name basis. I had setbacks along the way but once the infection started to subside, over weeks and months I regained most of my vigour.

As time passed, it would be my mates from the Applecross Cricket Club who dragged me out of it. Friends from the regiment called regularly to see how I was, but I was convinced that deep down they thought I was a fuck-up. The cricket guys, on the other hand, couldn't have been more proud of me. Guys like Steve Coyle, Chris Teede and Cameron Stirling came over for a chat, and I was trying to persuade them what a failure I was.

Stirlo, in particular, would tee off: 'Fuck off, Harry, stop that bullshit, you're a top bloke. You've achieved more than any of us can even imagine.'

When I really opened my eyes and ears to them, I saw that they weren't just stroking my ego. They meant it.

By October, Stirlo wanted me to go with him on a cricket fan's trip of a lifetime: to see Australia play a Test match in India. A larger group of Applecross players was going to play some matches against an under-18 team from Karnataka state, the capital of which, Bengaluru, was hosting one of the two Test matches. I wrestled with the idea. I was back at the unit, doing rehab each morning, and was surrounded by reminders of my mates who were still in Afghanistan. When they were fighting a war, how could I contemplate something as flippant as going off to India to watch cricket?

One evening, as I was sitting on the steps at the Moffitt Cricket Ground, my backyard cricket field, Stirlo rang me.

'Harry, you're killing yourself, mate. This self-pity has got to end. You don't owe anyone anything, no one thinks you are to blame or that you are a fuck-up. You need to forget all of that SAS bullshit and war crap, and forget about anyone who thinks you are to blame, they can get fucked. As your standing Second XI Captain, I order you to be sitting beside me at M. Chinnaswamy Stadium in Bengaluru and that's it. I won't hear another word.'

For better or worse, I agreed to go to India. It turned out very much for the better. I still carried the guilt and shame, but my civilian mates had an endless appetite for hearing stories about what I had done in the services, and this alone helped me feel better. I played in and enjoyed the games, hobbling around the field against the local juniors. I continued my rehab in the hotel gym. During breaks in play, I stretched and worked on breaking down my scarring—I followed the doctors' orders to the letter. Best of all, I was with Stirlo, Teedey, Shandy the Mangy Cat, Big Al Cheese and others from Applecross.

Sitting in the grandstand in Bengaluru, gradually unwinding, talking about cricket and life with these guys who only wanted the best for me, released something that had been trapped inside me.

During day two of the Test match, having watched Ricky Ponting craft the first century for the series in a big partnership with Simon Katich the day before, I grew restless. I complained to Stirlo that we had no radio station to listen to. Like many keen cricket fans, I was used to listening to the dulcet tones of the ABC's Jim Maxwell. I had brought my transistor with me, but the ground did not allow a broadcast. We were sitting in front of the media area. I could see the television box, mostly full of hairdressers and make-up artists, and just beyond that the ABC Grandstand box.

'I'm going for a recce,' I said to Stirlo. 'There has to be a way to listen to the cricket here, for fuck's sake.' I limped towards the armed security manning the media area. To my surprise, the guard was shaping to let me through, obviously thinking I was media. To cement myself in his mind, I told him what a great job he was doing and shook his hand in the most ingratiating manner. I cracked a joke and looked deep into his eyes as we laughed—insertion method and passage-of-lines secured!

I made my way up the stairs leading to the commentary boxes, past the commercial TV box that looked more like a hairdressing salon, along to the ABC box at the very end. There was the great man plying his trade. I quickly realised that the room was partitioned in two, and the non-ABC side was empty. I went in there, and nobody cared.

Here I was, living a boyhood dream, sitting behind the bowler's arm while in the same room Jim Maxwell commentated on Test match cricket. It had been three months since Sean's death. I rubbed my right knee, which was still achy and very weak. Should I really be here? I decided to suspend that thought, relax and enjoy a few overs.

I went back and got Stirlo. 'Let's go, just follow my lead, act like you own the place.'

'Where are we going, Harry?'

'I have a surprise for you.'

We headed back past the guard with whom I was famous now, and took a seat. We sat there as pleased as twelve-year-old boys who had just found their fathers' *Playboy* stash. I took my copy of the *Laws of Cricket*, which I carry at every Test match, from my breast pocket and tore a page from the rear. I wrote a note to Jim Maxwell, briefly explaining who we were, and passed it to him during a break between overs. We watched Michael Hussey make his only Test hundred in India, were interviewed by Jim Maxwell live on radio, and ate lunch with the media pack, getting into a long discussion with the veteran cricket writer Mike Coward about geopolitics and the role of the town of Quetta around the border regions of Pakistan and Afghanistan.

This surreal and beautiful experience took me right out of myself. I listened for the commentator in my head, the one who had been telling me what a fuck-up I was, who had told me I should probably kill myself. That voice seemed to be a little kinder and softer.

I truly appreciated the importance of having civilian mates outside of the SAS. It is now the number one piece of advice I have for young operators: have something outside the unit. Don't let the SAS define you. Spend time with civilians, as they will give you a greater sense of identity.

'How good is this, Harry?' Stirlo beamed. 'Glad you came?'

'Brilliant, mate. Just what the doctor ordered.'

———

By the time I returned to work full-time, and began to prepare for the 2009 deployment back to Afghanistan, I had lost much of my fear and anxiety. Nobody at work treated me like a fuck-up or a failure, and there was no explicit impact on my job. As far as the unit was concerned, I had been wounded in action (WIA) and now I was fit again. End of story.

But it would never really be the end of the story for me. I have never fully accepted that I was not responsible for Sean's death, and much of what I have achieved since that time is in part driven by my need to compensate—perhaps overcompensate—for that guilt.

In early- to mid-2009, the memories no longer rendered me unfit for service, but I would never forget Sean. It's just that I became a person who could work again. I attribute my recovery to the people in the regiment, to my mates at the cricket club, to my wife and family, and ultimately to the healing properties of talking and time.

BAT VIII

THE GENERAL SPIN

AFGHANISTAN, 2009/10

As tough as it was, that year after Sean McCarthy's death turned me into the person I am. I had to confront all my insecurities about my place in the regiment and my self-worth, go into a very dark place to battle with them, and somehow get out the other side. Not everybody receives that opportunity. I would never be thankful for the circumstances that brought on my ordeal, but I do, in hindsight, appreciate its value. In many ways, Sean McCarthy is the most important person I have met.

One of the developments that came out of that year was the Wanderers' Education Program. When I was suffering from the infection and the doctors said they might have to amputate my leg, I was ripped apart by anxiety. My working life had been centred on my physical abilities. I wasn't a desk worker or an intellectual. I was, frankly, terrified by the thought of physical impairment.

But should I have been? I was studying for my psychology degree at Edith Cowan University, well on my way towards a qualification, and was loving it. I finished my bachelor's degree and made the cut for the extra year's honours course. Why shouldn't a person from a working-class background see themselves as a thinker?

This type of questioning worked against an atmosphere of prejudice from the military hierarchy. It was all very well for the officer class to gain university qualifications, but to provide those chances for grunts was seen as a waste. The military spends considerable public money on sending senior officers to educational courses around the world. When you work with some of them, you wonder where all the learning went. We in the ranks, meanwhile, received a few weeks here and there in the jungle, living on rations, learning how to operate a machine gun. That was all we were seen as good for. Self-educating soldiers were even seen as 'soft' by some of their fellow operators, who thought we didn't need smart soldiers, just war fighters. Staring down the barrel of the end of my career and the prospect of losing a leg, I knew these attitudes were complete bullshit.

During my time WIA, I decided to put my natural instincts as a disruptor and a rebel to good use. A few years earlier I had written a long document on the value of educating soldiers. I revised and sent it to many senior officers and warrant officers, receiving few responses. One of the more considered came from Colonel 'JJ' Irish, without doubt the best officer I ever served under, indeed one of the best leaders of men that I know. Many would agree. He listened and gave a fuck, genuinely. But I realised that the military would not listen to a 'DUM digger' and that I would have to develop my ideas myself.

The inspiration didn't come from a vacuum. Big Duke had planted the seed years before, telling me not to wait for the unit to do things for me when it came to education but to take the initiative myself. I had done that, but I'd had a very special person in Danielle encouraging and enabling me along the way. What did other soldiers have? There had been some senior members of the unit who also developed the idea, writing that 'A smarter soldier, and one who allows himself to be smart, gives himself permission', but they had run into resistance from the system too.

Inspired by David Stirling's mandate to be 'daring', and armed with those voices who said, 'Do it yourself', I turned my paper into a five-year plan for an educational program. In 2012, I organised meetings with universities in Western Australia, and after months of knockbacks and hearing 'What do you want to educate soldiers for?' I met Michele Roberts, who was the Program Director at the University of Western Australia Business School. She thought my idea was so cunning it might just work, and I think she liked its 'Who Dares Wins' spirit. Given that soldiers were still taking university education covertly, Michele showed courage to support us.

I rang the philanthropist Todd Bennett, who had contributed to welfare programs for SAS soldiers, told him of my plan and asked for $30,000 to support the pilot and first cohort. Around the same time, Mark Donaldson introduced me to the financier Chris Joye, who in turn connected me with a hedge fund manager, Rob Luciano. I said we would have to do it behind the defence force's back. This was a first of its kind in Australia and, I think, the world. They liked that enough to give the program $150,000.

In 2013, we put four SAS operators into a pilot program we titled the Wanderers' Education Program (WEP). One of our program's great advantages was that each course an applicant wanted to enrol in was independently assessed between the unit and the applicant. When education was funded by the military itself, by contrast, it had to be directly relevant to your work. They were always questioning why I needed to study psychology, and I funded half of that myself, as the military didn't consider it 'strictly relevant'. I still carry a HECS debt from it. I wanted all soldiers to be able to study whatever they wanted and, past a period of returned service, when they wanted. Those people who were telling me it was a waste of time didn't realise they were only firing me up. Over the years, we have had dozens of members of the SAS studying everything from medicine to public leadership, from sports science to physics, from business administration to small business. I was proudest of all, I think, of guys who applied for money to go to TAFE and finish their final year of high school, determined to complete that task before they let themselves progress to university, which testified to the type of person the SAS seeks to select.

The WEP is an incentive-based scheme, working retroactively: the soldiers pay their fees, and when they finish their course—*only* if they finish their course, to an agreed pass mark—we reimburse them. It's tough but, I think, fair: if they fail or drop out, they get nothing from us. We had no intention of turning them into welfare recipients, as some veterans' programs tend to do. It remains my ambition to see soldiers educated, and to have their worth recognised by the wing of the military they are working for. I strongly believe that education, and the pathways it opens up, will see a decrease in the mental health and transition problems that plague the veterans' community. I am proud to say that the program has inspired similar initiatives both inside and outside defence. And it all came out of those dark days in 2008 and 2009.

———————

That year also gave me a chance to re-establish a connection with Timor-Leste, a country that had meant so much to me.

Georgia was fourteen years old and very similar to me: passionate, sociable, personable, also forgetful and messy. I had been at home through her early life, not re-joining the regiment until she was six, and as a result we were, and are, very close. Now I was keen for her to have a 'crucible' experience growing up, though the choice was rather extreme: I had the idea to send her to the Timor-Leste highlands to spend a couple of months with the Salesian Sisters of Don Bosco. An ex-regiment bloke had sent his daughters there. The difference was, we would send Georgia alone—for three months!— to experience life without running water, electricity or phones. She would be staying at a girls' college with duties to assist the nuns in their domestic and agricultural tasks, as well as teaching the girls in the college. One of her main jobs was assisting with the computer lessons, using the college's one and only solar-powered desktop computer.

Danielle, Henry and I saw her off at the airport. Danielle and I had our arms around each other, thinking, *What have we done? We have just sent our fourteen-year-old girl to the remote highlands of a poverty-stricken country on the brink of revolution and civil war! To live in a subsistence village . . . What the fuck are we thinking?*

A friend of mine in Timor, Ashley Rees, the expat Australian owner of the Hotel Esplanada in Dili, would help Georgia settle in and visit her to check she was all right. I'd first met Ashley during my 2006 deployment when, at the end of one very long and difficult day, he had saved the team's lives by providing some desperately needed cold beer. I'd had many other memorable nights at Ash's hotel, including watching the infamous 2006 FIFA World Cup match when Australia got knocked out by Italy after a questionable refereeing decision. We'd remained good mates ever since.

During Georgia's stay, Ash found out that the locals believed she was his niece. He happily allowed this rumour to spread unchallenged. Save for a few accidents falling out of trees and off fences in the search for ripe mangoes, and having to assist in slaughtering and butchering her own food, her experience was amazing, and I hope she will keep drawing on it throughout her life. I have continued the connection with the country, visiting there with Danielle, and I hope Henry will go there one day too.

———

Another bright moment during my recovery was Mark Donaldson receiving the Victoria Cross. His feats on that 2008 deployment, along with those of many of our mates, were the stuff that gave our regiment its high reputation in Australia and around the world. Donno is one of the most humble, grounded people I have ever met, and was completely unchanged by being the first Australian to receive our highest military award in four decades. In fact, his initial instinct was to refuse the VC, as there had been a tradition of taking recipients out of the front line, putting them in cottonwool and saving them for ceremonial tasks. Donno, who had only been on his second deployment to Afghanistan in 2008, wanted none of that. It was only after the chief of the army promised him that he could stay in his rank—he was a lance-corporal—remain with his troop and keep going on deployments like he would have gone on anyway, that he consented to receive the VC. That attitude, I felt, was SAS through and through.

The ceremony in 2009 was in Canberra, and Donno insisted that the team all be there. Amid the pomp and ceremony, he was gracious in accepting the award, while some anonymous officers received their required share of the reflected glory. Cynicism aside, these moments are important, as they gave us a chance to reflect on where we had come from. I remembered a similar event in 2002, after we arrived back from our first deployment to Afghanistan, when we received a Meritorious Unit Citation. Prime Minister John Howard, a favourite in the unit for committing Australia to a major international conflict, entered the tent erected at Campbell Barracks for the event. As he stepped onto the stage, a huge roar of approval shook the tent. I had goosebumps. My mind flooded with inspirational memories. I had joined the SAS in 1990 proud and strong; reached burnout and despair in 1994 and left the unit; spent seven years having children while seeking a direction for myself; re-joined the unit in 2002; and now, after I had thought I would never achieve anything in the SAS, Donno's VC helped us all feel like we had arrived. He was incredibly generous in making sure we shared in his moment.

But the cheeky disruptor was always lurking, ready to seize his chance. I took my 2008 Gray-Nicolls Excalibur to the investiture, anticipating the opportunity to get Prime Minister Kevin Rudd and Governor-General Quentin Bryce to sign it, which they did. After the photos and presentation at Government House at Yarralumla, we were moved into the dining room for lunch. I was at a round table with nine other SAS boys, towards the back of the room. As we sat down, the waiters were serving champagne for toasting and so on. However, the din from our table for beer grew to a point that I could not contain myself and headed for the kitchen. The sympathetic head chef sorted me out with a tray of ten Crownies. Perfect. As I re-entered the dining room I felt a bit self-conscious at the looks that were coming my way, but a welcoming smile from the GG quelled any concerns.

When I got back to the table, one K. Rudd was occupying my seat. Sensing the opportunity for a bit of fun, feigning outrage I walked around the table and punched him hard on the upper arm. He jumped out of his skin, grabbing his arm in shock and possibly (I hit him quite hard) pain.

'You right, mate?' I asked, pretending outrage. 'You're in my seat!'

The table erupted in laughter—all except the PM, who got up, blushing with, I suspected, as much anger as embarrassment. I shared the beers around the table and said, 'Only joking, Sir! Please sit down—and here, have this!'

I shoved a Crownie in his hand. I think that smoothed it over. I needed to use the bathroom anyway. Famous for being an 'away dumper', I left K. Rudd with the boys and headed off in search of a toilet. I ended up upstairs where, finding myself in one of the GG's private bathrooms, I took a most luxurious dump.

To commemorate the moment, I got on the phone to Stirlo, back in Perth. 'Hey, you'll never guess where I'm having a dump right now. The GG's ensuite!'

'You're kidding!' He laughed.

'Yeah, and I might leave a reverse kanga!' I said, referring to the disgusting habit of facing back-to-front on a mate's toilet bowl so as to leave a skid mark on the front edge and, more intriguingly, a question for the next person as to how you managed to achieve it.

I was starting to feel more like myself again.

————

Almost a year to the day after leaving for that ill-fated 2008 deployment, I left with a new team for Afghanistan. This was early in what we called the 'never-ending summer', when we were cycling in and out of Afghanistan for a northern hemisphere summer, to return to Perth for ours. Some of these deployments I couldn't wait to get home from, while others I wished could have gone on forever. Both the good and bad ones strained my abilities to be a husband and father.

The 2009 deployment was a security job. We were living in Kabul, and I ran a detachment that was babysitting senior Coalition and Afghan officers and diplomats. Politicians, businesspeople and, I suspect, bad guys would come to visit the bureaucrats to discuss the war, and we had to make sure they weren't packing guns or explosives in their turbans, though they had already been cleared at checkpoints. For the most part, it was fairly mundane in practice.

Our team lived on the edge of the Green Zone in downtown Kabul, not far from the US and UK embassies, but we spent a lot of time out in the suburbs. There were several bases and Australian personnel in different places around the city, and we would act as their couriers and street experts. We were regularly visiting shopping districts, travelling in armoured but unmarked cars, and moved freely through the city, which I grew to know well.

Kabul is a big city of four or five million, with the relatively well-off areas in the western part. Downtown was like any third-world city, low-rise with a handful of taller buildings. The dangers didn't need overstating. Often we passed a convoy that had been hit by an IED. Bad guys frequently penetrated the Green Zone and 'cooked off', or exploded a bomb. Once, a car came in what we called the 'back entrance', an area we had previously highlighted as a security risk to the base officer, and made it to the front gate of the Coalition headquarters, where it detonated. Several people died and, as usual, it was the lowly paid local private security contractors and civilians who took the brunt of it. In another attack, senior local politicians and businesspeople were meeting just around the corner from us, and an insurgent got through the security scan with a turban full of explosives and cooked himself off, killing a dozen senior peacemakers. Suicide bombings were so commonplace that, in the seconds after a roadside bomb had detonated, cars just drove around the scene to get out of the area before a secondary attacker arrived and caused the roads to be blocked off for hours. For many Afghans, avoiding these scenes was as customary a part of daily life as avoiding roadworks in an Australian city.

Because we did things unconventionally but effectively, we were often called on to get shit done where it might otherwise be stifled by regular hierarchies. For example, we could pick people up and drop them off at the airport, more safely and punctually, in our low-key armoured 4WDs, which attracted no attention, whereas regular forces would have taken them in a 'Rhino', a *Mad Max* kind of bus that was heavily protected but also a conspicuous and popular target. Plus, we had highly trained SAS drivers who were excellent at dominating the roads and keeping on top of roadblocks and other obstacles. We had the travel times and alternative routes down to a fine art.

Complex attacks, where an IED is detonated to start an ambush on Coalition forces and emergency responders, were not uncommon. More regular were simple armed attacks on care agencies, schools and hospitals. There were also many assaults on hotels, restaurants and bars where westerners hung out.

Kabul had quite a thriving underground social scene, with the added edge that you weren't certain of getting through the night in one piece.

Given our freedom of movement, various Australian and Coalition people asked us to buy alcohol for them. The isolation and banality of much of the day-to-day work in the headquarters meant that a few beers or a bottle of whiskey went a long way. Even the highest-ranking people were interested, and we didn't discriminate. Though there was some emotional reporting in the press about isolated incidents, the immutable fact is that, throughout history, wherever there have been soldiers and war there have been booze, sex workers and a thriving black market. I can honestly say, hand on heart, that I never saw anything get out of hand, save a little nude darts or a farting competition, and a few beers off shift were a good thing from a psychological perspective—I think.

We occasionally organised a SOF-only meeting with our Canadian, New Zealand, British and American counterparts over a few relaxing beers. Once, in the basement of a 5-Eyes HQ, our meeting ended up in a four-hour knockout world championship of scissors-paper-rock. One of my favourite photos is of 'Wodonga' Russell playing paper to his Canadian opponent's rock, a microsecond before the room exploded in euphoria, beer cans smashing into the roof, like the winning run had been scored in an Ashes series. For all its bad press, a few beers can certainly normalise things for a moment.

How did the booze get into our military facilities? Until around 2009, it was sent to Afghanistan in the mail. Sometimes it was smuggled through inspections at Bagram Air Base in weapons and top-secret storage trunks. That did not always work out, such as when one idiot filled an entire trunk with grog—a bottle broke and the smell and leakage had the inspectors in raptures. From that point on, they inspected all mail.

With the SAS leading the way, we had to improvise. Danielle came up with some great solutions for us, and I know she enjoyed the challenge. She would fill those little pop-tops, the mini-sized juices kids use for school lunches, with bourbon or scotch and hide them inside biscuit cartons. Some spouses were excellent at the job of posting 'morale' into foreign theatres of operation through standard mail. Nancy Wake would have been proud. Most of Danielle's efforts succeeded. She once sent a home-brew kit, each part individually packaged, which we set up in clever and surreptitious ways. Most of the home brews, though, made us sick. I only tasted a few successful ones, and one of the best was a moonshine made with potatoes, the old-fashioned way.

Danielle was far from the only home supplier. The mother of one of the guys sent a 'pickling' kit over. On opening it, the recipient discovered a book on pickling, a jar full of vinegar (real vinegar) and other bits and pieces, including a box of tissues. No alcohol, apparently.

'What the fuck was your mum thinking, Slick?'

'I don't know, maybe we can do something with the vinegar.'

This got us thinking of what we might do; after all, alcohol *was* very rare. Some time later, one of the lads asked for a tissue, to discover a half bottle of vodka hidden in the Kleenex box. The vinegar was a decoy. Brilliant.

I also remember Pigpen opening his mail to find a very large, one-litre bottle of shampoo. He opened it, and to our great joy it was full of bourbon. When it came time to consume it, however, we discovered that his loved one had failed to wash out the shampoo bottle before pouring the booze in. Spoiled for choice given the stockpile we had accumulated, the group decided to throw the shampoo-contaminated stock into the bin. I furtively grabbed the bottle and hid it in my foot locker. Sure as shit, the next time we were lamenting the lack of grog after finishing a job, I pulled out the contaminated bottle. There were a few grimaces to start with, but the full litre was consumed gleefully over the night, with a few blokes even growing to like its pearly, sheeny character, especially Hawkeye, who remarked: 'At least we won't get dandruff in our mouths!'

In Afghanistan, alcohol was also a valuable diplomatic tool. If you wanted to win hearts and minds in Kabul, a good bottle of scotch and a couple of packets of western cigarettes tended to help.

In Kabul, and throughout Afghanistan on later deployments, smuggling booze became less necessary, as it was quite freely available. Very late in the week we would get a text saying, 'Flowers' or 'Gandy's', to signal where the meet-up would be. There was a war going on in the hills, but meanwhile a loose party scene was developing in the restaurants and bars where the diplomatic and care agency crowds went to unwind. The food was so good that you willingly rolled the dice on whether you would wake up shitting through the eye of a needle the next morning. The best-known bars included L'Atmosphere, Flower Street Café and Gandamak's, named after a village outside Jalalabad where the British occupiers made their last stand. The pub was underneath an old colonial-era house, done up as an old tavern, with memorabilia on display, including the evocative painting *Last Stand of the 44th at Gandamak*.

A personal favourite of mine was the Raven's Nest, owned by Canadian Dave, who ran a private security company among other enterprises. In the basement of his headquarters-slash-home, he had set up a bar and club with live music. Open every fortnight or on demand, it attracted civilian care agency workers, security contractors and embassy staff, who would sneak out into the night for a dance and a few beers. Guns were checked at the door, unless Dave's security allowed you in armed. Whatever live band was playing, no matter its personnel, was called 'The Internationals'. Indeed, it was so international, one of the nights I played I could not communicate with the German guitarist or the Italian singer other than by showing them the chords or writing down letters.

Since we were not involved in war fighting out in the provinces on that trip, the tension had a different kind of edge, but it was still apparent. The anxiety produced by random bombings and the danger on the streets, mixed with tedium and fatigue, high-stress jobs around the city and late nights, made for a more combustible atmosphere than when we were out chasing targets from Tarin Kowt. One example of how the tension blew up involved the wonderful little Maton F10 guitar, circa 1968, the year I was born, that I often took on deployments. I had written about one hundred and fifty songs on it and it went everywhere with me. It was resilient, reliable and never lost its tune. One night, after a couple of beers, I'd just finished playing my Maton and put it on a chair. At the crux of a song we were listening to, one of my teammates, for no apparent reason, and accidentally I have to assume, punched the guitar straight through where the neck met the body. He was a big strong man and he destroyed my guitar. Without thinking, I got up and punched him in the head as hard as I could. I picked up the pieces of my Maton and carried it back to my room. Danielle can still remember my tearful call. This was, in an unlikely sense, one of the most regrettable moments of my life. That guitar and I had been through so much, and though I have mostly forgiven my mate, our relationship has never been the same. He has never been able to explain his brain fade. I always wondered if it was the stress of the place, the cabin fever. He replaced the Maton with a nice Canadian Maple guitar, and I have since spent a lot of time with it. Being vintage, the F10 was irreplaceable and I miss it.

The weird happenings after dark took place against a background of relentless work, mostly outside the wire on the streets, in a city on edge. Out in the shopping streets and markets, there were metal detectors and checkpoints for guns, and criminals and terrorists were everywhere. There was nothing stopping someone running up and shooting us, but they were mostly occupied with their own business feuds. I didn't feel particularly vulnerable. I had a grey, mullah-type of beard, and Afghan people revere 'grey beards'. Thinking I was a distinguished old man, people were too shy and deferential to make eye contact with me.

More dangerous than shopping was driving. Driving in Kabul was strange because there were no lines marked on the roads and the only operational set of lights in the whole city, in front of the university, was purely for show. Traffic could all flow one way or the other, on the same road, depending on the volume of cars and the time of day. In the morning, a street would flow one way, and in the afternoon it would go the other. There was no prearranged time when this would change, no traffic cops. If you got caught going the wrong way, you had to stop and wait an hour. Plenty of accidents resulted.

Near the city's Ghazi Stadium, where the Taliban had executed women, my car was T-boned by a truck one day. It was quite a substantial collision, and left me sitting in the car, stunned, my head and hand bleeding. People came and banged at the window saying it was my fault. I thought, *We are in big trouble here, this angry mob won't let us go, they might drag us out of the car and whack us right here. Or some terrorist is going to cook us off.* It was probably my scariest moment of that deployment. Fortunately the other car was not far behind. It came past, grabbed us and all our kit, and we left in that car. We had no choice but to leave the other car on the side of the road, knowing that abandoned cars were soon picked over for parts.

Once you knew where the culverts and drains were—a big obstacle to traffic—you could find your way around Kabul. It's a well laid out town with a university and some big hospitals that the Taliban converted into madrasas, which were now being turned back into their proposed function.

About an hour east of Kabul was the golf course, ranked the most dangerous on the planet at the time. The middle of the fairways had been de-mined. You had to be careful to walk between the white rocks but not stray outside the red rocks. During one round, my caddy was ten or twelve years old with half of one of his arms missing. The owner said this caddy had lost his arm clearing mines on the course, which may or may not have been true. We would take people we needed to stay on good terms with for nine holes, building rapport just like a corporate golf day at home, only you had to let the caddies walk first. They had branch-off runs so that if you hit the ball wide of the fairway, they would step out there on footpads. I lost countless balls, and the ball that came back with the caddy was never the one I had hit. I am a particularly shit golfer. I enjoy it, but I refuse to leave the fairway to look for balls. Instead I place a new one roughly where I think the lost one should have landed on the fairway. Nor do I keep score, which infuriates my mates. As a result, I have scored pars and birdies on nearly every hole I have played, including all nine in Kabul.

We also played that course when the heavy winter snow fell. Snow could shut Kabul down suddenly. We could only travel on the main roads, which choked up. Sometimes we got around that by using interpreters or the local taxi network, good drivers who knew what side of the road to drive on. Using taxis, however, came with risk. As soon as you got in, they would know you were foreigners. So you were putting your life in the hands of someone who slept in his car, owned nothing, and had little reason not to take some cash to get you into trouble.

You couldn't help feeling like a target. One of our roles was to escort military people, diplomats and VIPs around the Kabul tourist spots, so they could say they'd been outside the wire. An attraction was Swimming Pool Hill, a popular place for a photo. It took five minutes to drive to the top of the hill, which was used by the Russians as a lookout, as it dominated the city. They had built an Olympic-sized pool with a high diving platform. But there were issues filling the pool, and it never really got going. When the Taliban took over, they took intellectuals and politicians up there and forced them to jump off the diving platform into the empty pool in secretive executions. The locals said they could smell the dead and rotting bodies. I thought it was a pretty macabre place to have your photo taken, and driving important foreigners up there always made me feel uneasy: what a stupid job to risk your life for. Luckily, none of our trips met with any incident.

Four years into Australia's second stint in Afghanistan, we were quite proud of the reputation as good fighters that our countrymen

had built. One useful job we realised we could do was to collect
and forward intelligence from headquarters to the combat guys
out in the provinces. On one occasion, Mullah Muhammed Omar,
the Taliban leader, issued an order to his commanders to avoid the
'Soor Talibs', or 'Red Students', the name they gave to Australian
soldiers because we had 'red beards'. (An old cricket coach of mine
used to say many men had red in their beards, but nowhere else on
their bodies: 'The red man lives in all of us, my boy.') Mullah Omar
wrote to his commanders in Uruzgan Province that they wished
the Dutch and Americans had remained, because the Australians
were very fierce fighters and did not give in. The translation of his
order to commanders was 'to attack American soldiers' because
'their cumbersome vehicles make them easy to target'. The Soor
Talibs, the Australians, on the other hand, identifiable by the 'red
rat' (or kangaroo) painted on the side of our camouflaged vehicles,
were 'very difficult to see and could move quickly with the use of
their motorbikes'. Yet it was our beards that most impressed the
Taliban and AQ, and coming from them with their meticulously
well-kempt facial hair, this was a huge compliment.

———————

For me, this trip was about getting back physically and mentally.
It helped that this was quite a sedentary gig, mostly in offices
and cars. Using a gym in the Green Zone, I got my weight back
to 85 kilos and my strength and fitness as strong as it had ever
been, which was a good recovery considering I had lost a centi-
metre of length off my right leg and about 20 degrees' range of

movement from my right knee and ankle. In time, I would work on those too.

For morale, cricket again came to the rescue. Driving around the city, we could see games being played on the streets and the big maidans, the pitches marked out in the dirt. Their stumps were rope and cane, all in one piece on a stand, and their bats were fashioned out of a piece of wood. It was heartening to see the people so joyfully taking up a pastime that the Taliban had forbidden.

Although I did try to bring a bat from Australia, I was unable to get it through customs. Not to worry: I was able to buy a much better one, along with a box of six-stitcher cricket balls and tennis balls, from a shop called Kabul Sports. Most items from that shop were pretty poor quality, such as the boxing gloves that exploded on our hands the first time we used them. But the cricket bats, imported from Pakistan and India, were beautiful. The one I bought, a 'CA' brand, had twelve perfect parallel lines of grain running down the face. Even though it had a big knot in the back of the blade, it was every bit a $500 bat or more in Australia, but in Kabul we got it for US$50. It was a ripping piece of willow and I used it to death.

I had a surreptitious personal goal behind my cricket on that trip. The last competitive fixture I had played for Applecross was back in early 2008, before Sean's death and my injuries. That game was a Second XI final at Bassendean, on turf, against Swanbourne. It was the closest a suburban cricketer like me got to playing a Test match: four days of eighty-over-an-innings cricket played over a nine-day stretch. That final was the crowning glory of my career: we won the match and took home a felt pennant. I can still remember man-dancing like Fred Astaire and Ginger Rogers through the night in the never-ending puddle with Stirlo and Teedey, and drinking on the clubhouse steps until sunrise. The celebrations might have gone for a few days, if I remember correctly. It seemed a lifetime ago. Since then, I had been blown up and spent a year off in rehab and recovery, gone through that terrible period, and then redeployed. We were due home in January 2010, and I figured that if I played all the remaining games for Applecross on my return, I might just qualify for the finals. The club was going well, so my chances were good if I could teach myself how to play again.

The first thing I did after visiting Kabul Sports was set up a ball on a string outside an accommodation block at the base in the Green Zone. I pulled open the stitching on one of the balls and buried inside it a length of hoochie cord. Once the cord was buried into the stitching and very firmly tightened, I could loop another longer cord through the loop I'd left protruding from the stitching, and suspend the ball from the concrete ceiling so that the ball hung at a drivable height above the ground. The ceiling being concrete meant that I could hit it hard. The struck ball would swing up to hit the ceiling, and then, like a vertical version of Totem Tennis, bounce back to its original position, where I would belt it again, over and over and over. I spent hours hitting that ball, often pissing off the guards who were sleeping in the daytime in preparation for their night shift. I'm sure the thousands of red cherries are still on the ceiling.

I was predominantly a bowler though, and that was another issue. I took a bunch of balls down to the headquarters to bowl on the artificial turf tennis courts. The court area was big enough to get a reasonable run-up and to push through my action, and I bowled at one or two teammates I persuaded to come down with me. Often, I would just bowl at nothing. Though I made a strange sight, my 'net sessions' would attract Coalition people who had never seen a game of cricket. They thought we were mad, hurling very hard balls at each other with little protection—though we did manage to get our hands on a protector.

Whenever we went out on jobs, I always took a cricket ball with me, polishing or spinning it to keep my hands busy. We played impromptu games with local Nepalese guards at our accommodation, which had a little garden and a grassed area, and on the streets with Afghan kids.

When it came to obtaining signatures for that bat, I would be dirty at missing out on getting Julia Gillard to sign it back in Australia. If I had, I would have had a sacked PM and a sacked general on the same bat.

The sacked general was Stanley McChrystal, the American officer who headed the Joint Special Operations Command running the war in Afghanistan. He was known to speak the truth without fear, and this would cost him his job in mid-2010 when he said some disparaging things about the Obama administration, US diplomats and Vice-President Joe Biden to *Rolling Stone* magazine. When I was there, McChrystal was still very much in charge, and appeared to be deeply respected in the ranks.

Towards the end of my trip, quite focused on the collection of bats I was building, I went to General McChrystal's office in the Green Zone to ask if he would sign my CA stick. His assistant took the bat and said, 'Yes, I'm sure the general will help out someone from the SAS.'

That was the last I saw of it. I went back a few times, and they kept saying they had sent it to the general and were waiting for him to sign it. Clearly, I figured, they'd lost it.

I spent the last two weeks of my deployment feeling peeved about another disappeared bat. For one, I really loved that stick; I had re-learned how to bat with it. And for another, I was increasingly attached to my collection. The bat had many other signatures on it, from the men and women I had worked with on that deployment. I did my best to forget about it. It's a war. Things get lost.

Two months after the trip finished, I was walking across the parade ground at Swanbourne when my teammate Billy 'Ashtray' Cooper came by in a car. He wound down the window and shouted: 'Moff, I've got something for ya!'

Out through the window came the bat—with McChrystal's signature on it.

Ashtray had found it in an assault bag on a load coming back from Kabul. We knew nothing of where it had been or what scenes it had witnessed. If only cricket bats could talk. As I held it gratefully in my hands, cradling it like a long-lost friend, I thought I was getting a message from somewhere. My collection was preserved. Some benign force was watching over it.

THE SURGE

AFGHANISTAN, 2010

Who is 'Harry' Moffitt? I'd often wondered, ever since Ken Studley saddled me with the nickname in 1991. It was my SAS identity, but my name is Anthony and I'd never felt 100 per cent comfortable as 'Harry' until one night before the 2010 deployment to Afghanistan.

I was lying in bed at home reading Patrick Lindsay's book *Fromelles* when, *bang*, there it was. Lieutenant Harry Moffitt, an accountant from Bendigo, Adjutant to Lieutenant Colonel Ignatius Norris, had enlisted into the 53rd battalion. A shiver ran down my spine: he was killed while going to Norris's aid on the evening of 19 July 1916, the darkest day of Australia's military history. I felt a kindred spirit. My heart pounded as I reached for my computer and started surfing the net for Harry Lowry Moffitt. I discovered he was killed instantly by heavy machine-gun fire having just topped the bags, and his body was never retrieved. His memorial was at the VC Corner Australian Cemetery and Memorial, just outside Fromelles.

As luck had it, I was due to travel to the UK to observe a British SAS counter-terrorism exercise. On arrival at Heathrow, I realised that I could be at Fromelles in three hours, not much more than a surfing mission from Perth to Margaret River. Off I went, arriving at the prettiest war cemetery you could imagine. From there I walked to VC Corner, searched for what felt like an hour, and there he was: Moffitt, HL. From that moment, the nickname Harry Moffitt became a badge of honour. I rambled around the World War I battle sites contemplating the other Harry Moffitt. Later that night I found myself at Menin Gate in Ypres, listening to the nightly changing of the guard and Australian national anthem. I will never forget that night; my nickname of Harry Moffitt underwent a metamorphosis to become my identity. After twenty years as a soldier, something clicked into place: my heritage.

———

One very hot Perth evening, at home after training at the Applecross Cricket Club, I was sitting on the steps that led up to the Moffitt Cricket Ground (MCG): my backyard cricket colosseum. The members' and ladies' stands had been built, piece by piece, over a ten-year period. During the planning stage, my mate Streaky Bacon, with whom I shared a car for weeks in the deserts of Afghanistan, and who was also renovating his home, would kill time with me by dreaming of the homes we were building back in Australia. With the toes of our boots as our drafting pencils, we drew scale maps of the rooms in the Afghan dirt and walked around them discussing what would go where, the ergonomic flow, all the big ideas. Between deployments, I had dug every post, hammered in every nail and slapped down every stroke of paint to complete the 'members' stand'; and while I was away, Danielle and our neighbour and good friend Kylie had built the 'ladies' stand'. We had built our house on the site, and the MCG was the finishing touch.

Matches at the MCG were seven-a-side, played over five hours, homage to the five days of a Test match. They had two innings and a complex set of rules, mostly obeying my dog-eared copy of the *Laws of Cricket* but with some local variations. You had to hit the ball onto the grass or else you were out, a hit ball was one run, and reaching the boundary (made of old helicopter fast-ropes) was two runs. The chicken pen in the north-west corner was at leg-slip, and if you hit it in there you were out. LBWs were assessed by the central and square umpires (must pitch in line, hit in line, and strike the batsman behind the batting crease), therefore were always controversial. We might not have had video technology to settle disputes, but we had lights, and even played the occasional day-nighter.

On the evening in question, I was flicking through my phone returning a few texts to the captains of the Applecross grade teams as they were sorting out their final sides and availability for the weekend. It's something that will bring a groan of recognition from any suburban cricket captain—the Thursday–Friday night selection panic to move players around as people drop out. Applecross was a large club of seven and sometimes eight teams, so the logistics were a weekly challenge.

As I was returning the texts, I recalled a similar night when I came across Matt Locke's phone number soon after his death. I read some of the texts we had shared: him calling me a 'soft Freefall poof who should have gone to water', banter about drinking beer. For some reason I rang his number, even though he had passed away. At the sound of his voicemail, I tried to leave him a message, but was overcome by emotion. I will never forget that. I felt as if I had betrayed something or someone by hearing him, indulging the momentary fantasy that he was still with us. Yet it was strangely comforting. I had enormous respect for him as a professional soldier. He was everything a 'Watery' could and should be, critical and clinical, but compassionate in his dealings with everyone he met. He was a great loss to the SAS, the army and the nation.

That night, after a few more beers in the glorious Perth evening, the Fremantle doctor eventually tickled the tops of our backyard trees. I looked through my contacts and found Dave 'Unreal' O'Neill, Craig 'Crackers' Linacre and Mick 'Macca' McAvoy, three SAS mates who had been killed in a car accident near Swan Island in Victoria after a training exercise in 2007. I sent each of them a text of farewell and regret. I have a photograph that I love: myself, Streaky, Matt and Dave sitting out the back of the residence we lived in during our 2004/05 deployment to Baghdad, drinking coffee and smoking tobacco from a shisha, or hookah pipe. In the background is the cricket pitch. Neither Dave nor Matt were particularly good at cricket, but they were enthusiastic participants and enjoyed humouring me. Craig and Macca, on the other hand, were very handy, and competitive as well. All top blokes who I miss deeply.

This photo triggered an appreciation of how much the game of cricket had given me. My involvement with Applecross started when one of my closest mates, Steve Coyle, a civilian, invited me down to the club for a few beers. 'Why don't you come have a game?' he suggested. I don't do things by halves. I signed up the next week and really enjoyed the escape. In the next few years, sitting and having a post-game beer after coming back from Afghanistan, the relief was exhilarating. Much as I loved the unit, it was a place where the pressure was high level and unrelenting. Daily service in the SAS really did feel like living inside a pressure cooker. Cricket was my sanctuary, giving me a feeling of freedom I needed more viscerally than ever as the deployments mounted.

Applecross played the equivalent of subdistrict cricket, the level below Premier Cricket. Our better players went up to Melville, our nearest Premier Cricket club. Our top three grades were pretty competitive. In the Suburban Turf Cricket Association we were thought of as silvertails, as we were from a leafy riverside suburb of old money, BMWs and Mercedes, although the blokes I played with were far from silvertails, many of them suburban guys who worked in or around the mining industry that propped up Perth and Western Australia. Hardly any lived in Applecross. In fact, always up for a piss-take, I had Applecross blazers made. They became popular, and were worn to big games such as finals. It gave us a little psychological edge, and it showed that we could laugh at ourselves. It couldn't lead to us shaking off our tag as finals chokers, though. That had more to do with the fact that our teams could be found at the clubhouse bar, or on the steps, until three o'clock in the morning the night before the finals. Perennial early celebrators!

I only ever played one game of A-grade cricket, in which my great achievements were to take a catch on the boundary and one wicket. I played most of my cricket at the club in either the 'thirsty third' eleven, or the seconds, who played on turf, which was everyone's aspiration. During these years I made lifelong friends and realised something important: I could trust civilians just as much as I could fellow soldiers. I knew these guys would keep an eye out for my family when I was away. I had now officially spent more time at a single address than ever before, and felt embedded in the community.

I was the only military person regularly playing at Applecross. Regiment guys tended not to play cricket. Rugby union is the primary sport in the military, often driven by the officer ranks, and SAS rugby players turned out for the Associates club at Swanbourne. I even played a handful of games on the wing for the Associates, or turned up to watch my mates play. As we were not meant to be taking risks by playing such a tough contact sport, rugby injuries were routinely reported to the regiment as 'accidents at home'. The regiment guys maintained an elite level of fitness; they might have lacked skill but they could run other teams into the dirt. Every time the club made the finals, they would come knocking at our door to see who was available.

Over the whole time I was at Applecross, only a handful of SAS guys played cricket regularly. Others would make occasional appearances under the names of 'P. Sundries' or 'Twelfth Man'.

For me, cricket was a great sport if you weren't meant to be playing sport. You could quietly get permission from the commanding officer, who might not be so keen to let you play football. Yes, it's true that in my first year at Applecross, every second bloke would introduce me as the guy who could kill someone with my little finger, which gave me the shits at first, but soon I became just Moff who got hit around the ground or Moff who bowled the occasional good spell.

Due to my schedule, some seasons I played just one game and other seasons as many as fifteen. I tried to make up for my sporadic attendance by getting heavily involved in the administration of the club, to Danielle's distraction. Cricket sometimes took me away from the family when I was at home, but she conceded that it was a necessary release for me. It might sound strange not to want to spend every available minute with your family when you are away for so long, but the pressure of my job required some kind of aggressive release, which competitive cricket provided. If you think your family can provide that counterbalance to a life of war fighting, I would say that you might be expecting too much from them. I was extremely fortunate that Danielle understood this and gave me the necessary time to get rid of all that pent-up energy and frustration.

I've only recently been able to persuade Danielle to enjoy Test matches. It was a long project. With Rowdy and his partner, we went to the Adelaide Test match between Australia and India after Phil Hughes died in November 2014. Danielle found the routine of getting up late in the morning, going shopping, hanging out at the hotel and then joining us for the last session of play and a

G and T quite enjoyable! That good old Test match rhythm. That said, getting her to enjoy Test cricket with me every season is still a work in progress.

———

In 2010, as a decisive move to end the eight-year conflict in Afghanistan, US President Barack Obama ordered a 'surge' of 30,000 troops into the country. Australia's contribution was to deploy a second of its three SAS squadrons in support of the one that was already there, a combination that was unprecedented in the unit's history. This had important consequences. Normally, while one squadron was away, there would be two in Australia: one on duty and one on reset. The doubling of our squadrons in Afghanistan meant that no operators were able to take time off to be with their families at home.

As a member of 3 Squadron, I was among those swung into training in early 2010. We had known that the order was coming, and went to Bindoon for drills, Standard Operating Procedures (SOPs) and individual skills training in JTAC, heavy weapons and explosives. The deployments had become so routine that the preparations were somewhat cookie-cutter in nature.

Our role had become almost exclusively a helicopter-borne assault force, more like a conventional commando team than the traditional SAS surveillance or special reconnaissance role; a departure that caused me increasing disquiet.

As a Freefall specialist, I took a large team to the alpine region around Mount Hotham in Victoria, which had the highest above sea level landing strip in Australia, to prepare. It had become fairly routine, but I have to say that leading a combat equipment, freefall descent into mountain terrain at night is about the most technically, physically and psychologically challenging thing I have ever done. I had some exceptional colleagues who assisted in making it all look pretty easy from a distance, but it never was.

On the particular training night I am recalling, we were flying in a single-engine PAC P-750, a lightweight aircraft that could fit about six people once all our kit was on. It was dark, with only the lights of the dashboard allowing us to continue our checks. We communicated in sign language. We had a full load, and military rigs and equipment were not exactly the easiest gear to move around in, let alone with our guns that seemed to always add a degree of difficulty no matter how we packed and prepared them. We had a smaller load this night, and our guns were plastic, as we were prohibited from taking real guns on civilian planes.

We checked our altimeters with each other's and the pilot's. This was particularly important tonight because we had taken off from high in the mountains and were dropping into another remote area that was slightly lower. If you don't have your maths right, you can get into serious trouble. After a week of reverse-cycle (sleeping by day and working at night), very late nights and early mornings in planning and preparations, we were at the edges of our endurance.

Next we checked our AADs (auto activating devices), the failsafe mechanisms that deploy your canopy if you have passed out from lack of oxygen or a knock on the head during or after your exit—all of which happen.

Our final check was our pins, reserve and main, making sure they were seated correctly and would work when needed, all the more important tonight because a 'hard pull' on a poorly set pin, or a late deployment of your canopy, might put you into the trees at a dangerous speed.

As team leader, my most critical check was morale. A quick thumbs-up, a deliberate stare into each bloke's eyes and a wink: no matter how many times guys have jumped, let alone into an unfamiliar drop zone at night, many, including myself, get anxious. A bit of humour—a good fart in the back of the plane—was always a good way to lighten the mood. For some reason, farts at altitude were especially putrid and funny.

At twenty minutes to exit, I got a yell from the pilot. Some in the team were dozing, while others were pantomiming drills. One bloke was picking his nose and wiping it on his mate's arm. After a long period in the plane all you want to do is get out.

At six minutes, we made our final checks and adjustments. At three minutes, there was a type of buddy check and we started to take a collective shape for exit. Flickering eye contacts and positive body language suggested readiness. At one minute, the door opened and that shape started to take on a life of its own, the team becoming a single entity. Individual navigation devices were activated, though I hadn't seen one person turn them on—it was automatic.

The red light switched to orange, and we stacked ourselves on the open side door of the aircraft. The interior was tiny, barely able to fit five burly kit-laden men. No need to herd people into position. It was as simple as rolling over in bed. I looked around.

The early days of the 'MCG', 2006. One of the chickens is fielding at short gully.

Our Timor team at RAAF Base Darwin, just before flying to Dili in 2006.

Maubisse, Timor Leste, 2006. A game of cricket at Alfredo Reinado's hideout. I am in the foreground, right, with my back to the camera.

Reinado and me at Maubisse, 2006.

The House, Campbell Barracks, Swanbourne, Western Australia. Henry, Danielle and Georgia with Prime Minister John Howard at the investiture of the Unit Citation for Gallantry awarded to the SAS and 4RAR in 2006, in recognition of acts of extraordinary gallantry in action.

Swanbourne, Western Australia, 2007. In the driveway of the house in 'The Village'. Danielle and I are off to the Applecross Cricket Club awards night. Danielle loved to drive the Kombi!

Narrandera, New South Wales, 2007. Night combat equipment jump—that's me getting the laundry out at around 6000 feet above sea level.

Forward Operating Base Locke, Afghanistan, 2008. Sean McCarthy took this photo of Sammi bowling to me the night before Sean was killed. Tiny (first to the scene) and Midsouth (also in the car) are fielding.

The morning before we took off on that fateful patrol. Sean is in the front row, on the right. I am in the back row, first left.

Me, Sean and Sammi preparing the vehicle, moments before we drove south to TK and into the ambush.

Chora Valley, Afghanistan, 2008. The aftermath of the IED strike that killed Sean McCarthy. Multiple vehicle tracks can be seen, adding to the confusion over which track we were supposed to be on.

Bengaluru, India, 2008. After my recovery from the ambush I went to India with the Applecross Cricket Club international touring side. Here we are with the Karnataka Under-23 cricket team—they belted us! I am in the middle row, fourth from the left. The Mangy Cat is notably absent.

Kabul, Afghanistan, 2009. Swimming Pool Hill, where extreme Taliban would bring people to be executed by, according to locals, forcing them to jump off the top platform into the empty pool.

Operating out of Tarin Kowt, 2009. These flying squad operations were designed to disrupt the movement of the bad guys along rat lines from the border to Helmand Province.

Me singing in The Internationals band at the Raven's Nest in Kabul, 2009. This was one of only a few places that humanitarian and embassy staff could go to break their isolation. Some people spent years in places like this.

Western Australia, 2009. Though we were not on deployment, we spent the same amount of time training to keep our skills sharp and to keep up with the rate of change in technology and capability.

Targeting operations out of Tarin Kowt, 2010. Just after inserting, we lie in wait, observing the village before approaching and starting our clearance. This is the most vulnerable period, giving the bad guys a chance to set up while we position ourselves.

Operating out of Tarin Kowt, 2010, taking a short break after hours of assaulting, before moving to helo extraction.

Awaiting extraction after a long day.

Conducting a recon for one of the special reconnaissance jobs we proposed to disrupt the bad guys. I was always keen to come up with ways to create psychological pressure and force them to make mistakes.

Relaxing after a day raid.

After eight hours of clearances we are about to be picked up by Black Hawks to return to base. We were an almost two-hour flight north of TK.

Mount Hotham, Victoria, 2010. An afternoon of para serials—day team jumps—rehearsing for the night serials.

Operating out of Tarin Kowt, 2011. In transit in a C-130 for an operational night jump.

Exhausted before we even begin, I am taking a nap beside a mate as we wait for the helos to pick us up to insert us on another mission. You have to take opportunities for sleep whenever you can, including on your way to a gunfight.

Helo and crew familiarisation training in between direct action against high-value targets, Tarin Kowt, 2011.

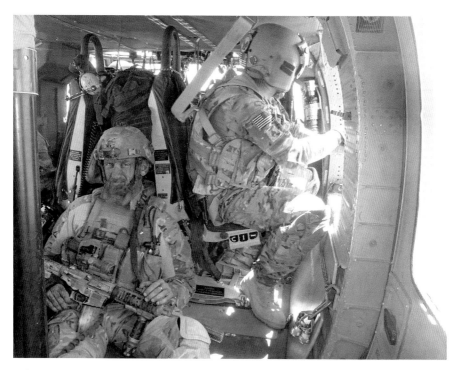

Afghanistan, 2011. Tired and keen to get home after my last ever combat mission.

Swanbourne, Western Australia, 2011.
Henry has a cheeky photo while he
waits for the Duke of Edinburgh to
stop talking and sign the bat.

The House, Campbell Barracks, Swanbourne, Western Australia. Former Prince Henry (Harry) signing the bat. Henry Moffitt (centre, facing away) is waiting to get it back. Even the women couldn't get in the way of the smitten operators, who were more giddy than the other punters.

Kabul Golf Course, 2012. Golf in the snow during some downtime.

Other than the eleven bats, these are my favourite souvenirs of my years of service: the marble tile from Saddam Hussein's palace, the brick from Usama Bin Laden's hideout, and my combat helmet and fatigues.

Speaking in the Melbourne Cricket Ground's Members Dining Room, 2018, while displaying the bats and telling their stories.

Even though it was something we trained for, this was still one of those truly incredible moments of life. With hundreds of kilograms of equipment and rigging, noses and eyes millimetres apart in the deafening roar of the aircraft engine and the bitter cold of the passing alpine air, the team sucked in as if we shared a single set of lungs. I checked my altimeter and my GPS—all good. I gave the pilot a disciplined stare, waiting for him to give the thumbs-up.

Thumb, green light, go. I pivoted and nodded three times. On the third nod, the team entered its fall.

It was a 'hop and pop' jump, which means we counted to two or three before deploying our chutes. In small teams, you could rely on a natural variation in separation to avoid opening your chutes on top of each other. In bigger teams of twenty or so, you needed to give everyone a precisely coordinated count time.

In leading the descent, it was my responsibility to watch the entire team exit, not only to maintain situational awareness but to ensure that I would be the lowest, and therefore in the best position to lead the team to the ground. As I pulled my handle to release my main canopy, I noticed one of the guys had had trouble with his deployment sequence, and he quickly fell below the group. I spent the first ten seconds under canopy on my front risers to increase my rate of descent, spiralling down below him, which was cause for a little anxiety. Simultaneously, I relied on him working hard to decrease his rate of descent until the team caught up. The team, now dispersed over approximately 200 metres, communicated in complete silence through nuanced movements and directional changes with our canopies. We were ready to start tracking towards our target.

I swear my feet flicked through the top of the trees as I flew down through the alpine valley. There are few views more beautiful than mountains, at night, under canopy. You see the snow and the trees through your NVGs, not to mention the thrill of looking back up at the team all nicely in the saddle, flying behind you. I imagine it is as close as we mortals get to an astronaut's view, sitting by themselves and contemplating planet earth.

The moment was fleeting. It was time to set up for landing. Our plan this night was unconventional. We approached from the north-east and north of the DZ (drop zone), in a counter-clockwise direction, crossing the wind line—almost directly over the DZ—before flying back around clockwise from the south: a figure eight of sorts, which is not best practice normally as it can create the conditions for a possible canopy clash, which accounts for a significant number of parachuting fatalities. Yet we were confident in our ability. It was by necessity, as the valley was steep on both sides, and there was little room for us to stack up on any particular side. This was the most technical part of the entire jump.

Once I landed, I turned immediately, expecting to see the other canopies following me in. Teams landing are often spread out over more than 50 metres, a safe approach at night, but this time we all landed within whispering distance of each other, as near to perfection as you could hope for. I could not have been happier.

Ashtray was the last one in, close enough that I touched his boot as he flew over me. We checked we were all okay, and started to prep our guns and stores for our move.

'Best jump ever!' I whispered loudly. 'And best grouping ever too!'

'Hey, Harry, what time you got?' Ashtray asked.

'Twenty to eight, mate. Why?'

'I booked us into the Mount Hotham darts comp tonight. We're on at eight thirty!'

We laughed, picked up our kit and ran to the waiting ambulance to take us to the General Hotel. And we did okay at the darts.

———

Most of the training took place in Western Australia, around the SAS's barracks next to Swanbourne Beach, which is not only a nudist beach but a well-known gay hook-up location. Many hours I spent on sentry post for live-fire activities (to stop civilians from walking along the beach behind the range), I would see beachgoers flirting and messing about. It was a little disconcerting, as some would deliberately come up only metres from the sentry tower and have sex right in front of you, as if daring you to do something. The really brazen ones even threw out verbal invitations. It was a curious juxtaposition: Australia's most secretive tough men operating alongside gay exhibitionists. As far as I was concerned, it was a free country, and as long as they didn't root in the danger zone, each to his own.

The attitude in the barracks was not always tolerant. Some mornings we used to go for a PT run as a troop through the sand dunes, in order to scare the local denizens away.

We were very lucky to be in arguably the best barracks for any military unit on the planet. We were the only unit on the base, beside one of the cleanest and most beautiful stretches of coast in Australia, and it was very, very quiet. We ran on Swanbourne

Beach many mornings and were usually the only people for miles around. The massive sand dunes were a great natural resource for fitness work, and our living accommodation, dining halls and boozer were minutes away. We could be shooting and training in the live-fire range minutes after arriving at work, and then duck up for lunch and back, losing very little time. Additionally, those who lived in the SAS 'village', or 'marriage patch', in one of the nicest suburbs in Australia, were housed just a few minutes' walk from work and the beach.

The only downside of living in the 'village' was noise from the exercises. We used many types of ammunition and weapons, including machine guns, short and long distance, as well as doing fast driving, roping, parachuting, and explosives training. Up to the start of the 2000s we could use up to a few hundred grams of explosive. After complaints about fine china being rattled off the walls in the nearby private houses, we cut it back to less than one hundred grams, which didn't make much difference. We had dogs, language, communications and other specialty training in the base. We were and still are self-sufficient, and a recent half-billion-dollar refurb has confirmed Swanbourne as the world's best Special Operations base. There was, back in the early 2000s, a rumour that Defence wanted to move our barracks to North Head in Sydney. If they had, half of the unit would have left, I reckon. We like Perth, Perth likes us, and it is the perfect place to keep the unit.

A great benefit of that location is how its natural gifts can be used to raise morale. On the eve of the 2010 deployment, I was concerned about a number of things, not least fatigue as a result of the revolving door of deployments, and as team leader I was determined to make it as enjoyable a trip as possible. We had finished the build-up training at Bindoon and on base, and were only days away from deploying on the surge. I called the team and said we would all meet up at Scarborough Beach and go for a surf. A few blokes from other teams came along as well, as did my daughter, Georgia, who at fifteen had only done a little surfing.

It was a full tide and the usual Perth straight-handers were rolling in at about shoulder-height on the sets. It was quite difficult to paddle out in these conditions, but we got in the water and were on our way. I was first out the back, followed by a couple of the other guys. I saw Georgia struggling through the whitewater. I wasn't concerned for her safety, as she was a strong swimmer and was surrounded by half-a-dozen SAS guys, but for a few moments I lost sight of her. As I sat up on my board, tracking everyone to see who was where, Georgia burst out of the back of a sizeable wave right beside me, laughing when she realised she had beaten several of those tough SAS guys out.

We surfed for a good couple of hours. A surf before a deployment was the last thing I did before going, and the first when arriving back, a psychological moment in the process that came to mean a lot over the years. Driving away from the beach afterwards, feeling and smelling the way only a surfer can, I thought, *Goodbye, beach, I hope to be back and fit to surf.* I was already looking forward to that wonderful feeling of return: parking, putting on a wetsuit and paddling out, having cheated death again, getting to wash off the residue of the most recent deployment in mother nature's magnificent waves. My mind was already in Afghanistan.

While our deployment during the surge was only to last three weeks, several bigger-picture issues started to worry me, and I was not the only one.

The SAS's principal purpose had always been special reconnaissance. We had developed our equipment, tactics and procedures over decades. We had well-defined SOPs and processes for risk management. Even our callout and application for external support, such as helicopters and air firepower, was a thoroughly developed exercise putting to use the experience and lessons learned since the 1960s.

Early in my career, we were encouraged to come up with daring plans. Our core business was to operate through daring and by stealth. Often, if you had to fire a shot, it meant that you had failed or been compromised. We were world-renowned for being able to do special reconnaissance work behind enemy lines to a level beyond what any other force could do, in any conditions and for any length of time.

Our parent unit was 22 SAS, the British World War II unit. Historically, Special Operations Forces had been generally spun up to react to a particular threat or problem outside the realms of normal military capability. Once the job was done, that particular team was disbanded; every job was unique and required people with unique skills. From the 1950s, the advent of jet aircraft, computers and the nuclear bomb had added additional layers of complexity and uncertainty to the world and its politics. Accordingly, the British Military decided in 1950 to create a permanent unconventional warfare unit. There would always be friction between these unconventional units and the broader military machine in which they exist, but the idea was worth persisting with. Seven years later, our unit was formed in Australia, and another seven years on, in 1964, we became a fully fledged regiment.

In all this, it was understood that the SAS would never be used to do conventional operations, given the resources that had gone into selecting, training and maintaining us to perform highly specialised tasks. But during the Afghanistan campaign, year by year this was changing. We were in some ways a victim of our reputation: because we were good, we were seen as capable of doing anything and everything, and were therefore in danger of believing this. During the 2000s, our role gradually expanded from reconnaissance to all-purpose fighting. Where we had been trained for unconventional work, now we were increasingly being sent in as an elite commando force to sledgehammer an enemy with high risk and high casualties, relatively conventional operations that over time were conducted in full daylight, robbing us of our advantages to dominate the enemy.

From then, I believed we were no longer playing to our strengths. Don't get me wrong: we had become very good at what we did. Our operations centre was an efficient production line optimised to get us from our bunks to our helos as quickly as possible. And we had become excellent at 'hunting the man' and our now controversial 'kill-capture' missions. We had become highly skilled in the art of researching targets and took an almost surgical approach to each job. This meant, however, that we were increasingly being influenced by by an increasingly conventionalised command who I sensed enjoyed the prestige of having the SAS under them, and we were lumped in with other units, occasionally looking more like infantry than Special Operations.

This trend, what I called 'creeping conventionalism' in a paper I was to write not long after, was evident during the surge. We were now co-located with the conventional ADF military, and a conventional elite commando unit. The arrangement was problematic. It brought mostly regular soldiers into contact with us, and our cultural differences—such as our more relaxed attitude, dress and bearing—exacerbated existing tensions. For example, having to share already limited resources, or using ranges (we could need them any time day or night to prep for a mission) became contentious, especially when preparing for sensitive missions. A lot was being made up as they went along. The tension between conventional forces and SOF was a good reason why they had always been kept apart, but this separation was breaking down and becoming confusing, both for them and for us. Many in the various conventional units appeared to resent us, which led to communication issues.

Trying to combine our operations with the existing commandoes of 4RAR, in particular, was bound to be complicated. My view is, give me a company of commandoes and I will give you Afghanistan. It is almost that simple. They are one of the great fighting forces on the planet. However, being part of the regular army, they were constrained by resources, hierarchical decision-making, and political will. They had been created to be a conventional elite special forces unit to bridge the gap between SAS and the ADF, as well as provide an elite counter-terrorist capability on the east coast of Australia. However, in time I would come to learn that their command were told that they were to be the equivalent of the SAS. It was an ill-advised message at the time and I think unfair for a newly forming unit. In time, the commandoes would become equal, and indeed superior, to the SAS in many regards, but they play a different role. The confusion resulted in great animosity in the officer class, as well as among the two groups of operators, leading to fruitless contests over who would play what role.

These problems were on open display once we arrived in Tarin Kowt, and later written about by self-serving journalists.

The deployment during the surge was swift, well choreographed and well executed. We flew straight into TK, with one short stopover at the US Indian Ocean base on Diego Garcia. We were on the ground and straight into preparation within twenty-four hours of leaving Perth. In TK, because Camp Russell was full, we were kept in a stinking-hot hangar in the Q store, but that was okay. We had been in worse.

What was more vexing than the conditions was the collective mindset of all the special forces inside the camp. On our first morning there, I woke up early, anxious to get the day going, and headed for the ops room to start briefing. On my way, I noticed several guys who would be accompanying us on the mission hitting the gym or going for a run. That was the last thing I would be doing on the morning of an insertion during which we might be fighting for hours and would need every ounce of our energy. Would an opening bowler go for a 10-kilometre run or a heavy gym workout on the morning of a Test match? In my mind, it suggested people were too comfortable. I went to the ops room and started researching the target area and the people we were hunting. Later in the morning I went to the dining hall for a coffee. I'm not a big breakfast eater, particularly in the nervous hours before a mission. I prefer to carry food in my pockets. I could not help noticing that the dining hall was overloaded with food and condiments. It was straight-out luxury.

Soldiers came in, fresh from a gym session and a hot shower. Many had shaved, some only to man-scape their beards—who were they hoping to bump into out here, some hot chick? Or maybe they thought they were going to be on camera, even though they had Protected Identity Status. This was all starting to look and feel, I thought to myself, like a dangerous parody. Or maybe I was just getting old and losing touch with the new generation of operators and officers.

This worrying theme continued during the formal briefing. I detected a disregard for the enemy, as if we expected to win absolutely everything we went into. We did have a good record, owing in part to the massive overmatch between our capability and that of the poorly trained and under-resourced enemy forces. They were often referred to as 'farmers', and it was true that some of them bore arms because their families were being held as ransom or otherwise threatened. But for all that, they had killed and injured enough of us to warrant some respect, and occasionally we came across battle-hardened forces. I was used to performing thorough analyses of the enemy and using our briefings to talk about them, but by 2010 this was a rarity. When officers and operators talked of knowing our enemy already and therefore not having to go into much depth, it smacked of complacency to me, and we all knew where complacency led.

An indicator of this mentality was the bandying around of the word 'warrior' when referring to ourselves. This was poor language in my view. I don't mind if it is used in the context of studying the psychology of combat. But it was being rolled out in particular by a small number of arse-slapping officers and senior operators. I was far from the only one to feel uneasy. As a senior officer was about to commence a fifteen-minute address that day, Rowdy pulled up beside me and murmured, 'How many times is he going to use the word "warrior" this time?' I counted. The answer was fifteen.

Just after this self-indulgent address, we moved outside for a staged photo shoot. I got that it was history-making that the two SAS squadrons were there, but this was ridiculous. Several of the senior ranks and officers stayed back after the group shot for solo photos. I found a rock, lit a cigarette, and stopped to watch what I can only describe as grown men having photos taken of themselves like they were landed gentry, striking every pose in the great white hunter handbook. In one photo a very senior officer put his hand in his vest *à la* Napoleon Bonaparte. The ironic thing is that he would not go outside the wire to fight at any stage during his deployment. I was up for comedy and skylarking as much as the next guy, but this was sheer hubris from this small group.

When I went back to the briefing room, I was just in time to watch a bomb being dropped on a target being tracked across a river. We had a full live video feed of the man walking down a track, and there were many communications about whether this person was the correct target or not. Even though the decision was not in our hands, a small group had gathered around the TV, barracking and shouting like it was the Super Bowl.

I'm not placing myself above this. The barracking was infectious, and I caught myself joining in. But when I reflected on it, I wondered: if it was that easy to take out targets, what were we doing here? In Iraq I had seen Special Operations Forces unleashed in the street to triangulate an individual, placing a laser target on the room or building he was in to guide a missile. Here, it was done using video-guided munitions. This ease of killing might have been contributing to the arrogance bubbling up inside the wire. Looking back, I wonder if such dehumanising experiences day after day, month after month, year after year, engendered a type of indifference to killing in some quarters. I had never been that way myself, but I felt it, and it made me uncomfortable.

Was fatigue causing this uncharacteristic, sometimes unprofessional behaviour? For all the facilities and food and personal grooming, there was an underlying weariness in the scene. We had been at war, without a break, for nearly ten years. A few hundred soldiers had been on high rotation during the toughest times, and some were now up to their tenth deployment. I could see fatigue permeating people's relationships, shown in a lack of openness to others' ideas, bullying and rank-pulling when decisions had to be made, which was unusual given how we prided ourselves on our flat, or collective, decision-making. During that deployment I saw mates arguing with mates, not just professional disagreements but personal. On our first mission in the surge, there were several times where an impasse was reached between team commanders, both of whom refused to give way.

This was by no means an everyday occurrence, but the signs were there, and my psychology training had made me quite sensitive to 'weak signals' and symptoms of greater than normal stress in individuals as well as in teams and organisations.

The surge was the first time I saw the strong characteristics of people selected for the SAS working against us. Determination and belief were turning to stubbornness and intransigence. These guys were tough enough to push through barriers of fatigue, stress and complexity, like bulls smashing down any resistance, but in doing so, they were just paying the inevitable consequences forward. I would leave the surge with some serious reservations about where the unit, and SOCOMO, was heading. I chose, however, to keep my thoughts to myself.

Our first insertion was via Chinook helicopter—the CH-47. I had never flown a mission in a conventional 'chook' before, only the USSOF version, which was awesome. They only flew at night, with big machine guns hanging off the sides, no windows, up-armoured to protect them from ground fire. On this occasion, we were loaded into two ordinary chooks and headed east to a known anti-Coalition militia stronghold. Our job was to deploy from the helo in the north, and spread out across a valley floor to provide 'cut-off' for the force that would land to the south and drive towards the enemy positions, therefore squeezing the enemy forces to fight or surrender.

As we hit the ground, we heard gunfire. It was not aimed at us, or if it was it was ineffective. We took position on the western side of the valley, which was about 500 metres wide at this point, and started moving south through several compounds, searching people as we went, but finding nothing significant. There was a lot of good nervous tension, as we were a fresh team with young members on their first gig. The tension was amplified by sporadic gunfire to our front and reports over our comms of contacts and enemy KIAs (killed in actions) as the southern teams found hostile positions.

About an hour into our clearance, we came upon a compound that was very quiet. Our scout, an experienced operator with high combat intuition, paused. I didn't need to ask what he was doing. I gave the rest of the team the thumbs-down and proceeded slowly to cover the scout. He had moved into an open position to see as deeply as possible into the compound. As I crept forward, I manoeuvred the team into position to cover unseen approaches and be ready for any attack from our flanks. We kept our eyes and ears on the scout to see if he started firing. The comms went silent, and I remember thinking something big was about to kick off.

I was now on the team's left flank in a gutter of knee-deep water. I could see past the compound, over its walls into the adjacent orchards. I could cover both the scout and the rest of the team, who were focused on the compound. It was a fantastic position, so I held.

Just then, a massive wild dog appeared from nowhere. It stood in the doorway of the compound, bracing and growling. Then it started towards the approaching team. At first it walked, but then it broke into a run, and bunched its shoulders as if to attack. The scout did not take his gun and eyes off the compound. He was thinking that if the dog came at him, he would just punt it through the head and chest. It was as large a dog as you will ever see on the Australian streets, about waist-high and easily 50 kilograms. Ned, our Rhodesian ridgeback at home, was a big dog at 45 kilos, but these Afghan animals were much bigger, fiercer and most likely dogs of war: tough, unforgiving and not animals you would want to mess with.

Then, without warning, one of the lads shot it. His bullet only wounded it, however, and it charged at the team. One of the other blokes on the right flank started firing at it. As it ran through the team, who were now spread about 10 metres apart in a line of advance towards the compound, he continued firing, which brought me into the background of his line of fire. The dog was directly between me and the young operator. A round fizzed past my head, so close I felt its breeze. I was down low in the aqueduct, camouflaged against the backdrop of trees and the field, and the bullet thumped into the mud wall of the gutter beside me. The young operator didn't even realise.

'Check fire, check fire!' I yelled.

The operator stopped firing and the dog ran off. We continued to the compound. Perhaps the gunfire had scared them off, but there were no baddies within. There were, however, some interesting individuals who seemed completely out of place. Perhaps the dog had tripped an ambush, or perhaps we, a new team, were on edge. We did not have time to go through an exhaustive search, as our job was to keep moving south to close off any escape out of the valley and support the teams that were in contact with the enemy. It was a close call for sure, and the first shots fired in anger by this team . . . all because of a dog.

———

For all the strains in that deployment, the Tarin Kowt base did present a fantastic cricket pitch. In the hot and sweaty hangar, we cleared out all the equipment and marked a pitch. The concrete floor, poured by locals, had plenty of natural variation. For a set of stumps, I found a 44-gallon drum, which gave the bowlers an advantage, but we lost and busted a couple of balls early and had to revert to the gaffer tape variant. You had to beware of fielding too close, because it hurt if you got hit by a 'stand and deliver' slog across the line.

For a bat, I used an 'SF' brand blade I had bought from Kabul Sports on the 2009 trip. We loved the brand name of course, and I had used this bat for games at Applecross. It was a nice-looking piece of willow, with a dark cross-grain, but it had a very hard-to-locate middle. In fact, I wondered if it had any middle at all. I remember one of my cricket mates, Teedey, telling me my middle was the outside edge of my bat, so maybe it was just me. But I rued using it every time I went out to bat. The handle was poorly balanced, and every time you hit a ball, your hands were ringing. I never let anyone at Applecross know this, of course. 'Nah, she's a beaut, mate, great middle . . . plenty of runs in her.' Plenty? I probably made a few dozen, even after a lot of practice.

In the hangar at TK, that SF bat didn't make too many runs either. We were only there for three weeks and the occasional hit of cricket was a good way for the young team to relax between missions.

The overall mission was pretty uneventful for us. The teams further south got all the action. Some individuals, well, the action finds them. Happily, I have never been one of those. While we had some missions looking for explosives traffickers around the town of Tarin Kowt, of which there were plenty, we used our time to understand the environment and do some preparation for the next deployment, six months later, which would be much longer.

We returned to Perth for the middle of winter. We had only been away a month, but it was particularly good to see the kids and Danielle. I had survived my third near-death experience and a voice was calling from deep inside, 'What are you doing, Harry?'

The day after I returned, it dawned unusually warm for winter. I hadn't slept much the night before and spent a bit of time on the steps of the MCG, looking at our new house, which was everything we wanted. We had just enough money to put Henry and Georgia through good schools, and life could not have been better. It was about four thirty in the morning and I crept out to the garage, grabbed my surfboard and wetsuit and made my way past our pool to my VW Kombi. I looked back at the house and felt very contented with what we had achieved. But I could not help feeling that something was missing. Or perhaps something was wrong. I headed off to the beach as the sun rose behind me.

My favourite spot to surf the small waves of Perth was called Sand Tracks, the first beach north of the entrance to the Swan River. There was rarely anyone there, and to be honest rarely a decent wave. On this morning there was a nice little A-frame rolling in. I paddled out and sat there. The water was cold and the waves enjoyable. I bobbed up and down, contemplating my life. Surely, I had more in me. Surely, I was more than just a gun-toting operator. There was a time that I thought that being an operator was all I needed in life. I had suffered the imposter years to finally feel like I belonged in the unit, and now I had done the imposter years as a team commander and finally felt like an established and respected member of the SAS. I was doing my part to leave the place and people better than I had found them. I had achieved everything I set out to achieve. So why didn't it feel like I'd hoped it would? Was I going to see my days out to retirement and then build the ranch and die tending to the garden, listening to talkback radio and country music with my lovely wife by my side?

I didn't feel satisfied at all. If anything, I felt a calling elsewhere, but what that was, I wasn't sure.

Another set loomed and I paddled into a waist-high left-hander. One thing I love about surfing is that each new wave brings on an instant flow state. I gave in to the water and allowed it to wash away any thoughts about Afghanistan, the SAS and the future.

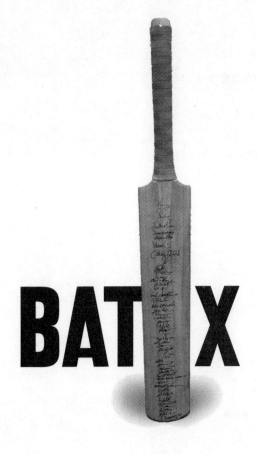

BAT X

RETIREMENT CALLING

AFGHANISTAN, 2011

When you go on a deployment with the SAS, family farewells
don't happen the way they do in the regular military, where there
are hugs and kisses with family at an airport or on the docks or
airfields of Australia, as TV cameras record your departure. Many
deployments of regular forces would leave with bands playing
on the docks, politicians everywhere, family and friends waving
goodbye like it was a luxury cruise, and then receive the same treatment when they came home. For my eleven overseas deployments
between 2002 and 2012, my usual farewell was to sneak into the
kids' bedrooms and give them a kiss while they were asleep. At
best, they might come in their pyjamas to wave from the front door
as I hopped onto a bus with blacked-out windows. For Danielle,
it might get as far as her giving me a lift to the barracks in the

middle of the night while Kylie, our neighbour, sat with the kids. I went to work like it was any day—except that I would be away for up to six months. It's pretty strange, looking back, to be dropped off on Friday night in Perth, to resurface in Kabul, one of the most dangerous cities on the planet, for breakfast on Sunday.

Our welcome home was also low-key. To my great relief, Danielle always came to Campbell Barracks to pick me up, and inside the house, or occasionally placed in the window so I could see it as we pulled up, was a sign saying, 'WELCOME HOME DAD'.

During my first days home, Henry would follow me around, scared I was leaving again. When I left a room, say to go to the toilet, I would come out to find him waiting for me. Whenever I had to leave the house he would ask, 'Where are you going, Dad?' Georgia, being older, was more focused on her own life, which also held me at a distance. My family all had their own lives. I was a ghost father.

Recognition and reward, such as the presentation of medals, were also low-key. In the beginning, a medal had been kind of a big deal, certainly for the 'head shed' if not for all military personnel. If you worked inside a big army base in Iraq, say the international airport, you received the same medal as an SAS operator working behind enemy lines. I had no problem with any of that, but I sensed medals might be driving decision-making in the broader armed services, and small corners of the regiment. However, for most of us operators they went straight in the back of the bedside table.

In 2010, while visiting the toilet in the barracks, I broke into a conversation with 'Sydney' Bill Duckham in the cubicle beside me.

'How's the family going, mate?' I asked him.

'Yeah, the kids are good thanks, Harry, but the missus has just about had enough I think. I might be on my final year or two, I reckon. Can't keep this up forever. Peter Pan has to grow up, eh?'

As I stepped from the cubicle and was doing my belt up, Clyde Farmer stuck his head in. He was the Support Squadron Sergeant Major, responsible for awards and ceremonies.

'Harry! Is Bill in here?'

'Yeah, he's just backing one out in that one.' I pointed to his cubicle.

'Hey!' Clyde called.

'What do you want?'

'Got something for you.'

Clyde produced from his pocket the Afghanistan medal, awarded for recognition of service in warlike operations, of which Sydney Bill was a multiple veteran. Grasping the medal's protective box, Clyde bent down and slid it underneath the cubicle door, and stated drily: 'Congratulations. Well done. Your nation is very fucken thankful for your service.' And walked out.

Those years were a relentless series of back-to-back operations in Afghanistan, Iraq, Afghanistan, Timor-Leste and Afghanistan again. As a senior leader, with a lot of responsibility for training others, constantly leaving my family and coming back to try to get to know them again, I was suffering death by a thousand cuts. Over time, as an involuntary defence mechanism, I went into a sleepwalking mode where I went away and came home and went away and came home and we all carried on as if it wasn't a big deal. For the kids, as they entered adolescence, it became, 'Dad's gone away again, life goes on.' Another day, another deployment.

I was far from the only Australian soldier spending so long away from home, and I wasn't alone in feeling torn between emotions. I absolutely hated leaving Danielle, Georgia and Henry; but when I went away, I couldn't deny that I was excited and highly motivated about what was ahead of me. When I came back, anxious to make up for lost time, I took Georgia and Henry with me to the cricket club, often to work with me at the barracks, and nearly everywhere else I went. When we went on a family break together, Danielle joked that I was trying to turn it into a 'Holiday Olympics', racing from activity to activity to meet my schedule when the others just wanted to hang out and not do much. I was a very energetic and involved dad in those few months. But they were always only a few months, or even weeks, wedged between some unimaginably high-stress jobs.

Danielle saw through to the heart of this potent mixture of very positive and very negative feelings. I admired her unreservedly for her independence. She's such an impressive human being, I won the lottery the day I met her. She would never have guessed that my involvement with the regiment would lead to so much prolonged time apart. From 2002 I was away for six months one year, eight the next, even ten or eleven months in one calendar year. At its most extreme, I spent thirteen of fifteen months away, either on deployment or on training. This left her to raise the kids on her own while continuing to work full-time as a teacher. Fortunately, she had her family and a tight-knit group of work colleagues to support her.

One evening, Danielle and I were sitting watching telly, sipping our cups of tea.

'I have something to tell you,' I said. 'A confession. I have another family in Afghanistan. Fatimah and the kids. I'm sorry, it just happened over time.'

'You what?'

'I think it's turned out for the best. Fatimah is divorcing me. She's accusing me of rooting around on her.'

Danielle's shock gave way to a wry smile. 'Hawkeye's right, you are a complete dickhead.'

'Fatimah' has become our joke, but things were not always light-hearted. 'Mrs War' would always be the third party in our marriage. I wrote about her in an Externals song:

> You took advantage of my innocence,
>
> you left me high and dry, a fucking mess,
>
> You took my smiles you took my happiness,
>
> but still I'm going home with you
>
> You made me do those things a man should never do,
>
> and stole from me the things a man should never lose,
>
> I've done most everything to rid myself of you,
>
> but still I'm going home with you

It was true. We had all sacrificed so much for Mrs War.

Danielle's capability only put more focus on my shortcomings. She would say that sometimes my coming home was disruptive, a phenomenon that is quite common in families where one parent has to travel a lot. She had to be very regimented with household routines, and when I got home I would upset the applecart, buying spontaneous treats for the kids, or jumping out of bed in the morning and saying, 'Let's go here' or 'Let's do this'. Danielle was fortunate to have a supportive extended family, who helped her to be tolerant with me, though there were times when she couldn't suppress her frustration.

Steve Coyle, who had been just about my closest friend since high school, recently became a father for a second round at fifty, after having three kids in an earlier marriage. I said to him, 'I really envy your opportunity to have a second shot at being a dad because I feel I made a mess of it the first time.'

Maybe I shouldn't be so harsh on myself, but my sense of failure cuts deeply. I was so head-down arse-up in the regiment, I lost sight of the most important thing in life. There is no doubt about it. If you want to serve in the ADF, you need to be prepared to sacrifice family time. In the SAS, it went to a whole other level: you needed to be prepared to sacrifice your family, full stop. And many did. I am not sure anyone has done the numbers, but a lot of marriages and families suffered greatly during those times, and divorce—and its worst form, men returning home to 'Dear John' letters—was not uncommon.

I didn't believe I had to sacrifice my family, but the effects of time away and the foreignness of my work did that job for me. I felt that I let Henry, in particular, down. I was at home for Georgia's first six years, but only two and a half years for Henry. Georgia was strong academically, played sport and was determined and motivated. Henry was less academic, more creative and a 'go with the flow' kind of character. While we were pretty tight when he was little, we steadily grew apart and our relationship became difficult. I missed nine of his first twelve birthdays. It was entirely my fault and it still keeps me awake at night. As he got older, Henry picked up a lot of my own spirit of defiance. These are all normal things between fathers and sons, but ours were magnified by the fact that all of our interactions were compressed into a fragment of each year.

By the time of my 2011 deployment to Afghanistan, Henry was twelve years old. During a home break, in a forced attempt to overcompensate and make up time with him by doing something 'manly', I somehow convinced myself that he thought he was less of a bloke because he hadn't killed anything. I decided it would be a good idea if we went shooting, killed something and skinned and ate it. Steve Coyle and his son Mackenzie joined Henry and me for a trip to Exmouth, where my brother Robert and his son Jake were living. We spent a few days out shooting and didn't get much. It was too hot, and many of the animals had probably gone inland looking for waterholes. Finally, on the third evening, we came across a bunch of goats. I leapt out of the car, rifle in hand, before running in a crouch downwind and around the back of the goats. I raised my .22, but the goats saw me. I popped a few rounds at the biggest one, and they ran. I followed, stopping occasionally to fire a poorly aimed shot. As I came out of a creek line, gassed, my brother drove around a bend in the track and hit one of the goats front on, killing it.

Henry was looking from the back of the 4WD tray as my brother got out and, rolling a cigarette, said to me in his driest Moffitt western Queensland drawl, 'You come all that fucken way to shoot a goat and I end up running it over in a car for ya. You SAS cunts are as weak as piss.' He laughed as he took out his knife and started at the carcass. Henry was pissing himself too, fully aware of the fool

I had made of myself and my 'man hours' plan. Henry later told me he would have been happy just going to the movies with me.

———

Soon after we arrived in Tarin Kowt in 2011, we were watching TV, and an image of a father and a son set me off. I felt my sadness welling up, knowing it was another six months before I would see Henry—at a critical time, as he was entering high school. I found a phone and called him. There had been bullying at school and Henry was on the receiving end of some of it, probably for having similar personality traits to me. I felt so hopeless, being in Tarin Kowt when I could be helping him at home. Henry was and still is a gifted musician, and he offered to play the piano for me over the phone. I recorded it, just a forty-second sequence, but it was so precious. Later, I went to bed and played that audio over and over again. Now the tears came. What the fuck was I doing here? I lay awake worrying about Henry, not the next day's mission. As well as being difficult for me, it was a most dangerous mindset for the team. The last thing anyone in a team wants is one of their mates distracted by thoughts about their family when entering a compound potentially full of bad guys waiting to kill you.

As the deployment progressed, although I was involved in some of the most intense military operations Australia had been in since World War II (almost half of all the KIAs and casualties of the Afghan campaign 2001–2014 occurred during this twelve-month period, in which I was deployed twice). I was dangerously distracted. Near the end of that trip, I started to watch movies Henry was watching, such as *Spy Kids* and the *Harry Potter* series. I never made it through a movie without tears. To this day, whenever I see a movie with a father and son I well up over our loss. The fighting almost came as a welcome relief.

We were out on our first job quickly. Team leaders met in the morning, at around five o'clock, to build a list of the most likely targets for the day and how we would react if we found them. It was pretty much up to us team commanders to come up with a strategy to disrupt, capture or kill the bad guys. We had sound intelligence of many high-level Taliban and AQ operatives, whether from locals on the ground (when they passed on the information) or from our Coalition partners.

We knew that one target, call-sign Delta Tango, had come into Afghanistan from Pakistan. He was a senior Taliban commander responsible for trafficking people, guns, drugs, information and money, and also for organising IED components, explosives and deployment. Given Australia had lost around half a dozen soldiers in as many months recently, mainly to IEDs or roadside bombs, our focus on these bomb-makers was keen. In fact, eight Australians would be killed during this deployment, which made our fight all the more important. Nearly two dozen of the more than forty Australians killed during my time occurred during 2010/11, the most intense deployment period for me and my colleagues.

Delta Tango was on his usual route to a particular village. Once there, he would access one of the many phones he and his men had scattered along that route for a quick call before he moved again. We had been told where he was holing up the next night, and planned to launch on him there, when we could triangulate his phone calls with local intelligence. As this was a targeting night, we needed air support in the form of helicopters. We were on twenty minutes' notice to fly on any good information about our target.

While I was increasingly critical of our over-use of direct actions, I can't deny that I loved being part of them, and there was a real buzz in the standby room as we readied for these jobs. The standby room was basically a locker room, in which each of us had timber cabinets where our fighting kit was stored (as well as, in my case, cricket bat, ball and stumps). We would get into our gear and load up with 30 kilos' worth of body armour and stores. Rock music would be blasting, often AC/DC or the like, now and then The Externals. Once outfitted, the five of us would huddle over the map of where we were about to assault into, talk through our roles, then bump fists or shake hands and head to the helicopter. It was very much like a pro sports team about to take the field, except when we walked out, there were no stands full of thousands of cheering fans or TV cameras, only 50-degree heat and the Hindu Kush beckoning us to join the tens of thousands of other failed invaders. But, like soldiers immemorial, those last moments spent preparing before battle had a profound intensity and magnificence that is impossible to describe.

In four helicopters, we aimed to land at four points around our target. Generally speaking, half of the force would secure the immediate area and the other half would search for persons of interest. Flying in, we saw panic on the ground as the genuine locals ran away, a sign that they knew there was trouble headed for Delta Tango. Our scout took a few shots from the bird at some armed insurgents who were scattering for fire positions, which was not unusual and a good ploy, giving us the initiative and preventing them from arming IEDs or getting to the heavy machine guns they might have hidden in walls, underground or even wrapped up in plastic submerged in creeks. Before the helo touched the ground, we were out the door, hurdling metre-high walls and 3-metre ditches. This is where our elite level of fitness really came to the fore.

The team spread out and punched its way through the big cloud of dust left by the helicopters. I scanned left and right: they had made a perfect formation, commensurate with the ground, environment and threat. Our scout, who had been sprinting at full pace, came to a sudden halt and fired a few rounds at an enemy combatant I hadn't seen.

He then got to the wall of the target compound and said this was where we needed to be to cut off the bad guys. Without checking his navigation, I radioed the other teams: 'That's Harry at cut-off north.'

'But the bad guys are on our side of the target area, Moff,' the scout replied. 'We need to get to them in there before they get set.'

Which meant set with a big gun or IEDs. A heavy machine gun would change our plans immediately, as would an IED explosion. Along with our scout, I decided to move our team into the target area, not what we had planned, but I knew this would make the other three team commanders happy.

'That's Harry moving south into target area, eyes on enemy,' I said. 'Stand by.'

From behind the mud wall, we moved quickly across a road, which was fully exposed to potential enemy fire. As we made it to the compound of interest, we saw an insurgent, armed and holding a radio, dump a motorbike by the side of a road. We'd guessed he was either trying to get away or pick someone up. We knew we were on to someone big. Our target had what looked like a new bike and his own rider. We swung around to the east, organised ourselves as a team, and moved straight into the central nest of three walled compounds. There was no need to issue any quick orders. The five of us knew what we needed to do.

The scout and I moved swiftly beneath the line of a wall, with three team members to our rear. He had his gun trained on the corner of the compound and beyond. Over his shoulder, I saw another team moving towards the same area, but we would get there first.

'That's Harry moving east towards target area,' I said, 'friendly call-signs converging.'

As we breached the end of the wall, we saw what turned out to be a senior armed insurgent yelling commands into a radio, apparently organising his ground forces to attack us. It was then that I knew we had the drop on them. The scout engaged and killed him instantly. He turned out to be the top guy on the scene. The rest offered little resistance as we cleared and dominated the three compounds and set up security. We captured a number of apparent bad guys, and found a few guns and other weapons, clear indicators that we were in the right place. There was no Delta Tango, but we had caught them with their pants down, due to our tactical surprise and superior speed on the ground.

———

We had refined our operations down to a very fine art, but in doing so we had become extremely narrow in our focus. Everything was about direct action: short-duration 'crash actions'. Indeed, we were now at risk of not really being a Special Operations Force as we knew it. Once you become a hammer, everything is a nail. The SAS was renowned for its shape-shifting and nuanced stealth, or so I thought. Back home, this change had begun to permeate our recruiting: the selection course now felt like it was biased towards viewing each candidate's ability through the lens of how they would fit into a direct-action team. Our training now over-emphasised shooting and martial fighting skills. It was obvious that we needed to adapt to the fight we were in, but I thought the policies applying in some quarters of the regiment were too heavily biased towards martial actions.

In Tarin Kowt, this was the most contentious subject between me and some of my peers, and there was more than one robust discussion. Few team commanders were doing any of the special reconnaissance or guerrilla warfare operations for which the SAS had been renowned. I believed strongly in the ideas established by David Stirling, the initiator of the original British SAS unit. He set it up as a lean Spec Ops unit—the hungry dog runs faster, harder and longer—and its characteristics were subterfuge and cunning, thinking inventively, disrupting stale ideas. Stirling actually proposed his idea to one General Auchinleck, after breaking into his headquarters to illustrate the idea of creating cracks behind enemy lines, stealing in unobserved like a ghost. Even the original unit's deliberately misleading name—'L Detachment, Special Air Service Brigade'—was about invisibility, giving them the cloak of a parachute brigade when they were actually a collection of troublemaking individuals. As the story goes, their first operation was to liberate equipment and supplies from a New Zealand unit in the Middle East—a tent, a table and a piano—to create their first HQ, which included, of course, a bar.

In Afghanistan, by this late stage of the war, because my ideas and thinking were in the minority, I conceded that I might be the one who was wrong. Some officers and operators treated innovative ideas as if they were pests. We were all satisfied to sleep eight hours, get up and go to the gym, shower and eat a hot breakfast, brief up, get on a helicopter, go out and do a mission, come home, debrief, hot shower, hot dinner, gym, movie, beer, bed. We complained about the food, the gym and the dodgy cable television connection. It was a cookie-cutter, conventional approach, to my mind.

I was fine with the overall mission, which was to disrupt the enemy's freedom of movement. Once the team commander had updated the existing 'target packs', and worked their way through new and emerging targets, we just waited until a target presented himself, typically by talking on a phone that gave his position away or becoming known to someone in the network who was passing information back to us. We would work out where the target most probably was, and launch a helicopter-borne assault onto the 'X'. The cookie-cutter approach was to land the helicopters, cordon the area (usually a group of compounds), and launch assault teams upon the target. This complex choreography almost always meant that we had teams moving, assaulting, fighting towards each other, or across each other's front. The risk of blue-on-blue casualties was ever-present, almost inevitable, something we trained to mitigate, but I often worried about it even though I had supreme confidence in those around me. Some studies reported that up to one in twenty of our casualties were from friendly fire.

I remember one direct action that nearly had a catastrophic accidental result. Just after getting off the helo, we were in contact on the ground. In an extended line, we swept down a large valley, and I got slightly separated from the team so that I was just outside of eye contact with the next guy. Finding myself in an apple orchard, I took a knee and looked through the foliage, gun up, anxious, on high alert. My heart was pounding, my blood surging through my temples, my brain pulsating. I was breathing shallowly, and felt a slight tingling in my fingers. This was a normal stress response, and I controlled it through deep breathing, concentrating on my situational awareness, and took in my surrounds mindfully through all my senses. *What extra can I see? What extra can I hear? What extra can I smell?* When you are hyper-aware, everything you see, hear and smell is potentially the enemy.

I sucked myself in behind a larger apple tree and scanned back to where I thought the team were. I could just make out one of them and decided to draw back in closer as we advanced. As I came back around through some soft cover, I saw a human figure in a slightly elevated position looking back up the valley. It was clearly a fighting bay, with a bit of foliage laid over for cover. He had a blanket over him and I could see his gun sticking out from the blanket he was lying under. From my position it looked as if he was aiming at our team. Every instinct in my body screamed, *Kill him! If he kills one of the team, you will never forgive yourself, and you already have Sean's death on your conscience.*

As I drew closer, slowly and silently, I grew concerned by my tunnel vision. There might be someone else lining me up. I stopped to take a look around. I was pretty certain that this bloke had broken away from the bad guys we had encountered at touchdown, and was ready to ambush us. About 15 metres away now, I found cover behind a line of trees. *Just fucking shoot him, Harry, and get back to the team!* My heart was in my mouth. I had never been in this position. I was starting to second-guess myself. *Should I do it?* Right at that moment it came to me: *What if this is not one of the bad guys?*

I closed in on him. Once I was in hearing range, in a low tone and the worst possible Farsi translation, I said, '*Wo drezha,*' or 'Stop.'

The blanket started to shake uncontrollably. The opening moved. I crept up to see a boy no older than his early teens peering up at me. He was not holding a gun, but what must have been his goatherder's stick. He wasn't facing back up the valley towards the rest of the team. He was curled up in the foetal position. He was absolutely shitting himself. I felt huge relief. I just left him there with a wink and headed off to catch up with the boys. I was soaking with sweat and felt like I had just run a time trial. That was as close as it gets, my finger taking up the trigger pressure and the fucking mind games—but I had passed my test. Not that any of this would be measured. Direct actions were about hitting targets. There were no metrics for lives that you had saved through restraint.

―――――

For all my reservations, to see an SAS troop in full flight on a direct action was still something to behold. We conducted around one hundred missions on this trip, some of them multiple operations when we leap-frogged from one target to another in the same day or night. The coordination and team cognition could be as perfectly in sync as a ballet. I took a moment to appreciate the sight during one operation. Operators with their guns up, at the top of their game, absolutely switched on (nothing focuses the mind like the potential of being killed), no time for complaint or distraction by negative thoughts, nothing but the present moment, in the ultimate 'flow state'. Everyone trusted each other. We crossed a river, flying the X, and our helo came in from the south to provide the southern cut-off for the area of interest. The target, a senior enemy commander, was said to have a security detail of fifteen to twenty henchmen, a sizeable force given that we numbered around twenty-five. With such a large detail, he was likely to have heavy machine guns and RPGs, which were a game-changer both in the air and on the ground. It was not uncommon to see poorly aimed RPGs whizzing past the helos as they were landing or taking off.

As we were coming in to land, at about 200 feet in the air, one of the boys leaned out of the helo and fired a few rounds at an armed individual running south. He looked middle-aged; I even wondered if that was the senior commander himself, deserting his men at the sound of approaching helicopters. (Later intelligence confirmed that he was, and he was also a bigger deal in the local enemy operations than we'd thought.)

Our helo couldn't get into the landing spot we wanted, which was not unusual, so we went a little further east and had to run across the additional hundred metres. By this time, a couple of operators from another team, who had also seen old mate running from the target area, fired and hit him as he scrambled across the river and crawled into a bush. Our team moved back towards our landing spot and crossed the river to see if we could find him. Full of ice melt from the Hindu Kush, it had a significant current. I was almost swept away. Crossing a river is a highly vulnerable time, as we were fully exposed and moving slowly. The enemy and the possibility of drowning were equal threats. But we got across as a team, covering each other as we went, and moved down to where the combatant had last been seen.

In the bush he had crawled into, we discovered his body. He had ditched or lost his gun, but he had ammunition and a radio and was wearing a chest rig. He was older, with a thick grey beard and a significant leg wound from a past incident, which would confirm that he was our target.

We got on the radio and called 'Jackpot'. We took photos, some biometrics and some geographical metrics, and headed back across the river to meet up with the rest of the troop, who were now clearing the village. They had found two RPK machine guns wrapped in plastic sitting in an aqueduct.

The danger wasn't over. As we clambered back across the icy river, our scout slipped and went under, dropping like a stone with all the gear on his back. I was the only person who saw him. Almost stupidly, but instinctively, I dived in after him and tried to grab him. As I went under, he found his footing and got his head above the water. I, however, laden by equipment, was taken away by the fast-flowing river. I thought, *This is it!* It was, more than my other near-death experiences, intensely annoying. *Fuck me,* I was thinking, *after ten deployments, being shot at, blown up and nearly*

*killed so many times, doing all those dangerous things, I'm gunna
drown in a shitty Afghan rud [river]. This can't be it, for fucksake!*

Rivers had taken their share of SAS operators, four in fact: Ken
Hudson and Robert Moncrieff in the Sekayan River in Borneo,
Trev Irwin in Collie River in Western Australia, and Tony Smith
in Avon River in Western Australia. But not me. Suddenly I felt
the scout's hand on my kit as he dragged me to where my feet
could touch the stones. I struggled to the bank, tapped him on
the shoulder and said, 'Cheers, mate.'

He just stared out into the thick foliage and maize fields around
us. There was no time to discuss it. There might be machine guns
in those fields.

———

Even though we were very well organised, it was also true that the
enemy were not as strong in Uruzgan Province as they were further
west in Helmand, where the British were fighting, or up near the
Pakistani border, where the AQ hardcore fought the Americans.
Uruzgan was a crossroads for smugglers and petty criminals, and
after a decade of fighting, their standard was average to poor in
many cases. We would find guns, ammunition and other signs of
enemy forces just about everywhere we went, but most often they
would scatter as we were coming in to land, or had done so before
we got there. There were some who believed in fighting the infidel,
such as those who engaged the SAS at Bagh Koshak, Shah Wali Kot
and Tizak, but I suspect not as many as we liked to think. We didn't
know how many had been brainwashed, or coerced, into fighting

us, but either way they were not very organised or committed for the most part. In many ways this made fighting them all the more difficult, as many of them would rather throw down their guns and pick up a shovel if they had the choice.

But the hardcore were around, and they were real pieces of work. They would often enter a village and execute the youngest or oldest or both, murder women for trumped-up charges based on interpretations of the Quran, and lie in wait for young men returning from employment in the bigger towns such as Tarin Kowt and ambush them, cutting their heads off and leaving them on the sides of the roads a long way from their homes, making a burial inside traditional and religious laws impossible, a significant fact for devout family members. I saw evidence of all of these things. They would set up night checkpoints and wait for villagers, to rob them or take them hostage. I hatched a plan to interdict these checkpoints, and put up a CONOPS (concept of operations—the initial plan you take to the commander to get guidance and permission to develop the plan to a more advanced state, necessary for outside-the-box jobs such as this) until, finally, a mature plan was accepted. I cannot share too many details, but it was successful, and took place in the Khod Valley, the area both of the first 'outside the wire' cricket match we had played, and where Cameron Baird VC would lose his life in 2013.

But it was hard to get such operations going, as the hierarchy was hooked on the sexy big direct actions, which made for easy 'body count'–style reporting back to Australian political leaders. I put up a series of plans for special reconnaissance patrols, but received pushback from both the officers and the operators. The hierarchy were not keen for any more deaths in a theatre that they had an eye on winding down, and it appeared that some operators might not want to give up gym and mess time.

I put up more than a dozen CONOPS on this trip. One I regret not fighting harder for involved a specific target who I will call Kilo Whiskey (KW). He was about the biggest target on our list, almost during the entire campaign. He facilitated enemy movement in and around the Shah Wali Kot province across to Helmand, on several key rat lines linking Waziristan directly to Kabul and Kandahar, a city at that stage still considered under control of the enemy, or at least not under control of Coalition forces. The rat lines included Tizak, where one of the biggest battles of the war occurred. I still occasionally Google the terrain around there, looking at the places where we knew KW travelled and holed up. We knew a lot about him, as the USSOF were targeting him too. They had family details, which cricket club he played for, and which brand of toilet paper he used. We never had a photo of him, which said a lot about his personal 'operational security' and discipline.

On two occasions, I picked the time KW was passing through a little area just north of the Arghandab River near the eastern border of Kandahar province. Once was at Pay Narwah, where I went a few inches from losing my head to a sniper's 'out-swinging' bullet (some of their old guns fired ammunition from the early 1900s that, disconcertingly, didn't travel in a straight line). The other was at a little cave entrance in a steep ravine about 10 kilometres further west, on the Taliban Highway, not far from where, on an earlier deployment, I'd called in two Apache gunships to engage a cave full of bad guys who had been firing at us for a day.

After my plan was knocked back in favour of a direct action mission, which I thought only increased KW's chances of slipping away, I went to the operations room, borrowed the ISR feed (the footage beamed in from high-altitude aircraft that could track targets) and watched for him. Someone was at the cave entrance at the time and place I had anticipated. He had a donkey, as was Kilo Whiskey's modus operandi, and a henchman. For a moment my mind drifted, and I imagined what kind of people he and his offsider might be. Evil villains or just adventurers or buffoons? Or were they like me, veteran soldiers growing tired of being away from their families? I snapped back to reality. They stopped outside the cave, went in and then came back out before heading south, also as I'd anticipated.

Not having been given the opportunity to get him, I was disappointed to say the least. I put forward another plan: get a team up on a knoll overlooking the cave entrance for a week. It was highly defendable if we got into trouble, and perfect for an SAS team to sit on without being seen. Classic SAS tactics. We could operate under the decoy of a nearby US Green Beret base, be inserted 5 to 10 kilometres to the north, and make our way down to the knoll over two nights. We would conduct night vehicle checkpoints in response to intel. It would have been perfect.

Again, it was knocked back. KW actually went through that exact area twice in the week I wanted to do it. As a team commander, it tended to get personal, and so I harboured desires of catching him alive and being able to have a quick chat to introduce myself. 'Harry Moffitt, motherfucker,' I would say, before giving him a business card.

But it would remain a fantasy. My impression was that there was little appetite for traditional SAS work at this end of the war. It felt like we were just trying not to lose a wicket before stumps, and I was starting to feel like the night-watchman.

To deal with my frustrations, I was always trying to trick up jobs: setting up night vehicle checkpoints, doing reconnaissance for US forces, inserting via parachute, building covert observation posts on the border: more classic SAS stuff. After much persuasion, they eventually allowed me three types of 'out of the box' missions— 'Flying Squad', 'Crusty Posties' and 'Operation Strickland'.

Flying Squad missions came about as a result of missing some targets by a matter of moments. I remember one, when we received intel that a target was in a car underneath us. We missed him. I'm not proud of this, but I got angry and inserted the troop even though it was very dangerous. If someone had died that day, I would have been ashamed of how I'd been motivated by pride. Down on the ground, we broke into the compound we thought he was in, but found no target and no evidence, nothing. I tried to break into a door and when I couldn't, I put five rounds into the lock and wood. It still did nothing. In my anger I had let my team down, and there could have been kids or civilians on the other side. I know the lads thought a little less of me for that. It was a low light, while I was short on sleep, overworked and fed up. Getting this target had become unreasonably personal. I still cringe at my actions that day.

Flying Squad involved simply flying around an area known to be a transit region for bad guys and forcing them to worry that we were onto them, then give themselves away through movement or communications. We would set down randomly on a very busy intersection or a lonely piece of road and set up a checkpoint, for no other purpose than disrupting and fucking with them. My colleagues resisted it because it wasn't that sexy and some of the blokes thought it a waste of assets, which was arguable given the amount of dry holes we were going to. I enjoyed the Flying Squad, hoping that we were having an impact, which our intel told us we were. On one occasion, we set down about 50 kilometres south of TK, west of a village called Sorkhbid. We had set down there previously and got some useful maps from the locals. We closed off the road and caught about thirty people trafficking through. For a bit of fun, we distributed business cards saying 'You have been Flying Squadded', with details about reaching out to us if they had any information, and how we wanted to rid Afghanistan of the bad guys and make peace again. The usual fare. On that day at Sorkhbid, I was going through the pockets of a few locals and found Flying Squad cards from a few weeks previous. I was stoked, taking encouragement that our message was in the system and might be having some impact. Unfortunately, such experiments were not resourced well enough, nor given enough time to evolve, and Flying Squad was wound down.

The name 'Crusty Posties' derived from the motorbike performers the Crusty Demons; we looked more like posties on our little 50 cc local bikes. It was a successful mission that I can't talk too much about for operational reasons. The idea of getting ourselves dropped into the target area and disguising our approach through the use of the tinny, cheap bikes was an example of thinking outside the box that came from the men on the ground.

Operation Strickland was more classical SOF: an airborne para-chuting mission. Like any operation, it started with me giving orders. Even after years of doing this, giving a mission brief to a room full of hardened—and, at this stage of the deployment, grumpy—SAS operators, was still intimidating. They put their analytical hats on and were unafraid to tear the arse out of any plan. I've heard hedge funds talk about the 'radical honesty' they encourage, but somehow I doubt any boardroom was as radically honest as ours. My plan was putting their lives at risk, so it helped to be organised.

On this night, I got approval to jump twenty guys, a dog and an interpreter into an area not far from the target. From there, we would walk up and grab him. This job attracted an unusual amount of attention, not all good. While I was giving the orders to the parachute team, the rest of the troop and HQ staff, with some other team commanders crammed into the briefing room, I was heckled by a senior team leader, supposedly a good mate of mine. He mumbled about the value of parachute operations, then loudly scoffed at the mission objectives. I kept going, but you can imagine how it came across. In all seriousness, it was another sign to me that we were not fulfilling David Stirling's mandate. We were succumbing to the effects of a decade of unrelenting pace. I let it pass, asked if there were any questions and finished by telling the team, 'We want it done in one period of darkness and without firing a shot. This will be a job you won't forget.'

Afterwards, I grabbed the heckler. 'Mate! For fucksake! There were guys who were nervous enough about a night jump without you putting in your two bobs' worth,' I said. 'Next time you have issues, have the balls to come to me personally, don't stand up the back of a mission brief.' Let's just say that he and I have not shouted each other beers for a while.

In any case, the operation was a success, due in no small part to the hours of planning and organisation we had put in, not to mention the meticulous training back at home. A few smart-arse comments weren't going to get in the way of that.

We endured the uncomfortable flight in the C-130 with our 20-plus kilograms of unforgiving military parachutes, more than 30 kilograms of equipment attached to each individual, the low light and the altitude, which made it hard to breathe, and the freezing cold. Nonetheless, we were sweating like a glass blower's arse, squashed in with our dog and, just to make it really fun, we had a small audience of HQ staff watching. It took me back to years before, when I'd sustained my most significant back injury in a jump in Afghanistan, after an 'observer' in the back of the aircraft rushed past me in his excitement and got caught up in my equipment. The weight of my equipment combined with his panic to free himself wrenched my upper and lower bodies in opposite directions, bulging several lumbar discs as I fell to the floor of the aircraft. I completed the jump and landing, which didn't help my back at all, before commencing a forty-day patrol. While the 'SF bickies'—codeine painkillers—helped me get through that patrol, my back was never the same.

By the time H-hour arrived, I was itching to get out of the plane. Through my NVGs I located the 'spot' (a laser designation from an aircraft thousands of feet above us) where we were to land, and waited for the green light to come on. Once it was on, we went into the night. Just before the chop, I remember looking at the first guy in the 'stick' of nineteen parachutists. He had the Afghan interpreter strapped to his front. The interpreter had never jumped from a plane, let alone at night, let alone strapped to the front of someone else! Fair to say, he was shitting bricks.

I 'fell' (you can't jump like in the movies) off the ramp into the pitch-black sky, feeling immense relief to have the weight and effort stop, just for a few precious seconds, before I deployed my canopy. As usual, on deploying my canopy, I prayed that I had adequately adjusted my meat and two veg outside the crush of my leg straps.

I turned, as briefed, to the west away from the moon. I looked to my right, adjusted my NVGs and saw nineteen neatly deployed and stacked canopies spread at about two o'clock high over hundreds of metres. The moon was so bright, I counted every canopy. Against a backdrop of the snow-capped Hindu Kush mountains and a brilliant sparkling night sky, given a unique green glow by my NVGs, it was one of the most mesmerising sights I had ever witnessed. I wished I had a camera, or my family, to share such an exhilarating moment.

We were a short distance from FOB Locke, where Sean McCarthy had been part of that game we played on the eve of his death in 2008. I thought about that while I floated down under my canopy.

I was snapped out of it by the need to start leading in the team.

'That's Harry turning north in three, two, one . . . the moon is high and to my slight right, heading north at three thousand feet, turning east in three, two, one . . .'

Soon we were hitting the ground at 30 kilometres an hour, at an angle of 30 to 40 degrees. What a brutal return to reality! There was no 'bend-force-swing' like they teach you at parachute school; it was simply 'lock-it-in-and-eat-the-pain'. I have played a fair bit of

AFL, and one of these jumps results in the same aches and pains as you get from an entire match. Torn ligaments and broken legs were commonplace. Thankfully, nobody got hurt, aside from the obligatory bruises, cuts and grazes, as we hit the ground.

For operational reasons, I can't discuss the specifics of Operation Strickland. But it was a winner. I still talk about it with my good mate who co-led the mission. Indeed, many of the guys still tell me how they prize it as one of their most memorable missions.

———

As the name of that operation suggests, cricket was never too far from my mind. The location of my desk in the headquarters—like any other desk with two screens, access to several top-secret networks, and large maps of my areas of responsibility—was just about where the pitch from 2005 lay, on the old helo pad. I joked with the troop commander, Pup, a Victorian, a fellow cricket tragic and a good friend, that my seat was positioned exactly at mid-wicket for a right-hander, and that the couch was the crease where Rowdy had been clean bowled by the Chechen. Occasionally, Pup and I sat up late in the ops room watching cricket on TV, instead of the ISR feed. 'Let's turn the war off,' he'd say, 'and watch some real action for a while.'

I couldn't have agreed more. Everyone was tightly wound. I remarked that a good game of cricket would sort them out. Unfortunately, on this trip, cricket was not a priority. Much had changed since I had played cricket on this helo pad: the big defence force had come, and the character of the conflict had changed completely.

The combat zones of Afghanistan were full of reminders of previous cricket exploits. On one job, we drove over the very spot where the enemy sledged my bowling from the mountains around the Khod Valley. That night, I stopped to do a navigation check, and the flat piece of ground that had been so perfectly suited to a game was right in front of me.

Back home, I had left my Applecross teammates at a bad time. There is never a good time to be leaving your family, but this year I really let my cricket family down. In the Australian summer of 2010/11, I was playing regularly with the Applecross Third and Fourth XI. A personal highlight that season was being part of the team when Robert 'Don' Pulley played his 300th game. 'Don', nicknamed after Bradman, was a great cricketing mentor with an excellent cricket IQ, one of those rare players who claim to be an all-rounder but can actually back it up. A remarkable suburban cricketer, Don had just about done it all: a famed first grade opening bowler, a number three batsman, a captain, and a multiple record-holder with the club. His 300 games were mostly two-dayers, which he was quick to remind everyone. (To put that into perspective, I played for Applecross for twenty years, and did not even total 100 two-day games.) Don and I were quite close, especially when it came to our shared passion for the Hawthorn footy club. In the 2010/11 season, both the Thirds and the Fourths were set to play in the finals, but alas, going on deployment ruled me out. I was deeply upset about this.

Applecross was woven into my life now, to the point where I took it as seriously as anything I did with the regiment. If you asked my SAS mates, they might say even more seriously. One of my nicknames at the club was 'HBF', after a health insurance company, which originated in one of the very first matches I played for the club, at Henderson Park in Wembley. I was bowling for the Third XI on an astroturf deck, steaming in off my usual eleven large paces. It was late in their innings and there were starting to get on top of us. The big fella at the crease was hitting a few around. Some of my teammates started sledging him when I came on to bowl. He played and missed a couple outside off stump. A teammate, Brett 'Snake' McGregor, said, 'Take his fucken head off, Moff!' He also called me Sarge, which I appreciated, because I think Sergeant is the most important rank in the military and in life.

With a couple of balls left in the over, I winked at Snake and pushed the ball deep into my hand and across the seam. It was a very hot Perth Saturday afternoon and I was, unusually, bowling down breeze. Old mate was a lefty, and I was coming over the wicket and pushing the ball across him. I took off with additional purpose and hit the crease very hard, pitching it short. Old mate smacked it over square leg for four: a good shot to an average ball. I walked back to the top of the mark. Snake met me halfway, put his arm around me and said, 'Give it to him again.'

'Already with you, mate,' I replied. 'He's gonna eat this next one.'

I had white line fever. At the top of my mark I visualised my next delivery. I steamed in, bent my back, and let it go. It came beautifully out of the hand, and pitched on the perfect length. It rocketed up off the astro and straight into old mate's jaw with a similar thud to when a round hits an enemy combatant's torso. He went down like a shot roo. I felt a little sorry for him and went up to see if he was all right.

'You okay, mate?'

Dumb question really. He was spitting blood and picking at some dislodged teeth. That was the end of his innings for the day.

My teammates were proud. 'Fuck me, Moff, that was a ripping nut, he won't eat solids for months,' someone said. Snake was the only one not laughing. He pulled me aside, put his arm around me and said quietly, 'Top stuff, Moff, perfect, mate. I like a man who sticks to the plan. Your new nickname is HBF, 'cos they better have fucking health insurance if they're gunna face you. You mad SAS prick!'

I'm not sure what it says about me as a cricketer that I got into that frame of mind. But my teammates loved to think of me as that mad SAS prick who could be pulled out like a secret weapon when needed.

Going back to 2011, I was missing some games in Perth that I really wanted to play in. To make matters worse, during this deployment we mostly only played some hallway games, and desk games with a ruler as a bat and a taped-up ball of paper. Even though I took the bat out on the helicopters, I no longer had the freedom to strike up scratch games outside the wire. We were constantly busy with direct action jobs, and as a team leader I was swamped by responsibilities.

I had brought a bat with me, of course, a Gray-Nicolls I had used at Applecross. Not being a batsman, I rarely purchased a bat for myself, relying instead on hand-me-downs. Paul Wirth, a dear friend of mine since school, a freight-train opening bowler and handy lower-order bat, bought a new blade each year and occasionally passed his old ones to me, so I got great bats that had scored 400 or 500 runs, one of which was this Gray-Nic.

We only had time for an occasional game on the concrete pad of the Q store at Tarin Kowt. Now that I was consciously building a collection, I kept this bat clean all the way down the face. Many of my earlier bats were ugly, and then got covered in unruly texta by my assorted signatories. I got the Gray-Nic signed by many colleagues, some of them wounded in action (WIA), others the recipients of military awards. The most prominent were two I got once I was back at home.

Prince Harry was a regular visitor to Campbell Barracks, coming to visit the regiment and joining in with some activities whenever he was in Perth. Most of us respected him as a pretty competent fellow even before he backed it up with operational service. I had in fact met him several years before. We took him down the back of the unit to the shooting ranges and put him into a team that was training in the 'Killing House'. We were using simulated ammunition, which still fucking hurt when it hit you. We trumped it up so he entered the house first. My mate Mick Reagan and me, waiting just inside the door, laced him up with a magazine each. His minders were not happy, as we'd left a few welts and marks on him, particularly around his neck. But Harry loved it. He seemed a pretty good young fella, who was handy with a gun in his hands too.

A welcome function for him after our 2011 deployment was held at The House, the unit's pub and spiritual centre, where Harry received rock-star treatment from a crowd of more than a hundred and fifty. Every operator's wife, mother, and even a few grandmothers, as well as every woman who worked at the base, was there. I knew he was coming, and was determined to do whatever I could to get his signature on that bat. I took it to the function at The House and handed it to one of his minders. At the end of the function, the minder brought me the bat.

'What did he say?' I asked doubtfully.

'Well, he doesn't generally like to sign things,' the minder said. 'He's not really allowed to.' As my heart sank, he added: 'But with this, he said it looks like a very important bat, so he was happy to do it.'

I even got an amazing picture of Harry signing the bat with determined concentration as he was being swamped by women and quite a few swooning operators too, it has to be said. He had taken a moment to read a few of the signatures and would have seen a couple of WIAs against names, making it all the more poignant.

More problematic was the other member of the royal family who visited that year. Prince Philip, the Duke of Edinburgh, was in no way as obliging as his grandson. When he came to The House, the message was passed to me that he would not countenance signing my bat under any circumstance. I was with my son, Henry. Thinking, no matter how grumpy the old man is, surely he wouldn't knock back a request from a twelve-year-old boy, I said, 'Would you like to take the bat to Philip?'

Henry carried the prized blade eagerly up to Phil. Sure enough, the old man begrudgingly scrawled his signature on the top of the face while Henry took a covert selfie—neither action having Philip's approval. As we drove away, we celebrated. 'We got him!' After such a fraught year inside and outside the regiment, there could be no better way to finish it than pulling off such a cheeky stunt with my son. In many ways this is my favourite signature and my favourite 'SAS mission'. For a moment, the two things that had kept me away from my family, the unit and cricket, had brought the two of us together.

BAT XI

GANDAMAK'S LAST STAND

AFGHANISTAN, 2011/12

Our family home was on one of the highest spots in Perth, the so-called Melville Hump, where we receive the Fremantle doctor fresh in our faces on the front porch at the end of a long hot day.

In the front yard I'd built a swimming pool, which was both a place for family fun and a rehab pool for me. By age forty-five, it only took one game of football or cricket to leave me sore for a week.

In recent years, I had maniacally finished the pool and every other job around the house, completed my bachelor's degree in psychology, played seasons of local football and cricket, and worked both domestically and on deployment with the regiment. But any sense of satisfaction was undercut by the knowledge that our family had paid the price for my absences. And here I was, getting set to go off again.

One afternoon just before leaving, I swung into the driveway and hit the remote for the garage door, before parking in what was effectively my gym. The garage was a place where I had spent thousands of hours, either rehabbing or preparing for the next deployment, and this time was no different. I took a six-pack from the beer fridge and entered the empty house. Danielle and the kids were at her sister's place. I walked through the house to find Ned, our Rhodesian ridgeback, loyally waiting at the back door. Ned had been our war dog, of sorts: I had always taken comfort in the knowledge that he would provide security and psychological safety for the family in my absence, as well as being a kind of therapy for the kids. We loved him dearly. The day we would have him put to sleep, at the age of twelve, would be one of the saddest of our lives.

I opened the back door, patted Ned and walked across our new rear decking up the stairs onto the Moffitt Cricket Ground. I sat on the steps, opened a Coopers Pale Ale and lit a cigarette. I loved this time on the MCG, no talking, just me and my thoughts, which Ned always agreed with.

I pulled out my phone and texted Danielle.

'How far away are you?'

They would be a while. So I unwound, Ned lying on the perfectly cut grass beside me, and looked to the west. The last of the sun disappeared.

It had been a big few days. We had been conducting final briefings at Campbell Barracks related to the upcoming deployment—my eleventh in eleven years. During the briefings, I'd felt tired. I'd caught up with some of the guys, had a farewell surf with them, and left them to spend time with their families. We had all been through this before. We were heading back to Kabul—K Town—to take over as the security detail for Australian forces. I was confident that, take out a random bomb attack, we would have a straightforward trip. For a few of the blokes, this was their first deployment to Kabul, so I had to manage their anxieties and the roles expected of them. They were all quite experienced SAS operators so I was certain that they would settle in quickly and we would execute our task with the usual professionalism.

Although it was very routine by now, something inside me was different. The weariness sank right through my bones. For the first time ever, I'd had spells of really not wanting to go. As I looked over the MCG in the fading light, with Ned by my side, I consoled myself that I had provided well for my family, and that they were all better for having me. But I felt like an outsider at times. Recently, I'd heard them all laughing while poring over family photos on the TV, and I stood, unseen, at the door to the living room, stealing a peek at the three of them enjoying themselves. I took great comfort from the beautiful sight, but my joy turned to sadness as I slowly realised that I was not in any of the photos they were laughing at, and did not remember any of these events. I had not been here. I returned to bed and wept silently.

As I opened another beer, I wondered what I would miss out on this time? I was homesick before I'd even left.

I told the commentator in my head to fuck off. I had a job to do and again had several young operators' lives to worry about. The fight, in my mind, was still worthwhile: there were plenty of very bad people to help sort out in Afghanistan. It had been a particularly busy year in Kabul for insurgent attacks and bombings, one of the largest being an attack on the Inter-Continental Hotel that led to a five-hour gunfight between the insurgents and the New Zealand SAS. I couldn't wait to get their operators' debrief on how that mission had played out.

On my last night, Danielle, the kids and I went into Fremantle for fish 'n' chips and ice-cream, our ritual final family dinner, and returned home. I went into the kids' bedrooms, kissed them goodnight and told them I loved them and would miss them. Henry asked a few questions about how long I would be away and where I was going, but I suspect mostly just to keep me talking and delay going to sleep.

Later, Danielle and I sat out the back, shared a glass of wine and talked. A part of her looked forward to my leaving, so she could restore order to the house. We got quietly drunk and went to bed together one last time, falling asleep watching a rerun of *Midsomer Murders*.

In the morning, we all got into the car, the kids in their pyjamas and dressing-gowns, to head to the barracks. After our last hugs and kisses, I waved as they pulled out of the front gate and drove off down West Coast Highway. It is not over-dramatic to admit that I did contemplate whether it would be the last time I ever saw them. We were going for six months.

I walked across the barracks to the grots (our change rooms), where I picked up my two bags of equipment and loaded them into the vehicle taking us to the airport. We flew civilian aircraft this time, as there were only five of us in the group. It was surreal to be heading to one of the most dangerous places on the planet, where targeted killings and IEDs were up to a decade-long high, where the Taliban had released a new strategy to target government workers and western humanitarian organisations, alongside people going for work or pleasure to Europe.

In Dubai, we transferred onto a military aircraft to Kabul, where the SAS security detachment we were replacing picked us up at the airport and drove us the 5 kilometres to the Green Zone. My stress levels and vigilance shot up—they would remain high for months—as we went through the many checkpoints, as those were the most-targeted places in the city. Being in an armoured vehicle was not always a good thing, as we might as well have had a bullseye on us. The armour hadn't protected countless Coalition soldiers from injury and death.

But as time passed, I adapted. The general anxiety suited my high-energy personality. I imagined I could hear the words of the great Richie Benaud in my head: 'Welcome back.' As if we had just taken a lunch break and were getting on with the next session of play.

Within days of our arrival, a new campaign of brazen attacks brought heightened security and anxiety to the streets of Kabul. The traffic, already glacial, slowed even further, increasing the danger. One of the insurgents' methods was to drive, or walk, into traffic jams and detonate IEDs. The satchel bomb was a good way to surgically target a carful of westerners caught in a jam. That December, more than seventy people were killed in the suicide bombing of a Shiite shrine in central Kabul. The killers were a new group, an extremist Sunni cadre from Pakistan allied with the 'Islamic State' movement, which we were hearing about for the first time. This attack brought a more sinister edge, as Sunni attacks on

Shiites had been rare to this point. It signalled a broadening of the intra-Islam war. We had arrived at an interesting time.

We settled into our digs and had three days of briefings, area tours and the organisation of passes. The handover with the outgoing team was formulaic and slick. We had long lists of SOPs that we worked through meticulously, as well as the arduous accounting for every gun, bullet, blanket and biscuit. Most importantly, the handover included the keys to the beer fridge. The liveliness of the night scene and the availability of alcohol were now an open secret. As a high-profile unit, we kept it very in-house and only had a few beers when the occasion allowed. I always ran a beer baron in our team, someone in charge of supply and control, and duty drivers for the nights we drank so we always had someone who could respond to a serious issue if needed. The truth was, incidents rarely happened after dark, barring a few kidnappings; it seemed that the bad guys were strangely afraid to operate at night, or maybe they were out on the town too?! In any case, the handover was never complete until a full stocktake of the bar, and a tasting, was signed off.

I had always tried to build friendships with Afghan locals, who assisted us with everything from gardening and laundry to interpreting skills. The Australian military 'leased' interpreters for liaison, diplomacy, checkpoint negotiation and the like, as well as for shopping, local knowledge-gathering tours, and to teach us their customs and traditions. I had become particularly close friends with two of them, Khalid and John, who I still keep in touch with today. I had also befriended the guards of the two checkpoints that led into the Australian area. One checkpoint was guarded by Nepali ex-Gurkha soldiers who had taken up employment with a security company to make some extra dollars. Some of them remembered me from my previous deployment to Kabul in 2009. They knew I was one of the Australians who helped their colleagues after that fatal explosion in Baghdad in 2005. They remembered how I loved cricket, and it wasn't long before a game in the street around the checkpoint broke out.

In the first days after arriving, I went with Khalid to Kabul Sports to buy a bat. We were not expressly allowed to go on shopping trips without military approval, but I took our motto 'Who Dares Wins' quite seriously. I said I was going out 'to enhance security' and 'to conduct reconnaissance work'. In truth, we had enough freedom and sense of safety to walk into shops. Now that the Taliban had been out of power for a decade, cricket's popularity was surging. There were kids and adults playing everywhere on the streets, like in India. Afghanistan was building its own national team by this stage, playing their first official ICC one-day international against Pakistan in 2012. I bought an Indian-manufactured CA 'Hi Hit' bat, a beautiful piece of willow, although we would make a bit of a mess of it by dragging it through the streets and playing wherever we could, and it suffered water damage near the toe. Such is the life of a bat on deployment.

I set up my personal cricket 'facility' in Kabul the same as previously, hanging a cricket ball from the ceiling and whacking it on its swinging arc. I began belting away before I remembered that the off-shift Gurkhas were sleeping nearby. Once I'd woken them up (what a dickhead!), I apologised and negotiated practice times for when they weren't trying to sleep.

On this tour, my position as commander of our small detachment meant I was sometimes alone at the base while the guys were out. This didn't worry me: I could rely on the off-duty Gurkhas to come out and play with me. If I walked out the front of the accommodation with bat and ball, some Gurkhas would materialise. Only a few of them were cricket fanatics, but they were all happy for a distraction from the boredom. Hikmat, Samit, Chandra, Sandeep, Indy and Sanj, among others, would join me for a game, and exchange tips on cricket just as we did when running through security drills.

The games only lasted an hour or so, often coming to an abrupt end with the loss of the ball when one of the Gurkhas would smash it over the concrete security barriers, some 7 metres tall, out onto the street. I always had a couple of spare balls on standby. The good-natured Gurkhas somehow even took great joy when I tried to teach them some of my modest cricket skills. Watching me smash them to all parts, they would laugh and grin and celebrate even more than if they got me out. After many, many dropped catches, a ball would pitch on a good line and sneak through the gate, and they got me. Sorrowfully, they would accept their turn at bat. I felt torn between lobbing up 'pies' that they could hit and lose, and my competitive instincts to get them out and try to improve their games. If I ignored the fact that the moisture on the ball came from an open drain with who knew what bacteria on it, they were certainly some of the most enjoyable games of backyard cricket I have ever played. The Gurkha guards would interrupt security briefings to ask me when the next game was on, or even dip into their precious sleep time to play. The on-duty guards, during their shift changeovers, sat on the roadside behind the checkpoint brushing their teeth and smoking, watching and cheering our games as they got ready for either bed or work. It brought us all closer and made their job, and being away from home, a little more bearable.

I felt I owed them something for their goodwill and the gift they gave me by indulging my need for cricket. I also had strong memories of the aftermath of the blast that killed their colleagues in Baghdad in 2005, and how my requests to their employers to improve their security had fallen on deaf ears. In a few months, I would be going home to comfortable Perth, while they would be here for years. I successfully petitioned the Australian embassy and its British security company for a pay rise for the Gurkhas of around US$100 a month, a significant increase on the pittance they earned from greedy contractors. I was sometimes disgusted by the discriminatory culture among those businesses, and did all I could to claw something back for the Gurkhas. The contractors failed to train them properly or, in some instances, supply them with working guns and ammunition. After we tested everything for the guards and found massive deficiencies, we went to the company and asked for better equipment. Their response was to go to other checkpoints and swap out their best guns and ammo, just to placate us, leaving those other checkpoints in greater danger. To make up for this culpable treatment, we trained the Gurkhas, updating all of their SOPs, running drills in the night-time until they were up to speed, and conducted scenario drills for attacks during the day. We did these drills in full view of likely insurgents, who would go elsewhere once they perceived this particular checkpoint as too 'hard' or too well drilled to breach.

We weren't confined to our little block of the Green Zone, of course. The area had many rings of security. Our immediate compound was well guarded by Coalition troops, situated about 50 metres inside the Gurkha-guarded checkpoint. About 50 metres beyond that was an outer ring, manned by Afghan guards of questionable quality and loyalty. Beyond that, the streets were the streets. Occasionally we would feel secure enough to strike up a game of cricket outside, on whatever surface was smoothest—concrete, bitumen or dirt—with a rubbish bin as the wicket.

'Hey, Khalid,' I said one day. 'How secure do you reckon I am playing a game out there with the kids?'

'Harry, don't be crazy, mate. There are bad guys everywhere.'

'How about if I keep moving around? They hit it all over the place!'

It was dangerous, as there were no concrete barriers in that area, so we were open to sniper fire. There was plenty of that going on, with insurgents seizing vantage points overlooking the Green Zone. A good British friend of mine led a UK SOF assault team to fight several insurgents who had taken over a tall building from which they were firing into the zone. The team assaulted the building and fought their way up many flights of stairs, some climbing freestyle up the side of the building to make entry. We were disappointed we couldn't offer them a hand. They successfully completed the mission with only one casualty, a wounded dog.

The games I played with the street kids were entirely different from the games with the Gurkhas. The kids were altogether more serious about valuing their wicket and taking mine, and they could bowl everything. The more accomplished could bowl leggies with a tennis ball flighted well above the eye-line, deceiving me in the air, dipping and landing on a perfect tricky length, luring me into many a false shot. One kid had me out caught and bowled, flicked the ball sideways to one of his mates, and didn't break stride as he continued towards me to receive the bat. He'd worked me over perfectly, using a few deliveries to size up my weakness and then putting in a fizzing toppy leg-break out in front of me. I was mesmerised by how skilfully he did me, just like my dad used to do. (In Dad's case, he also added commentary, Bill Lawry style, 'Yeess, got him!')

I set the games up so I would always keep wicket when I wasn't bowling, as I didn't want to go chasing balls into neighbouring alleys. Also, wicketkeeping offered some protection from snipers, as I could crouch behind the bin and survey the surrounding rooftops and other possible vantage points.

Playing with the children yielded a good safety dividend too. I always thought that the best security agents were kids. If you are in with them, they will tell you who is new in town, who are the good and bad people, especially in built-up areas. I would not do this in rural or small town areas, as it would compromise the kids' safety. However, cricket was the perfect cover for casual conversations about who was who in the city.

Games in the street and the compound weren't the only places I used that CA Hi Hit bat. In Kabul, we played on the tennis courts in the Coalition HQ area, attracting crowds of quizzical American onlookers. But as the tour went on, my attention turned to the future. I had finished my psychology undergraduate degree earlier in 2011, with a high distinction average. This was important to my goal of making it into a Master's program and qualifying to practise as a psychologist. I had always wanted to be the quintessential bar-side psychologist, to blend my philosophy of life with a practical job that helps people. I felt a strong grounding in the physical and philosophical and my academic qualification would give me the psychosocial part.

My focus on this next career was a sign that I was coming to the end of my time as an operator. I'd had a great run and batted deep into what many say is the sexiest job in the world. This wasn't lost on me and I worked overtime to try to remain humble about the great privilege I had been afforded.

For most of this deployment, I wasn't the happy-go-lucky guy I used to be. I was used to having a 'one of the boys' leadership style, but I was drifting away. Deep down, I knew it was all coming to an end. Once, after I had handed over the running of the detachment to the 2IC, as I liked to do to help them develop professionally and personally, a quite serious attack on the Green Zone was taking place near our accommodation. I burst back in and took over the situation, when really I should have left him alone. He had it under control. My heavy-handed reaction caused a lot of angst. I felt I was losing something that I considered a good character trait of mine: my trust in others. I was also short-tempered with the team. I never usually lost my temper—other than occasionally with my kids, or generally with West Coast Eagles supporters—and my outburst was another sign that things were shifting inside me.

I was regularly asking myself questions about whether I really believed in the success of the mission. When I looked around

Afghanistan, I saw more death and destruction than when we first stepped off the truck in 2002. The same could be said of Iraq, which was a basket case sliding into bedlam. Indeed, Timor-Leste, for all the billions of dollars it was earning from its Petroleum Fund, remained one of the most poverty-stricken countries in the world. I could no longer hold on to an ideal that we were improving every country we went into. I questioned my purpose and our impact. I needed a new mission, and it had to be more about my family, more about fixing me and less about the unit and the war.

During the final weeks of this trip, I spent a lot of time by myself. I committed several plans to my journal. I wanted to travel with Danielle—to nice places, not war zones! I wanted to register as a psychologist, so first I had to complete my Master's. This meant writing the equivalent of a 40,000-word research thesis, on top of compulsory class work, which I could never do while continuing as an SAS soldier. I wanted to take my unique Wanderers' Education Program for SAS soldiers to the next level, so they could develop their own educational goals. I wanted to play some dedicated and unbroken football and cricket too, while I still had a few games left in my knees, hips and back. I also, somehow, wanted the impossible: to make up for the time I had lost with my kids. Finally, and most importantly, given I had been away for so long, I wanted to find out if Danielle and I were still in love. I know this sounds strange, but I had watched so many marriages and families crack under the pressure of life in the regiment that I truly wondered how our relationship would survive my leaving this pressure behind. There was only one way to find out.

The handover to the new team went smoothly. One morning, as I was in the lounge rolling up a few carpets I had bought during the trip, Khalid and John came in with a very large cloth-covered bundle.

'Got room for one more, Harry?' Khalid asked.

'Fuck yeah, always room for more rugs, eh?'

They unfurled it and lay it down. It was the most beautiful rug. At nearly four hundred knots per square inch, it was from the top shelf of what was on offer in K Town.

'Harry, you have made a great impact here,' Khalid said. 'You have secured pay rises for not only the guards, but all the staff who work here in the Australian military base. You have also outed the security company and forced them to provide better conditions and training for the base. Most of all, you have treated us with respect and dignity, cared for us and made us your friends. We have all put in some money to buy you this rug to show our appreciation.'

The carpet was amazing, better than any others that I owned. Even if I felt overwhelmed by their generosity, I knew they would not let me say no.

'This is a fucking expensive carpet, mate,' I said. 'How did you all afford this on your wages? This must be worth nearly ten grand US!'

'Let's just say there is the infidels' price and then there is the local price,' Khalid said. I knew that he and John probably chipped in the most. It is the kindest thing anyone has ever done for me.

In tears, I hugged Khalid and John and looked around to see the house helpers looking on. Through the window, several of the Gurkha guards were smiling. They had pooled some of their meagre earnings for me. I swallowed a lump in my throat, knowing I would never see them again, and aware of the danger I knew they would continue to find themselves in.

———

We left Kabul in May 2012, just after Barack Obama visited Afghanistan and the one-year anniversary of the death of Usama Bin Laden. In that month, multiple attacks were carried out across Kabul and the rest of the country. At times it really did feel like we had achieved nothing.

I hopped into the car going to Hamid Karzai International Airport, my CA Hi Hit bat in hand with fresh signatures adorning its face. I was unusually silent on the ride with the new team. The trip felt more edgy than the thousands of nervous rides I'd had in the preceding decade. As we turned left through Massoud Square and onto Airport Road, a Coalition convoy was holding up traffic, forcing everyone into one lane . . . making us cherry-ripe for a suicide IED attack. 'Ears!' one of the boys yelled, mocking a call that is made on a range just before an explosive is detonated. But I wasn't in a laughing mood. As we inched through the traffic, a bead of sweat trickled from under my helmet down the side of my face. The air-conditioning was switched on, working flat-out in the Afghan heat. Nearly one thousand days of combat ops and I was about to have a panic attack in the back of a car.

It must have been because I had made my mind up that this was the end. You can't die just when you've decided you're never coming back.

I knew I'd be content if I never held a gun and ran towards the enemy again. I had seen enough killing and destruction for a dozen lifetimes, enough torn flesh, dead children, lifeless soldiers, distraught families and other evidence of man's depravity. I had done all I could to fight the good fight and make the world a better place. But the truth is that we can't eliminate chaos, violence and injustice. On that trip to the airport, I heard the critic in my head telling me how badly I'd done, how shit I was, how useless I had been in those eleven years of deployments. I was hoping he hadn't ducked away the previous night while I was asleep and told the Taliban, 'There is this guy who has been fighting you all for eleven years, and you have one last chance to punish him for being so arrogant as to think he could bring about your downfall!'

The commentator in my head was running riot, screaming, 'You weak cunt, I told you! What about those blokes in the world wars, they never complained and here you are in the back of an air-conditioned car, nearly shitting your pants, you weak prick!'

For a moment I thought, *Maybe the suicide bomber is me—I am going to blow up in the back of this car.* My heart pounding, I found myself playing the explosion in my head. A bomb goes off and I'm thinking, *It can't all end like this, I have been through too much for this to happen to me, it's not fair to die in a burning wreck after all I have survived.*

We made it through the roadblock just before the military convoy, beside their broken-down car, began blocking off the entire road to provide themselves security. We drove along Airport Road to the penultimate checkpoint before entering the airport, which set me off again. It wasn't until we were inside the terminal, guarded by US and Coalition forces, that I began to unwind. My jaw was aching from grinding, my fists were sore from wringing tight, my palms were drenched with sweat that had run down my gun and cricket bat. You can still see the sweat marks on the bat to this day.

One of my teammates smiled knowingly at me and said, 'You made it, Harry. Ready to go?'

'Yes, mate. Let's get the fuck outta here.'

————

I was often asked, 'What is it like to be in a war zone one day and then back home the next?'

Forty-eight hours after that nerve-jangling drive to the airport, I was eating roast lamb with broccoli at our dining table.

I looked at Danielle, Georgia and Henry and said, 'I'm not going away anymore.'

They half-acknowledged me and continued arguing about what kind of dog the new lady up the road had. Life goes on. I was just glad to know I was back for good, and took some comfort from being one of the lucky few to retire on their own terms.

It was the middle of the school term, so a welcome-back family holiday was out of the question. I settled into late-season football and family life, and took some time off, which I spent working on our home.

Later that year, I did go away, but it was for a life-changing visit to Fort Bragg in the United States, the home of America's most elite Special Missions Unit. The trip introduced me to emerging ideas about military human performance that lit a fire in me that still burns brightly. I realised that, although I was on a 'transition trajectory', I did not have to be in a hurry to leave the unit.

I just needed to make a new job for myself that, when I came back home, I set about doing, successfully initiating the ADF's inaugural Human Performance Cell, SASR. We had to battle to bring everyone along with me at first, but I am happy to report that the legacy we aimed to create remains and has had a positive impact on future operators and their families, and the culture of the broader unit.

As I looked around Swanbourne, I saw some very tired people. It showed not only in the odd argument between long-time mates, and the palpable frustrations and disagreements within the command, but also in the management of people and materiel. A decade of on-the-run management, decisions to shuffle things around and 'sort it out later', all in the service of keeping up with the unbelievably stressful cadence on the operational hamster wheel, had taken its toll. From the junior operators right through to the top, no one had been able to stop and take stock in more than a decade. Years of ad hoc decision-making resulted in people being too often overlooked for career and professional development. Most worryingly, those who had transitioned out of the unit due to injury or fatigue were not being looked after properly, if at all. I counselled a number of soldiers then, and still do now, who suffer from mental health problems resulting from fatigue. This was no fault of the individual psychologists and physiotherapists; it was a Command cultural problem. At that time, if people didn't understand your reasons for leaving or moving to another squadron, you were seen as weak or an outsider. If you couldn't keep up, you fell by the wayside.

We selected tough and intelligent men, that is true. And we selected good blokes too. But in doing so, we took, and still take, for granted that a slap on the bum, a wink and a winged dagger plaque is all they need when they leave the unit. I am now committed to helping not just Special Operations units but mission-critical teams everywhere survive and thrive in service, and then recover. It is not too fine a point to make that my proud and amazing unit finds itself in a soul-searching place at the moment because the demand and tempo were so high, near breaking point, for so long. My hope is that we learn from this and get better at developing intelligent human performance programs that enhance the success, survivability and sustainability of operators. Critically, we need to help them process extreme experiences and cope better with long duration effort from a biopsychosocial perspective.

My emerging hypothesis about change in the unit firmed up not long after we opened the Human Performance Cell. After my trip to Fort Bragg, I met many scientists and researchers across many disciplines. Through this research, I began to envisage a different kind of operator in the future. Perhaps it is time for another David Stirling character to emerge, a young charger with the daring and intellect to disrupt the current paradigm, someone to jump the fence, like Stirling, after a few beers and go straight to the top brass, put the plan on the table, perhaps drawn on the inside of a VB carton, and say, 'Sir, I have a mad idea of how to really fuck 'em up!' I like to think she is training for selection right now.

But a cultural shift was needed first. In my high-performance role, I could see more clearly than most the weak signals of an emerging division in the unit, mostly along the direct-action-versus-special-reconnaissance lines. Nowhere was this more apparent than in our selection and development processes. It was particularly evident around the highly contentious issue of women in Special Operations. Many in the global SOF community were tackling the 'female issue', steadfastly ignoring the evidence, as it was somewhat unpalatable for those staunch operators trapped in the Spartan warrior mentality. Women were coming whether the old guard liked it or not. Haters would put up arguments like, 'The guys will be distracted and want to have sex with them all', or 'They can't kill when it counts', or 'They are not strong enough.' The Jergertroppen in Norway was already disproving these old prejudices, and giving us an insight into the future. And of course, when it comes to high performance in the physical realm, we only need look at elite women's sports to see professionalism and competence that matches and often exceeds the men's sports.

———

Being a soldier can be a selfish pursuit—you spend your most intense experiences with mates with whom you build very deep bonds through shared and privileged suffering. The fact that you have volunteered for it, so it's your interest rather than a burden imposed on you, makes that bond even stronger. The training and work are challenging and enjoyable, and very good for your self-confidence. Your family, friends and nation hold you in high regard. You are regularly reminded by photo opportunity–seeking politicians and so-called VIPs that you are the best at what you do and that your job is immensely important. Through the media and other national messaging, you are constantly told you are special. This can over-massage your ego if you don't keep it in check. You also travel to unique places and see some very inspiring things that the average person never gets to see. Some have referred to the SAS as a rock 'n' roll lifestyle, a never-ending footy club post-season trip. You work hard and play hard, having a great time in pubs, clubs and hotels all over the world, and it becomes addictive. And then there is the real addiction—combat operations with their danger and excitement. Amid the blood, sweat and tears of those extreme experiences there is a neurochemical high that is impossible to replicate. On top of the good times and the operational excitement, there is also a deep sense of solemn duty and purpose, as you regularly see your mates killed and hurt in service.

In short, being a Special Operations soldier means living in an iron bubble, which to the unaware can make a fertile ground for self-centredness, arrogance and ego. It is easy, and perhaps somewhat necessary, to become very selfish in prioritising your career above that of others, and above your family life.

I have a great amount of satisfaction and excitement about my career, but there is a dark regret in the middle. I ripped myself off as a father.

I retired as an operator with the intention of making up for everything, but the kids no longer needed me. Their childhood was gone. Georgia had moved to Sydney with her partner for work and study. I continued trying to rebuild my relationship with Henry, and it hasn't been easy, but I'm dogged about rediscovering what we share and asking him to forgive and accept me. He's studying health care at university, with the aim of maybe becoming a psychologist, which would restore some of our common ground. He's a beautiful handsome boy, six foot six, off on his own road.

Dad remarried, and has been with his second wife for more than twenty years. They're now a pair of grey nomads, chasing the sun around Australia. In the years when I was coming and going to and from deployments, I kept visiting Dad and Marlene when I could. He was always super-proud and would annoy Danielle about wanting to see me as soon as I came home. We had a rule that the first week I was back, none of my mates could visit. But Dad always snuck through for a chat and to check I was still in one piece. He had a lot of anxiety around what I was doing. When I was wounded in 2008, Dad endured a week of sleepless nights and then, when I finally got home, he burst into tears. It was tough on him. We love each other deeply.

We go to Dad's property at Serpentine, south-east of Perth, every Boxing Day, and it's never long before our Boxing Day Test match breaks out in his backyard, just like the old days: Paul bowling gentle offies, me keeping wicket, and Robert at a silly gully cracking jokes about Dad's bald head.

I still regularly visit Mum's grave whenever I am in Perth. When I was in the unit, I would spontaneously go and reflect for a moment. Sometimes Danielle would suggest we drop by and see Mum on our way somewhere else. Robert and Paul would also visit her, and we would 'talk to' each other via the flowers or other objects we left there.

Mum visits me almost every day, and in the noise of life I occasionally hear her voice, which used to make me sad. But I have learned to embrace her visits, a psychological skill I wish I had developed earlier.

Despite the burden I have placed on my family, we have stuck together, which is the thing I'm most proud of in my life. For all the trials and tribulations we've been through, with the time away amplifying our struggles as a family, Danielle and I have been married for twenty-five years now. That's a solid achievement in itself.

To say that I am profoundly indebted to her for her service to our family, and, via what she enabled me to do, her service to our nation, is a hopeless understatement. Her ability to keep the nucleus of our family grounded and functioning is testament to her personal fortitude, and a great example of the life that partners have led in our unique service. In my experience as a leader in combat operations, the hardest people to manage are those going through family and relationship issues. Whatever her struggles, Danielle never let such issues interfere with my ability to maintain a high level of performance while I was away. I owe her more than I can put into words. I tried my best at the Melbourne Cricket Club Members' Dinner in 2019, when I took the stage, shaking, to deliver a speech titled 'The War Bats'. When I looked up to the crowd, I could have heard a pin drop. Even the commentator in my head was unusually silent. My opening statement might have caught some of them by surprise. 'The greatest challenge of my service,' I said, 'is not to have come out the other side with my mind, body and soul intact. Rather, it is to have made it to the end with my family and my marriage intact.'

In 2015, knowing this was my final year in the unit, I became possessed by the urge to return to the UK, to the *Midsomer Murders* region of all places, and write my memoirs. Much to Danielle's concern, I proposed a twelve-week sabbatical in the Thames Valley. She said, 'How about eight weeks?' I needed a circuit-breaker away from everything and everyone, to draw a line between what had been and what was to come.

It was an inspired decision. I spent those eight weeks writing in The Bull Hotel in Wargrave, on the banks of the Thames.

While there I joined the Wargrave Cricket Club and played in many an enjoyable Saturday and mid-week fixture. I rode my pushbike to most games, occasionally on a unique 'only in England' village pitch. One memorable pitch was the Royal Ascot CC, whose home ground was literally in the middle of the famous racetrack. It was bizarre having the races going on around you as you were batting. You could hear and feel the horses thundering around the track. You got to see some great little gems, especially in the English countryside and villages.

My eleven bats, it turns out, are bookended by village cricket in England.

The timing of my sabbatical was not unintentional either, as the 2015 Ashes series was on. I got along to most games, including the Test between Australia and England at Sophia Gardens in Cardiff.

My time in Wargrave was brilliant for two reasons. I came back with a great sense of purpose for the next phase of my life, the confidence to push on and become what I wanted. Almost from nowhere, being a writer had entered my list of life objectives, a difficult ambition coming from the SAS, but I had great determination and some of the skills, including being a good typist. When I joined the army in 1986 and was sent off to learn how to touch-type . . . well, that ended up being one of the most valuable skills I learned. And to think I was upset about being lobbed in with a roomful of women when I wanted to join the SAS.

———

The day I discharged from the military, I was early to the ADF transition centre on Collins Street in Melbourne. It was a beautiful summer's morning and I was about to register as a psychologist, the end of a journey that started in earnest back in the double bunk that Matt Locke and I shared in Baghdad. The day before, I handed my Master of Psychology thesis—*Gender Equity in Elite Sports*—to the assessors. I had also registered my human performance company, Stotan. Once the business was up and running, I was aiming to work full-time with the Mission Critical Team Institute.

The Wanderers' Education Program (WEP) was an unmitigated success, with fifty scholars and $2 million placed. I'd now returned it to the unit and it was in the hands of a trusted colleague. I was eyeing off writing a book, which would involve my unique collection of cricket bats. I had a hunch that writing was something all veterans should do: tell their story before moving on to the next phase.

'Mr Moffitt, you're early.' A civilian woman welcomed me into the transition centre. 'Are you nervous? Last day and all?'

'It does feel a little strange, I must admit. But I think I'm ready.'

She took me through the transition process, which I was already passionate about improving. Transition shouldn't start this late, particularly for infantry and front-line soldiers. You need to start your transition from very early in your service career. This was the motivation behind the WEP.

'So, any questions?' she finished.

'Nah.'

'I'm afraid I have a little bit of bad news. Your certificate of service has not arrived, but if you wait here, the transition boss will be in with an interim one.'

Fuck me: they'd had thirty years to get a proper certificate together for me. An old warrant officer came in with an interim certificate of service. It reminded me of my year twelve school achievement certificate.

'Sorry, Sergeant Moffitt,' he said, embarrassed. 'The boss is still out at morning tea. I guess you'll want to get going? And I apologise for not having the real certificate here. Usual army stuff-up.'

I slipped the piece of paper into my transition file, which was essentially a bunch of contact numbers and brochures.

The commanding officer of the transition centre passed me on the street outside. I said nothing. I stood in the sun and looked at the photocopy of the certificate and thought, *Is this it?* I took out my phone and videoed a message to Danielle.

'8220663, Sergeant Anthony Wayne Moffitt . . . It is with great pleasure that I am able to send to you the enclosed Appreciation of Service Certificate. Regrettably, it is unfortunate that the certificate could not be presented to you on a more appropriate occasion, but be assured . . .' And so on. 'Thanks for coming, Harry,' I added with a note of sarcasm.

I should not have been surprised. When I left the SAS my farewell gift was the same memento I had presented to the mess on a previous occasion. Someone had forgotten! But this seemed different, a more final insult. Standing there on Collins Street, my new life before me, I felt a deep resentment. And what recognition would Danielle get? None. She could share my 'Army Achievement Certificate' with me.

Later that summer, I walked the leafy streets of Carlton North reading *Why Die?* by Graem Sims, about the enigmatic Australian visionary Percy Cerutty, whose 'Stotan' philosophy spoke to my future: 'I urge you to go onto your greatness if you believe it is in you. Think deeply and separate what you wish from what you are prepared to do.' Remarkably, at the age of 51, Percy transformed himself from a postman to one of the world's greatest ever athletics coaches. His unique consideration of physical, psychological, social and philosophical aspects of human performance deeply inspired me.

And so, at the age of 51, we began our transformation. With Danielle by my side, how could I fail?

TWELFTH MAN

'Three minutes!' yelled the door gunner of the Sikorsky UH-60 Black Hawk as he racked his dual M60 machine guns. The Black Hawk was flying low and fast, straight up the middle of the Khod Valley. I looked down onto the valley floor, the scene of many events in my life over the previous eleven years. Cricket games and practice, contacts and conversations with the enemy, night-time motorbike operations, and long-range vehicle patrol quizzes. This was my last time. I looked at one of the junior operators, Jumbuck, who had his eyes closed, relaxed and deep breathing. He wasn't scared, he just knew he needed plenty of oxygen in his brain to optimise his decision-making once we hit the ground. Everyone was box breathing, and I joined them.

'One minute!'

The doors opened and slid rearwards. I stuck my head out and looked ahead to try to see the village, our destination. I remembered how its early-morning call to prayer gave me an unexpected sense of peace back in 2005.

'Thirty seconds!'

The Black Hawk banked over the small group of compounds we were targeting and the scout pointed with his gun to several fighting-age males running into a creek line. One of them was armed. We released our strops and gave each other one last glance.

Before the pilot had a chance to touch down and the loadmaster give us the chop, the whole team left the bird and sprinted towards the enemy. I was running again, the hot dusty air burning my lungs. This was probably the last time I would run like this in my life. I could barely keep up with Jumbuck, who, mid-sprint, stopped, sucked in a quick deep breath, and released three rounds before sprinting off again. I battled on in pursuit.

Jumbuck had shot and killed someone who turned out to be a senior Taliban commander. The shot was amazing, the best I had ever seen: around 200 metres, with his heart pounding and breathing rate through the roof, standing unsupported, aiming at a moving target. Surgical. The new breed of operators were, at the end of the war, elite clinical machines.

By the time all the teams had got onto the ground, our team had found ourselves in a creek line guarding ten suspects we had gathered while exchanging sporadic fire with enemy who were concealed in the cluster of compounds. All of a sudden, an armed bad guy ran obliquely across our front from right to left. He was shot and killed instantly. He fell into an open patch of tilled dirt. I looked around for a better position, across the creek line on some more secure-looking higher ground. But when we moved, rounds cracked into the banks of earth around us, forcing Stuey Two-Up and the team back into the low ground. I thought this was a tactically unsound position. I could smell the enemy body, which had already started to decay in the heat. The situation felt bad. I had a sense that the enemy were reorganising to attack.

Just then, a boy of about fourteen and an old man who could have been his grandfather wandered out of some reeds further up the creek. The old man had a bleeding forearm, and the boy had a severe wound to his head and stumbled along, semiconscious, bleeding badly. His skull was open and his brain appeared to have been compromised. Under fire, our medic, Cuddles, ran out, grabbed the boy and went to work.

'How is he, Cuddles?' I asked.

'I think I see brain, and he's bleeding pretty heavily. We need to get him out of here.'

'Fuck, if we call in a bird they'll be a sitting duck. I think the enemy are reorganising and setting up to attack.'

The way forward was clear. Mission came first, and protection of the force a very close second. No civilian should trump either, and neither should I be contemplating exposing an Air Medical Evacuation team and helicopter. Or should I? What the fuck was I here to do? Protect the locals and make it safe for them to carry on their lives.

I got on the radio to Pup.

'Have a Pri 1 civcas, request approval to AME.'

This brought down a backlash from some in the troop, who disagreed with putting air assets and others in danger for an Afghan civilian.

'Fuck 'em, Harry,' someone said. 'We're in the middle of a gunfight. Let him go and let's get to a more secure position.'

I ignored the free advice and radioed HQ. I told them the situation, including the threat profile. The AME were happy to react and be updated once they were closer to the target. I had never really had a moral dilemma such as this. Put four helicopter operators and maybe a couple of SAS operators at risk for a civilian boy? It wasn't our job. But if protecting the Afghan population wasn't our job, what were we doing? Was it all about chasing bad guys? There were fucking bad guys everywhere. Where did it end? I decided that letting the boy die was not something I was willing to live with. I had to draw a line, and this was it.

Stuey Two-Up came over as I was finalising the details for the pick-up.

'Fuck, Harry, what are you doing, mate? We have a situation here, they look like they are re-orging.'

'Mate, we are getting him out of here. We can't save or kill everyone, but I'm fucked if we aren't gunna give this little bloke a good chance. If we don't, then we might as well pack up and go home.'

After that last gig, the team arrived in Perth quietly on a private flight before going into a hangar for our quarantine checks. Then we were put onto a bus with the curtains drawn. No crowds, no fanfare, no cameras, no cakes, no family. As we drove back to the serenity of Swanbourne, I looked out of the window at life going on in Perth, civilians blissfully unaware of the death, destruction and darkness we were returning from. I wondered if, had they known, they would have cared.

'I reckon you're getting a bit old for all this, eh Harry?' Stuey brought me out of my nostalgia. 'You looked a bit slow on that last gig. The pack looked a bit heavy?'

'Stu, I was humping packs in Baghdad while you were still in Dad's bag.'

The boys all laughed, and although Stuey was speaking tongue in cheek, he was right. I was too old for this.

It had been a long journey, but what sticks with me most is not the memory of confrontation but the humanity, humour and psychology of modern combat. I had listened intently to the veterans in the *World at War* television series early in my life, when they reminded us over and over again of the horrors and depravity of war. I was inspired from afar by their words about 'mates, family, and a sense of humour'. I'd been inspired, from afar, by people like David Stirling, Albert Jacka VC, Percy Cerutty, and the 'white mouse' Nancy Wake among others. But I was forged by men I worked alongside, like Rowdy Joe, Seadog, Streaky Bacon, G-Port, Cranky Frank, Chief Siaosi, JJ, Hawkeye, and of course Big Duke. I liked to think that a little of their excellence had rubbed off on me. Even if it hadn't, I was much the better for having met them, as they had all helped mould the curious, compassionate, determined and disciplined humanitarian spirit that my mother had instilled in me.

As I stared out of the bus into the Perth afternoon, I thought about how Mum still lived in me. I still often heard her, clear as day. Through the noise of that last afternoon in combat, it was

Mum's voice that had told me I had to put that young Afghan boy's life first.

––––––––

At the end of my military days, I realise I will always live with mixed feelings. I am sad for all the death and destruction, the killing and suffering. I am disappointed by the way the unit seemed to have lost its way and the current investigations that have brought disrepute to our fine name and reputation. I am angry at politicians, high-ranking officers and businessmen who seem to use warfare as their plaything, to advance their careers, to feed their egos and to make money. I am confused and still picking over the ideology of it all. I feel disappointed and a little betrayed that the Taliban is coming back to power in Afghanistan, and embarrassed by our greedy and Machiavellian role in keeping Timor-Leste impoverished. However, I am immensely proud to have served in an amazing unit and community, to have been considered worthy of joining its number. I am extremely proud of how the unit has reacted to the recent challenges and those individuals who have fought and are fighting for its integrity. I am proud and thankful for the amazing soldiers and operators with whom I have served and become dear friends.

I am happy that we have had some impact on lives somewhere. I take great pride that many, many children have had the chance to survive and thrive and maybe go on to effect great change due to the work we have done and sacrifices we have made. I have loved the adventure and the unique life lessons.

I am very happy to call myself an average SAS operator, not the best or the worst. I was happy to be a role-player, in support of those excellent operators around me, hoping that in time, if I played my role well, some of that excellence would rub off on me. And I like to think it did, improving me as a person and teaching me a lot along the way.

The world is a volatile, uncertain, complex and ambiguous place, and from what I have seen, so are humans. When I started, I was a keen-eyed optimist who was mad keen to fight the good fight. You couldn't have dragged me away. I am just thankful that I have made it and now have time to reflect. I encourage anyone to do the same. And there is nothing better than stopping to watch a session of cricket on a sunny Saturday afternoon, a cold beer in hand, and with someone you love, to reflect on everything.

Good cricket to all.

ACKNOWLEDGEMENTS

Behind every operator, there is a team of support staff who make it possible for them to do their job; who plan, prepare, organise, coordinate, facilitate, resource, pack, move, repair, issue, create, cook, count, liaise, distribute, inform, guide and advise—and so much more. Without these often underrated and always critical people it would not be possible for operators to do what they do. Writing a book is no different, and in doing so I would like to acknowledge the following people.

My wife, Danielle, for her continued love and support in our transition out of army and helping me to forge a new identity. Whilst writing this book, she has been my north point, ensuring I remained genuine and authentic, and honest with myself.

My children, Georgia and Henry, for keeping me grounded and showing me that, while it doesn't always feel like it, I did okay as their father.

My mother, Sandra Joy Moffitt, who, while not here in person, inspired me and continues to inspire me as a man and human.

My dad, Greg Moffitt, for leading the way, and my brothers, Robert and Paul, for reminding me that at the end of the day I am still just 'Anth', regardless of what I have done in my life.

My school friends—Raelene, Paul, Geoff, and Coylie—who continue to check in on me, no matter where I am in the world.

The Applecross Cricket Club, my second home away from home, for always being my 'Third Thing'.

Tom and the team at Allen & Unwin for being professional and making the process fun, the first principle of our agreement together.

Clare, Preston, Adrian, and John for their mentorship and guidance during my transition to civilian.

The men and women of SASR, my brothers and sisters in arms, whose stories are also woven into this book.

Finally, I would like to say thank you to Malcolm Knox who nurtured and polished my words and convinced me it was a story worth telling. It has been a great privilege to work with you and become your friend. Thank you, mate.